# Consistent Divergencies

## The Studio and Community Art of Hugh Merrill, 1969-2011

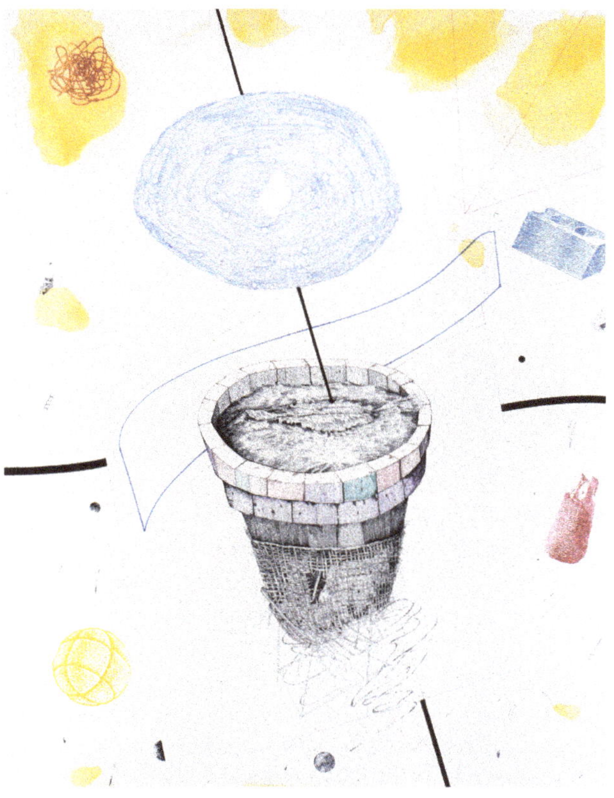

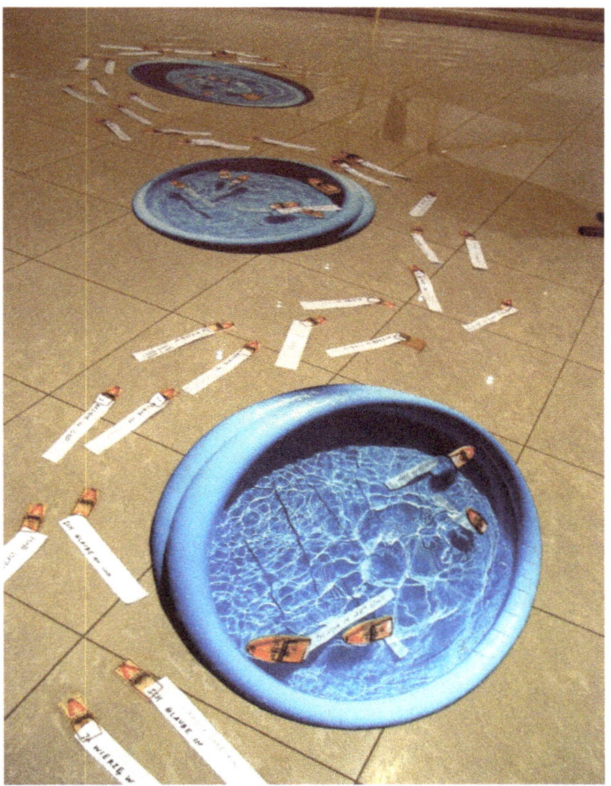

edited by Jeanette Powers

designed by Amanda Rehagen

Chameleon Press

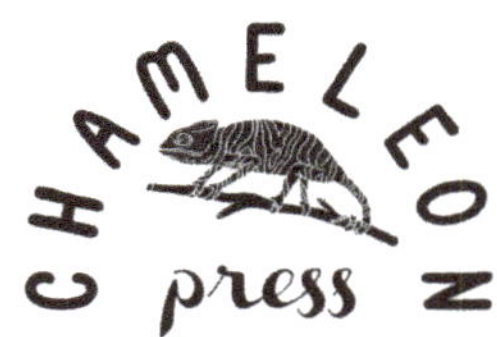


Kansas City, MO

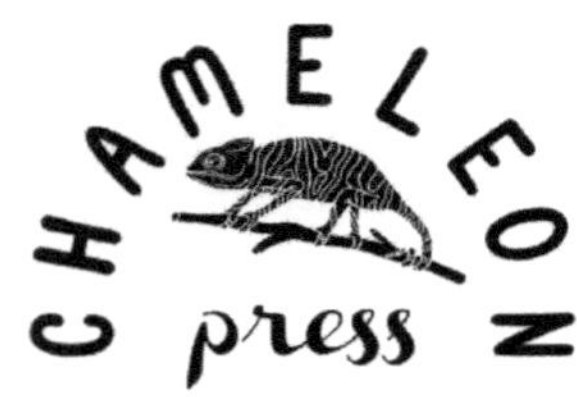

Chameleon Press
Kansas City, MO

2nd Edition: 11 7 5 3 2 1
© 2018 by Hugh Merrill
editor: Jeanette Powers

2nd Edition
ISBN: 9780999022238
Library of Congress Control Number:  2018932278



Cover, left: *Tern*, 2010, painting and digital print, 38"x23", collection of the artist.
Cover, right: *Pools of Belief*, 2005, installation, Academy of Fine Arts, Poznan, Poland.
Title page, left: *Inland Sea*, 2009, drawing, 60"x32", collection of Staci Pratt.

Photos in this book are by Emmett Merrill or personal family snapshots, unless otherwise noted.

1st Edition:
Leedy-Voulkos Art Center, Kansas City, MO 64108
© 2011 by Adelia Ganson
Proofreaders: Janell Meador and Susan Fiorello
All images of works by Hugh Merrill © 2011 by Hugh Merrill.

*To Hal...*

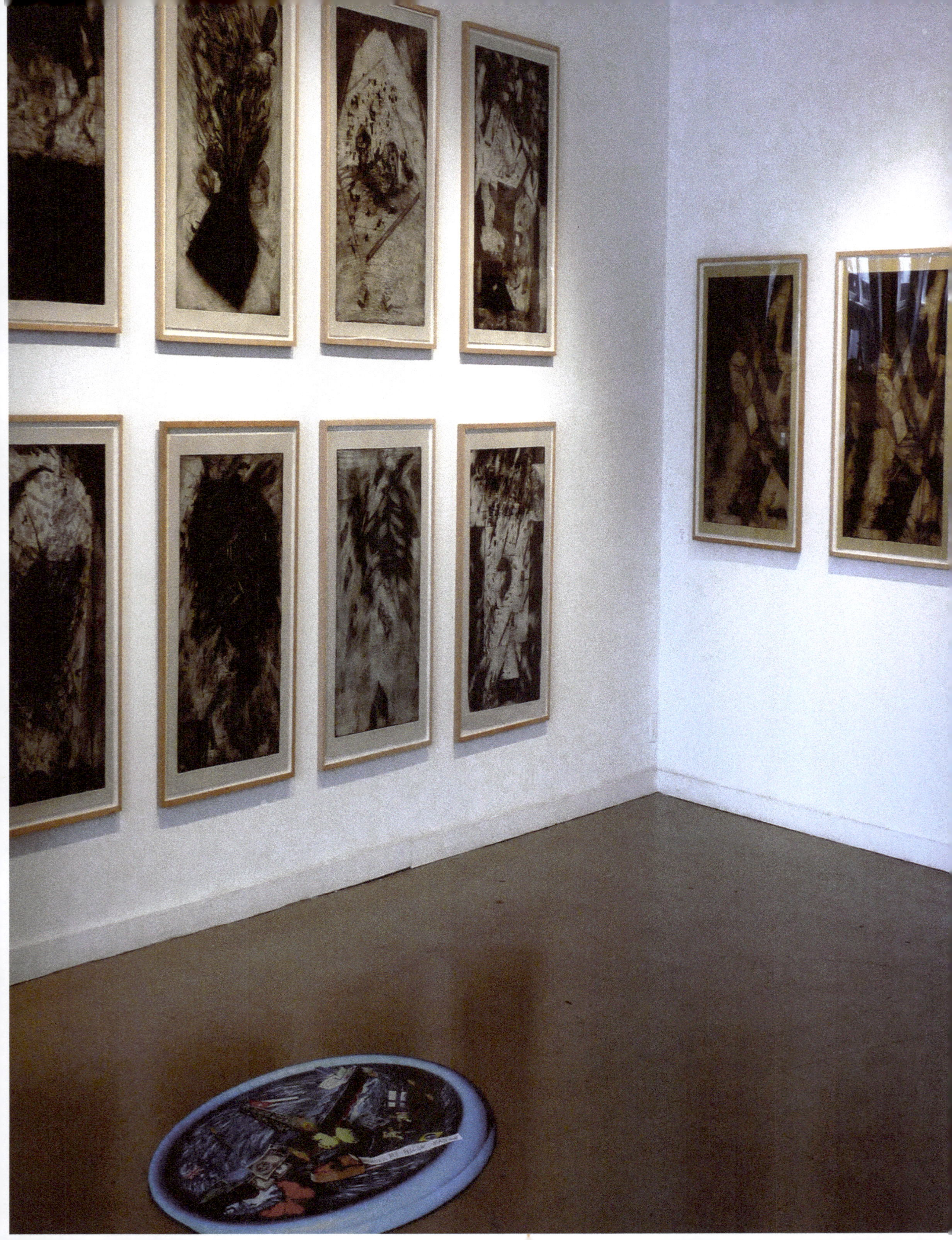

# Table of Contents



## Studio Art



## Community Art



Opposite Page:

**Divergent Consistencies**, *2009, installation, Leedy Voulkos Art Center, Kansas City, Missouri.*

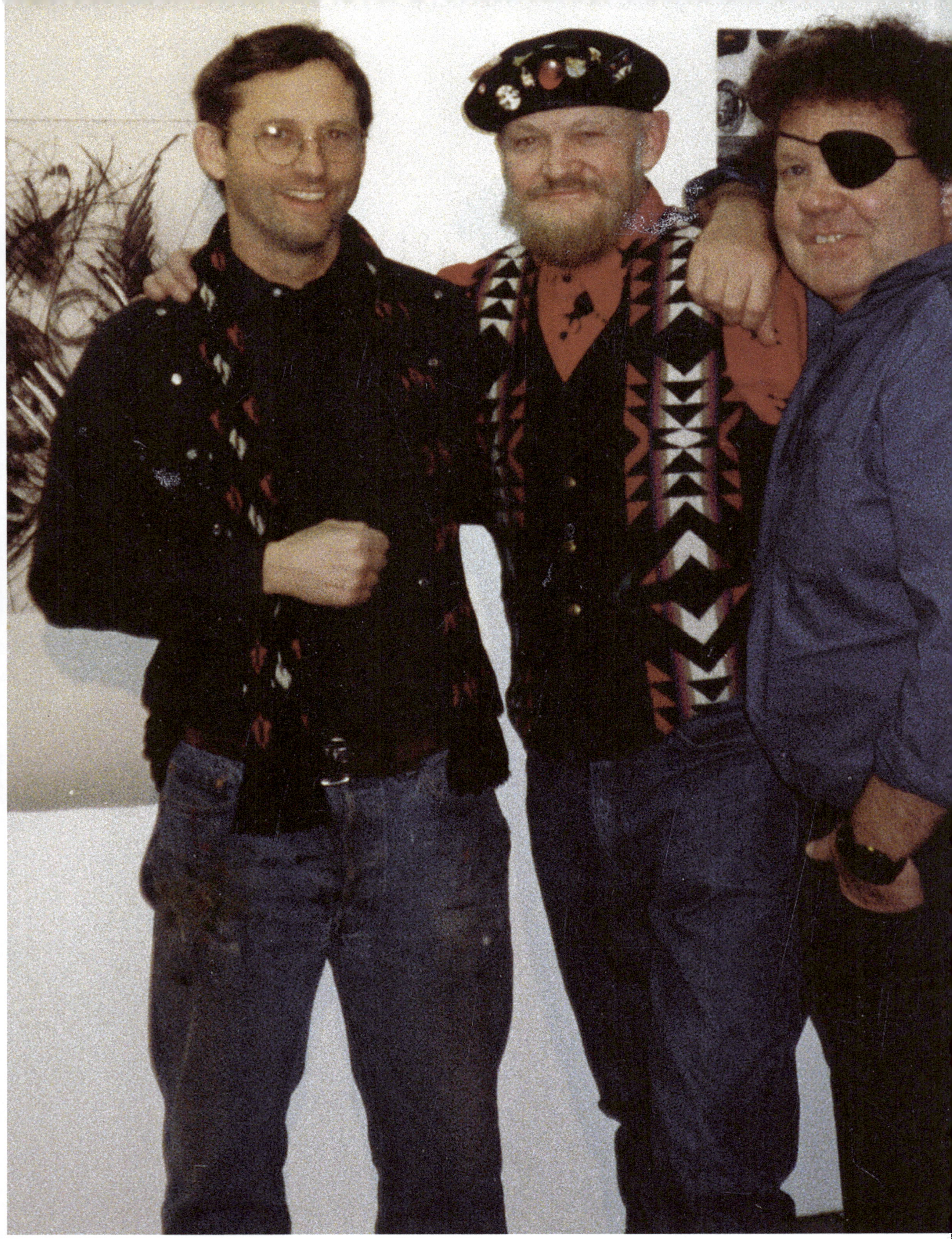

# **Acknowledgements**

Art has the unique ability and power to inspire us as human beings to see a new world, beyond the mundane and difficult challenges of daily lives. I have seen the effects of creative thought and action on children in Mother Teresa's Orphanages in Kenya and the Philippines. In Kansas City's homeless shelters and family court detention centers, art has transcended into the realm of magic. I have seen hundreds of students at the Kansas City Art Institute grow into vibrant creative professionals focused on using art to change society. In my own life, encounters with artists and art have made all the difference and are the forces that awaken and nurture me.

There are many who have provided guidance and support for my journey and growth as a person, artist and educator. I especially want to thank Jim Leedy for his mentorship, guidance and friendship over four decades. Jim, Molly, Stephanie, and Holly, the Leedy-Voulkos Art Center family, have been unwavering in their encouragement for my studio and community work. The *Divergent Consistencies* exhibition and book would not have been possible without their support. I must mention George McKenna, Curator of Prints, Drawings and Photography at the Nelson Atkins Museum; Ken Kerslake, artist/educator and past President of the Southern Graphics Council and Gabor Peterdi, my mentor and friend. These are just a few among many.

I especially offer my gratitude to all of the students and Community Arts kids that have taught me so much about life, perseverance, stamina, vision, and hope. Watching their lives change through art has added to my life in ways that are infinite and inexhaustible.

I would like to gratefully thank all of the Community Arts partners that have influenced my work and collaborated with me for decades: StoneLion Theatre, Hip Hop Academy, Cheryl Kimmi and the KC Fringe Fest, Mel Chin and his Fundred Dollar Bill Project, Staci Pratt and the Office of Homeless Liaison of the Kansas City, Kansas Public Schools. The Community Arts and Service Learning Program of the Kansas City Art Institute, Arts Incubator and INKubator Press, and the Kansas City Parks and Recreation Department have all provided underpinning for successful projects spanning many years and many participants.

I wish to thank the foundations that have consistently provided support to Chameleon Arts and Youth Development and my community arts programming, beginning with the Muriel McBrien Kauffman Foundation, H&R Block Foundation, Francis Families Foundation, R.A. Long Foundation, and the Sosland Foundation. Along with equable support from the Bank of America Foundation and the Oppenstein Brothers Foundation, these proponents reinforce the ability of at-risk youth to access arts programming that would have been impossible without their contributions.

Designer Amanda Rehagen and writer/editor Jeanette Powers were the driving forces and guiding spirits for the exhibition and then the book's 2nd edition. Their kindness, professionalism and friendship have made this creative journey a joy of discovery.

Special thanks to all those that contributed to the book: Heather Lustfeld, Eleanor Erskine, Richard Noyce, Max Skorwider, Patrick Moonasar, Staci Pratt, George McKenna, Rebecca Callaway, and Emmett Merrill.

Thanks to Staci Pratt, my beloved friend, whose love support and humor has made my life a living heaven.

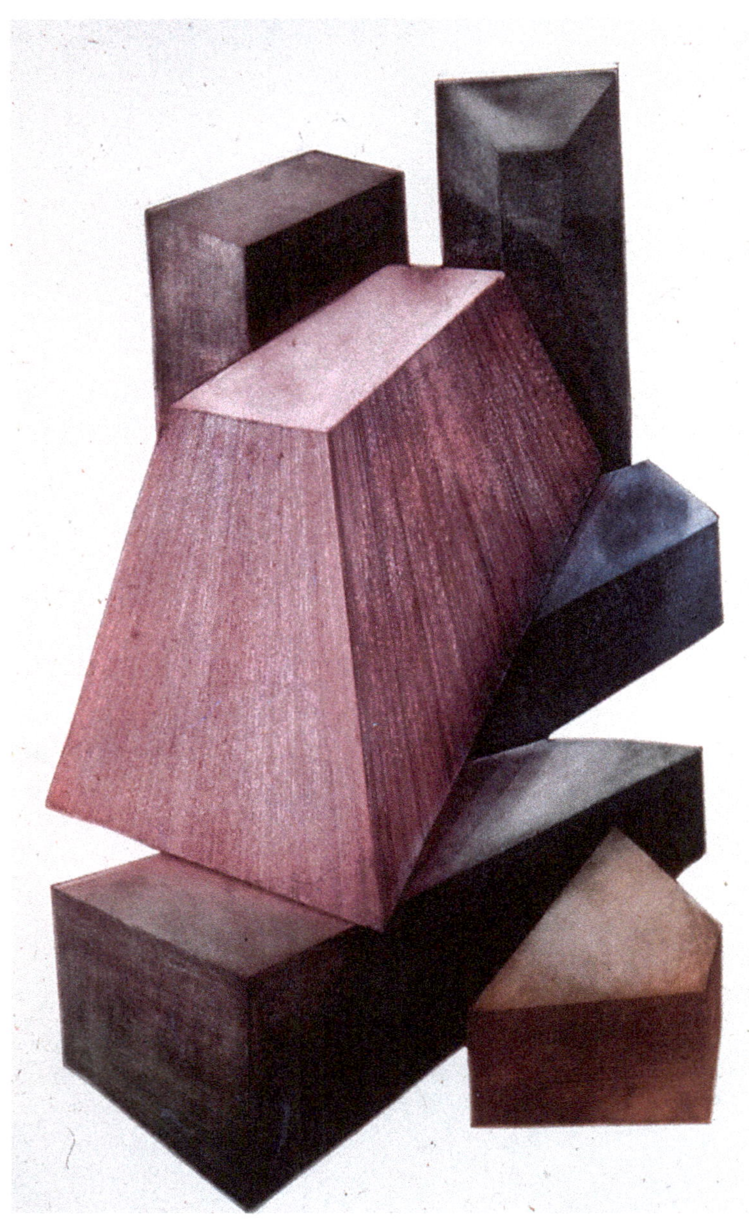

**Object**, *1975, etching, 24"x36", private collection.*

# Introduction

Hugh Merrill came into the Uptown Arts Bar in 2015, because he heard there were a ton of young people spontaneously creating art. It was irresistible to him, because he has a constantly curious and youthful heart which thrives on interacting with artists at all levels. We met and talked and hit it off instantly. I knew of Hugh Merrill as one of Kansas City's well regarded visual artists, a long-time faculty at the Kansas City Art Institute, a guy who had a one-person exhibition at the Nelson-Atkins Museum and that he was in the collections the other museums in town. Now, he was 67 and wanted to begin writing and performing poetry.

He told me about hanging out with Allen Ginsberg in the late 60's and John Cage, Divine, Robert Motherwell and the list seemed to go on and on. He once told me of meeting Robert Pinsky and how elegantly the future Poet Laureate had described poetry. Pinsky ruminated that poetry was meant to be first spoken, that it was the most physical of the arts because it came from inside the body. Pinksy quipped, "Poetry is our breath, its sound inseparable from the poet's being." Merrill tells me he thought dance was more physical "but who is going to argue the point with Robert Pinski on their first meeting?" This is the heart of Merrill, respecting a master while endlessly questioning the lecture.

He had come to read and was often the oldest poet in the room for Slam Poetry nights. His work was more beat than slam, but he was well received due to his wit and personal history of activism. He surprised the young audience constantly with his irreverence and humor; he was outlandish, funny, theatrical, brave, and silly all within the same reading at times. He was insightful and encouraged everyone, most especially me. He became a fixture of evenings and has served to nurture and mentor so many of the youth at Poetic Underground, never turning off his natural gift of teaching.

In that first year we began working on publishing his first book of verse, Nomadic? Rover by Days Singing These Gang Plank Songs of the Ambler, which was released in September of 2016 by 39 West Press. This charming little subversive romp incorporated Merrill's drawings which he doodled on the first galley copy and makes it a great representation of his layered style of working. It was shortly after this that Hugh came to me and told me of his cancer diagnosis.

The next year I bore witness to what survival means, what commitment and fearlessness mean. As the powerful and vibrant man I met waned before my eyes, to the months of hospital confinement, to the ever-present feeding tube, to the sadness of seeing an Irishman sober up, at every turn, he never said anything but, "it's no big deal." I kept a sense of humor all the time with him, making bawdy jokes at Death's limp knock and teasing about how his friends at the Arts Bar wouldn't have to worry about his long readings for a moment (we love those long extemporaneous performances), but I knew that he was in crushing and brutal pain.

The beauty that Merrill is turned Death's Door into a studio space. In between morphine dreams and chemo vomit he would roll over on the pallet on his floor to work on large scale drawings which are now in gorgeous frames and part of a featured exhibition. He connected with his deep family roots and discovered an ancestor's role in lynchings which set off a new project building monuments to those lives taken by lynchings. He wrote a new book of poetry, Dog Alley, and when the dying stopped, he returned to performing with Poetic Underground.

There's never enough time to do it all, but Merrill hasn't wasted a second of it.

Merrill came to Kansas City in 1976 to teach in the printmaking department at the Kansas City Art Institute. His interest always flowed easily from the personal to the political, and from the private studio voice to being a community activist. In the early 1980's community art was non-existent in Universities and Art Colleges, it seemed only the private studio voice mattered. But there was a ground swell of change building and Merrill was one of the few deeply involved from the beginning.

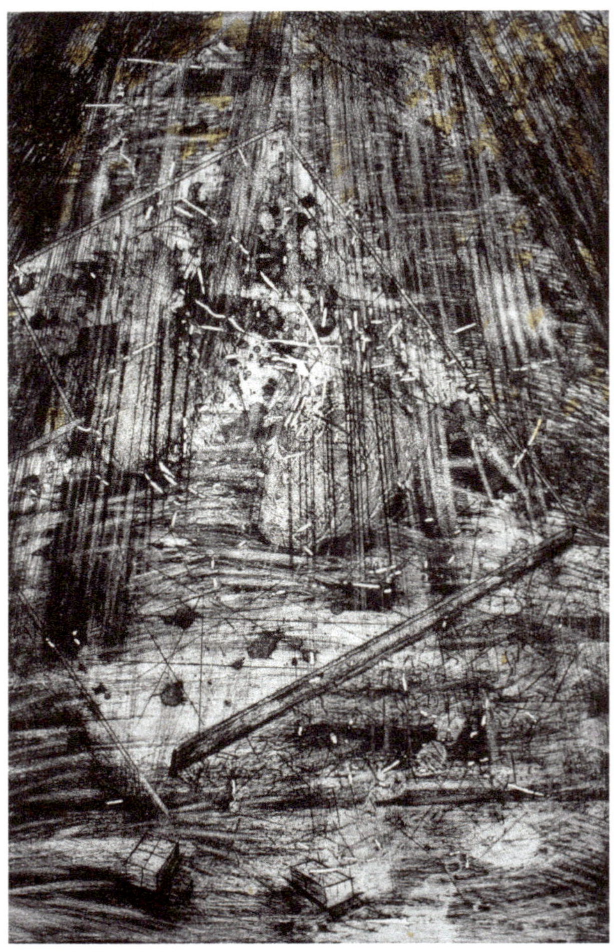

**Facts of Fictions**, *1990-1995, etching, private collection.*

He took over the not-for-profit agency the Childrens Community Theatre of Kansas City, doing business as Chameleon Theatre and turned it into Chameleon Arts Agency. The agency focused on using arts in the urban core to help children overcome the extreme difficulties of racism, poverty, systemic police profiling, gang violence and drugs in Kansas City. Chameleon in thirty years has done over one million dollars in arts programming in the inner city. He wrote grants to major foundations and received funding from the Francis Family Foundation, RA Long Foundation, Weiner Founda-

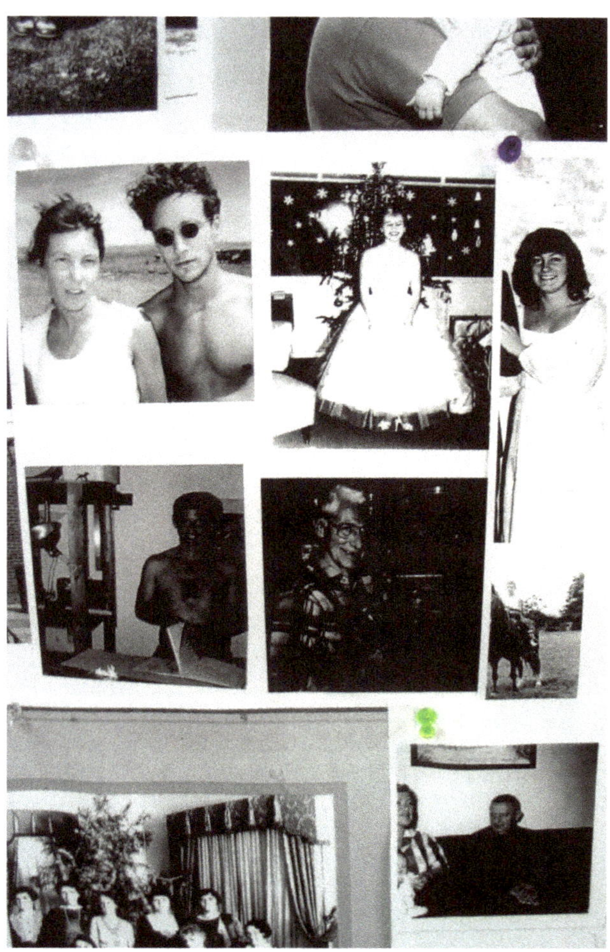

**Our City, Ourselves**, *1998, installation, Kemper Museum of Contemporary Art, Kansas City, Missouri.*

tion, Muriel McBrian Kauffman Foundation, Ewing Kauffman Foundation, Commerce Bank, and H&R Block Foundation.

He set up programming with the Kansas City Art Institute to train young artists to work in the community. He expanded the mission of Chameleon to provide creative opportunities to emerging and established artists, and poets. I worked closely with Merrill on this fantastic and historical non-profit and ensured the organization survived his illness. In 2018, we proudly handed Chameleon Arts off to the stunningly talented rising star, poet Samantha Slupski. Under her guidance, Chameleon focuses on bringing poetry to the people of Kansas City through workshops, features, outreach, slam and so much more.

This book is a survey of the studio and community work of Hugh Merrill from 1968 to 2011. Merrill's mantra is "I draw everyday," and he balances his role as an activist to work with amazing consistency in the privacy of his studio. His works have received numerous accolades and high recognition, including pieces in the collection of the Museum of Modern Art in New York.

A thread runs through his 50-year career of creating prints, drawings and paintings: his abstract and landscape forms seem to exist in a world of weightlessness, dislocation, and are inhabited by partly deteriorating structures of wood and stone.

He learned well the geometry of his mentors Al Held and Gabor Peterdi. Merrill sees mark making as the interplay of space and form shifting on the surface of the paper. The meaning the symbolic interpretation is secondary to the constant shift of planes and forms before the eyes of the viewer.

As a counterpoint to his studio investigations, Merrill's community work is based in time with an emphasis on social change. His projects, mostly aimed at high school aged, inner city youth either in the family court system or homeless, through schools and social service agencies. Merrill's goals are to advocate a space for youth to make sense of who and where they are and to provide creative outlets aimed at building self-esteem.

The methodologies include journaling, theatre,

dance, visual art and poetry to help youth build a foundation of successful experiences. Experiences that lead to daily creative exploration of their lives, renewed hope and conviction in their own ability to overcome racism, an economically unfair system and other issues faced by those most endangered by our present corporate capitalist system. The curricula he has developed has the potential to be life changing and can be assessed by its success on the young participants.

Consistent Divergencies: the studio and community work of Hugh Merrill is testament that the artist needs to both be deeply involved in the private world of their poetic studio life and simultaneously to be actively involved with their world at the street level.

Merrill's career is fashioned by an array of life and educational experience. From his family's southern racist political roots, his white privilege and access to politically powerful people to his stint as a homeless person in Baltimore. Merrill's varied life encompass his learning difficulties, bouts of depression and other struggles which are reflected in his art work and writings, reflecting a journey between imagery that reflects structural and social architecture and local and international culture.

Merrill's influence thrives in Kansas City as he mentors the street poets at Arts Bar, as he continues to nurture students at KCAI with his current foundations classes, and continues to work with mid-career artists. He encourages social practice, self expression and teaches the inestimable value of dedicated studio practice. His trickster humor, easy affability, expansive knowledge, and sense of ethics are a required course for any working artist.

*--Jeanette Powers*

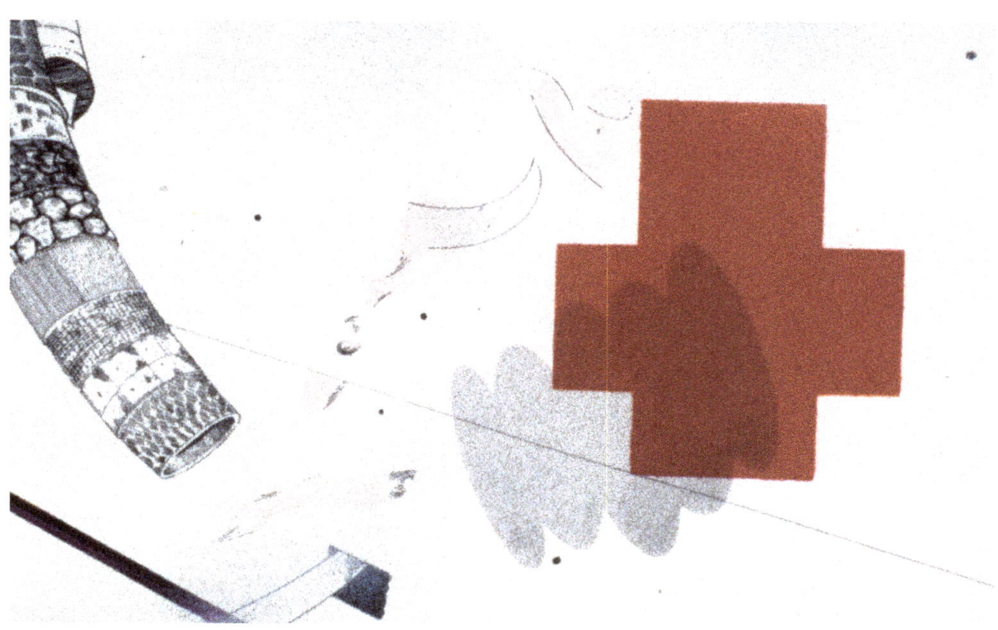

**Blood For** *(detail), 2005, collection of Jim and Molly Leedy.*

# Printmaking at the Edge

"Print is not an object, a technique, or a category, but it is a theoretical language of evolving ideas." This quotation, from Hugh Merrill's essay, *Educating the Next Generation of Printmakers*, can be seen as being central to his work both as a studio artist and as a community artist. He grew up in Washington, D.C. in the 1950s and '60s where his father worked in government, and was from an early age exposed to Democratic Party politics, meeting many of the major politicians of those decades. He studied art in Baltimore and at Yale, before going into teaching, moving to the Kansas City Art Institute in 1976 where he is now Professor of Printmaking and Community Arts. His broad vision of what art, and Printmaking in particular, can achieve has developed during his long career in the arts, beginning with the reductionist approach at Yale in the mid-1970s which revered artists such as Rothko, Sol Lewitt and Ellsworth Kelly, and moving on continuously from that beautiful but sterile point. Of the need to consider the changes in the art scene and the wider relevance and a deeper sense of engagement he now considers to be essential Merrill writes, "*Deconstructing Modernism* is asking art to take on new values and functions, asking for social content, communication and audience interaction."

Merrill's work as an educator is not limited to the Art Institute as he is also actively involved in community work, particularly in his close involvement with Chameleon, a multi-media arts project situated in a former factory in an industrial area of Kansas City.

The dynamic sense of vitality and creativity that runs through that centre is remarkable a is its production of dance, music and visual arts. He maintains a base in the centre because of his profound belief that his personal studio work and community projects are symbiotic. His work as a community artist began with having the opportunity to work with Christian Boltanski on a project at the Kemper Art Museum, a short distance from the Art Institute. This experience led to Merrill's *Portrait of Self* project in which community groups are guided in the production of "notebooks" that archive their recollections and experiences, so that they can be shared with and communicated to others. Through this approach, "art is no longer an activity; it is a method for children to learn, to think . . . freely, creatively, and critically about their world." He considers that instruction and education have very different functions–instruction to enable the development of skills and education to allow a process of thinking that leads to discovery.

In his personal work Merrill adopts a complex free-wheeling approach to the production of his "hybrid prints," which combine a wide variety of traditional and technological techniques. A typical sequence of processes might include a drawing on a zinc etching plate to produce an image which is then scanned into a computer and modified as part of a Photoshop® collage that is printed out on decal paper and adhered to a board. This is then altered first by the addition of screen-print and then again by the addition of further paper allowing the image to be drawn and painted into. In the artist's view the work remains a Print because his use of technology in the process allows him, 'to slow, stop, multiply, transform, produce variations and re-contextualise the image', techniques that are commonly used in Printmaking. This process is used in the *Columbia* series, in which photographic images from different periods are layered together to produce something like a movie that freezes time, allowing an "all-at-once-ness" experience of someone else's past, or like the fragments of fleeting landscape seen from a speeding train.

To come to a fuller appreciation of the dynamics within Hugh Merrill's personal work, or indeed his community work, requires an understanding of the importance he places on delay and variation, factors that are inherent in the Printmaking process. Delay comes between those moments of spontaneity that come with the stages in a drawing, or from a change of medium. It also comes from the need for reflection, and this in turn provokes the desire for variation and and progression in an enriching process of discovery.

*--Richard Noyce*

© *Richard Noyce, Printmaking at the Edge, 2006, A&C Black Publishers Ltd.*

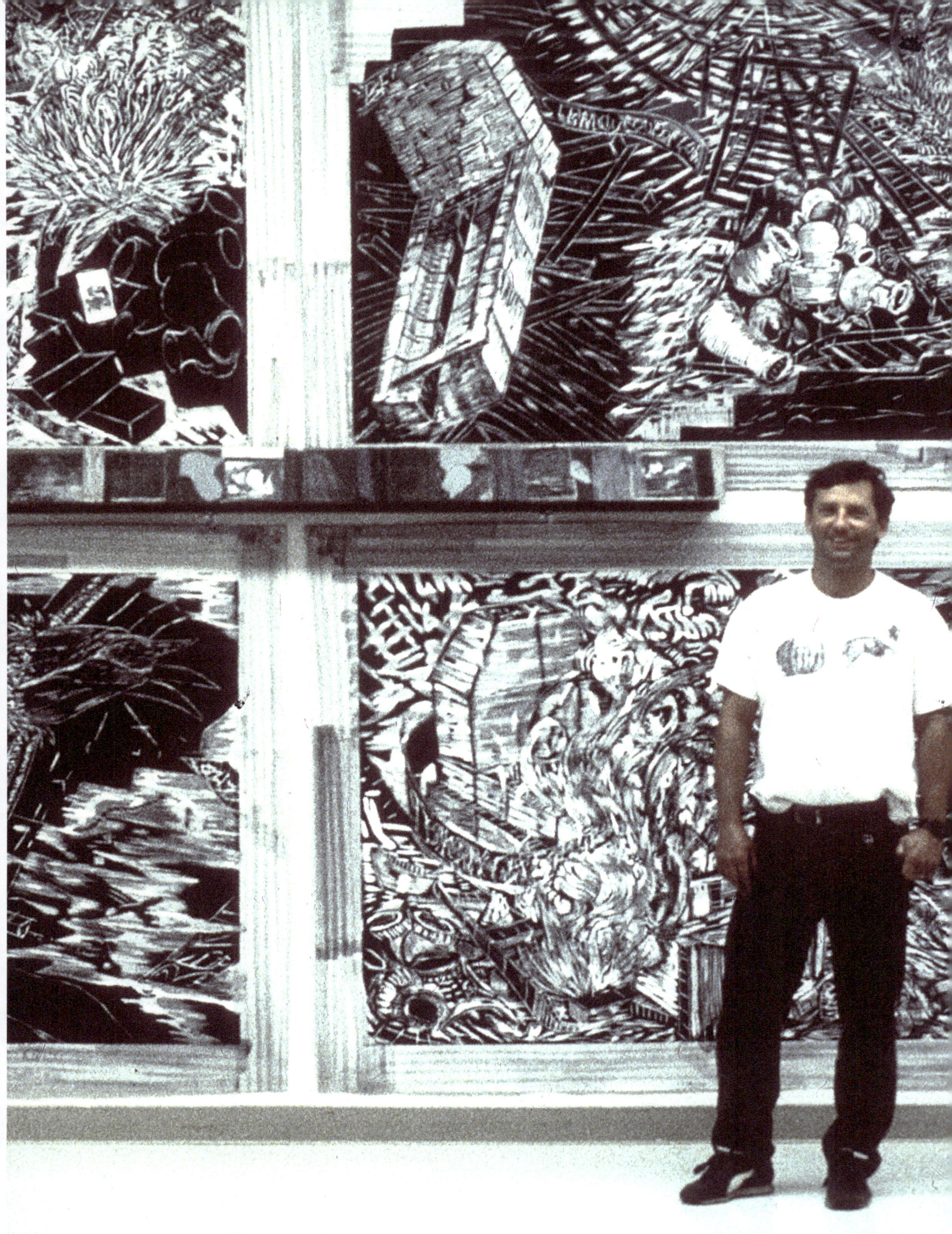

# Biography

Hugh Merrill began his artistic career in 1969 at the Maryland Institute College of Art in Baltimore, Maryland. Very quickly he found himself focused on printmaking, specifically working on etchings of the urban environment in the 1970's. He resisted the term landscape as a description of his work, feeling the term looked backward towards a time when the relationship between mankind and nature was dominated by romantic ideas of progress. Instead, Merrill referred to these etchings as real-estatescapes, a phrase meant to represent the dominance of society over nature. Nature had been divided up for the economic benefit of industrial corporations. Landscapes were for sale, and he wanted his prints and drawings to confront this reality. His early affinity for printmaking was due in part to an undiagnosed learning disability that made it extremely difficult for him to read. To his eyes, the white spaces of a page dominated the text and the entire page vibrated before him. He often saw words in reverse.

Not surprisingly, printmaking's reliance on the reversal of the drawn image became a natural area of investigation. He discovered a means to achieve his vision, and printmaking became his primary means of expression for the next four decades.

Within his first year at college, Merrill flunked out and ended up in Washington, D.C. as an office worker for Senator John Sparkman of Alabama. He returned to the Maryland Institute the following year and, despite continued academic difficulties, completed his undergraduate work and was accepted to Yale's School of Art & Architecture. While there, he studied with John Cage, Gabor Pederti, William Bailey, Alex Katz, Robert Motherwell, Al Held, and others, all of whom would have a profound impact on his thinking and work.

Merrill's early work was informed by the chaotic climate of the late 60's and early 70's, the rise of the environmental movement, the anti-war movement, and the struggle for civil rights. During this time, while coming to maturity as an artist, the art world viewed political imagery as illustrative and secondary to modernist abstract concerns. Like other artists of his generation, such as Louisa Chase, Judy Pfaff, and Jonathan Borofski, he searched for a personal narrative that could unlock the grip of minimalism and high modernism.

He sensed that his studio work, no matter how authentic, did not have a direct impact on the social and environmental concerns that interested him. He sought to balance his personal poetic studio voice with a more participatory process that involved disenfranchised communities. It was artists such as Joseph Beuys, Amalia Mesa-Bains, Felix Gonzalez-Torres, and Torres and David Hammons that helped Merrill define his work outside the traditional parameters of the studio artist. Their rejection of the commercial aesthetics of mainstream art production and their desire to reinvent art-making based on community values, social justice, and action provided a model for Merrill to move his own social justice instincts toward community art projects and social sculptures.

The underlying discourse for Merrill's work was fostered in childhood. He grew up in a political Yellow Dog Democratic family from Alabama caught between the Old South Jim Crow laws and the emerging fight for equality and cultural validation. His grandfather was a state judge and lieutenant governor of Alabama. His father worked with the Democratic Party advising Kennedy, Humphrey, and Johnson on agricultural issues. As the man in charge of peanuts at the Department of Agriculture in the 50's and early 60's, James Merrill would travel through the rural segregated south stopping in small towns where he gave talks on peanut allotments. His son often accompanied him on these trips and it was here the artist saw firsthand American apartheid, poverty, and the resilience of the African-American community.

After graduation from Yale University, Merrill taught at Wheaton College in Norton, Massachusetts before being hired to teach printmaking at the Kansas City Art Institute in 1976. Since then, Merrill has developed the printmaking program at the art institute into an internationally regarded undergraduate department. Merrill applied an educational concept

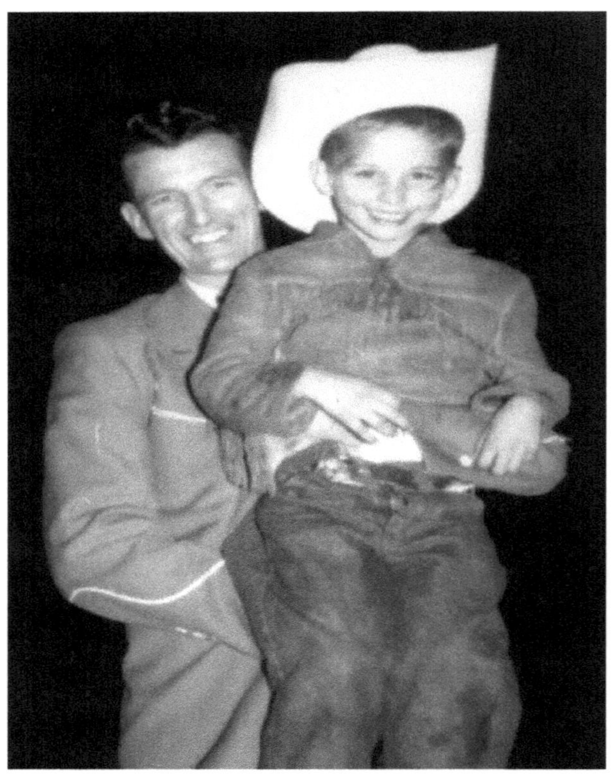

*The artist with country music singer, 1954, family photograph.*

that focused on the investigation of both traditional print processes and new conceptual territory. The students' competency flows between etching, lithography, relief printing and the use of new forms of print reproduction and print output. Undergraduate work is marked by an ability to explore a personal voice while navigating between consumer product creation, installation exhibits, and high and low cultural interactions to discover new artistic pathways.

During the late 1980's Merrill focused on sequential etching suites that had a social underpinning. The *Lucky Dragon Suite*, exhibited at the Nelson Atkins Museum of Art in 1985, and the Rosa Luxemburg and Raoul Wallenberg suites, exhibited at Printworks Gallery in Chicago. He became concerned that his prints and studio work were not having the direct impact on society he had been striving for. He began reading the writings of Lucy Lippard, Suzanne Lacy, Suzi Gablik, and the work of Tim Rollins and the Kids of Survival. These writers and artists laid out the belief that art strives for local context and cultural authenticity. This idea asks for art to come from the fabric of community and requires it be made within this context. Artists collect, listen, and collaborate before they create. After traveling to Poland, photographing and drawing in Krakow and Auschwitz, Merrill returned determined to begin a series of community arts actions. He saw the importance of continuing his studio work in a new light, one that balanced his studio vision with social actions.

In 1996, Merrill worked with the Kemper Museum as a visiting artist in conjunction with the Christian Boltanski exhibition *So Far*. He and Boltanski collaborated on the citywide community artwork *Our City, Ourselves*. With the help of designer Bruce McIntosh, Merrill created a tabloid publication insert in the Sunday Kansas City Star inviting the public to bring their family photographs and personal archives to the museum where they could pin them to the walls. Soon the gallery was filled from floor to ceiling with thousands of photocopies of family pictures and letters. The museum was in effect turned over to the local populace. The installation not only celebrated their lives, but served to render them insignificant through careful placement outside a familiar context.

In conjunction with the exhibit Merrill also created *Portrait of Self*, an arts and educational project to help young people process the many influences that create their sense of self. It is an archive of drawings, poetry, writing, photography, and other artistic practices collected in journal form. Since its inception, Merrill has gone on to use *Portrait of Self* in community arts projects in national and international locations including: Dania Beach, Florida; Sydney, Australia; and Dublin, Ireland. Other stops for the program include Colorado Springs, Colorado; Pittsburgh, Pennsylvania; and Portland, Oregon.

Building on these experiences, Merrill helped transform Chameleon Theatre, a small not-for-profit whose mission was to create dramatic plays about youth experience, into a broader Arts and Youth Development agency. Chameleon utilizes theater, hip-hop dance, and visual arts to transform the lives of homeless and at-risk kids. Merrill views himself as a social sculptor and does not see a divide between his continued printmaking and drawing efforts and his work as a community artist and director of an arts agency. In the past five years, Chameleon Arts and Youth Development has raised over 1 million dollars for community art and arts educational projects for homeless and at-risk youth communities in the urban core. Chameleon has also become a resource for small arts agencies including: StoneLion Puppet Theatre, I Am U Entertainment, Gospilunifics, Esoke African Drumming, Lewis Scenic Design, Happy Feet Dance, The Arts Incubator, and others.

Merrill's work as a community artist continues to grow and change with each new opportunity. In 2005, he was invited to produce a community arts action for the Impact Conference in Berlin, Germany and Poznan, Poland. The project, *Pools of Belief*, consisted of graphics of children's swimming pools laid out in a public square and filled with images of mousetraps shaped like boats. Trailing from the traps were narrow sheets of paper with the text "I believe in the New York Stock Exchange" and other statements. The public was asked to participate by writing their own answers to the phrase "I believe in . . . " on a narrow sheet of paper, which they then attached to the work. *Pools* has gone on to be exhibited at the Dalarnas Museum for the Falun Print Triennial in Falun, Sweden; Colorado College; and the National Conference of Environmental Educators.

Most recently, Merrill has worked with Director Staci Pratt of the Office of Homeless Liaison, Kansas City Kansas Public Schools, to facilitate a number of community arts projects, including *Faces of the Homeless*. *Faces* was a collaboration with Patrick Moonasar and Matt Hilger which produced a series of posters of homeless children showing not their need but their value. Merrill says "They are simply amazing and resilient children, no different on the surface than any child in any school. They represent not want but possibility and opportunity." *Faces of the Homeless* has been exhibited nationally, including at the conference for the National Association of Educators of Homeless Children and Youth in Washington, D.C. in 2008.

Since his introduction to printmaking Merrill has become a leader in the international printmaking community and has written articles on the redefinition of art, printmaking and education. Merrill has taught and lectured on printmaking at over 75 universities, colleges and schools worldwide. He collaborated with Doug Baker and Dan Younger in Kansas City to open Squadron Press in the 1970's, one of the first art businesses and studios in the now famous Kansas City Crossroads Arts

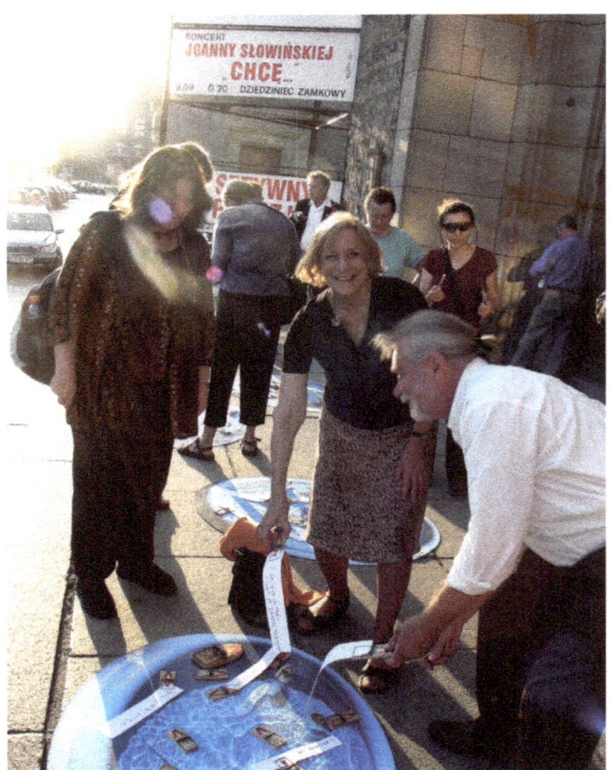


**Pools of Belief**, *2005, digital print installation, 4'x4', Poznan, Poland.*

District. In 2008 he was invited by the Nelson Atkins Museum to curate the print exhibition, *Print Lovers at Thirty*, in recognition of the Nelson Print Society and the contribution of George McKenna, long time print and photography curator for the museum.

Merrill has been a speaker at numerous conferences including: The College Art Association, The Southern Graphics Council (of which he was president in the early 1990's), and The National Association of Educators of Homeless Children and Youth. He has been awarded a number of grants, including a regional NEA grant, a Melon Foundation award, and a Yaddo Fellowship. In 2007 he received the distinguished education award from the Southern Graphics Council. His artwork has been exhibited internationally and collected by major

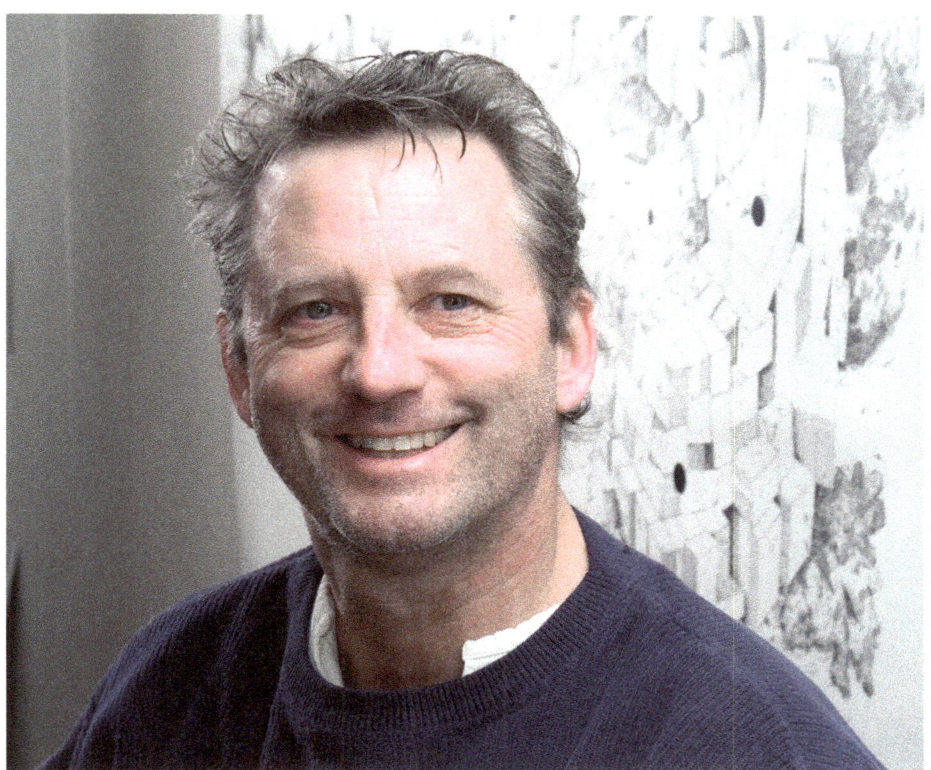

*Hugh Merrill, 2005.*

museums including: The Museum of Modern Art, the Daum Museum, the Harvard Art Museums, the Cranbrook Museum, the Minneapolis Museum of Art, and the Nelson Atkins Museum of Art.

Merrill has a long history of community involvement in Kansas City. He was president of the Kansas City Jewish Museum Foundation in the late 1990's, and has been an artist invited on Kansas City Medical Missions trips to the Philippines, Guatemala, and Cuba. He presently works with Soulfari Kenya, a social services organization building an orphanage in western Kenya. Merrill is on the board of United Inner City Services, working to use the arts in early childhood development, and he is on the steering committee of Inkubator Press at the Arts Incubator, an organization that assists emerging artists in finding and developing their artistic voices. Merrill continues to work with other artists and small arts agencies to bring arts events and programming to not-for-profit social service agencies.

*--Rebekah Callaway, 2011*

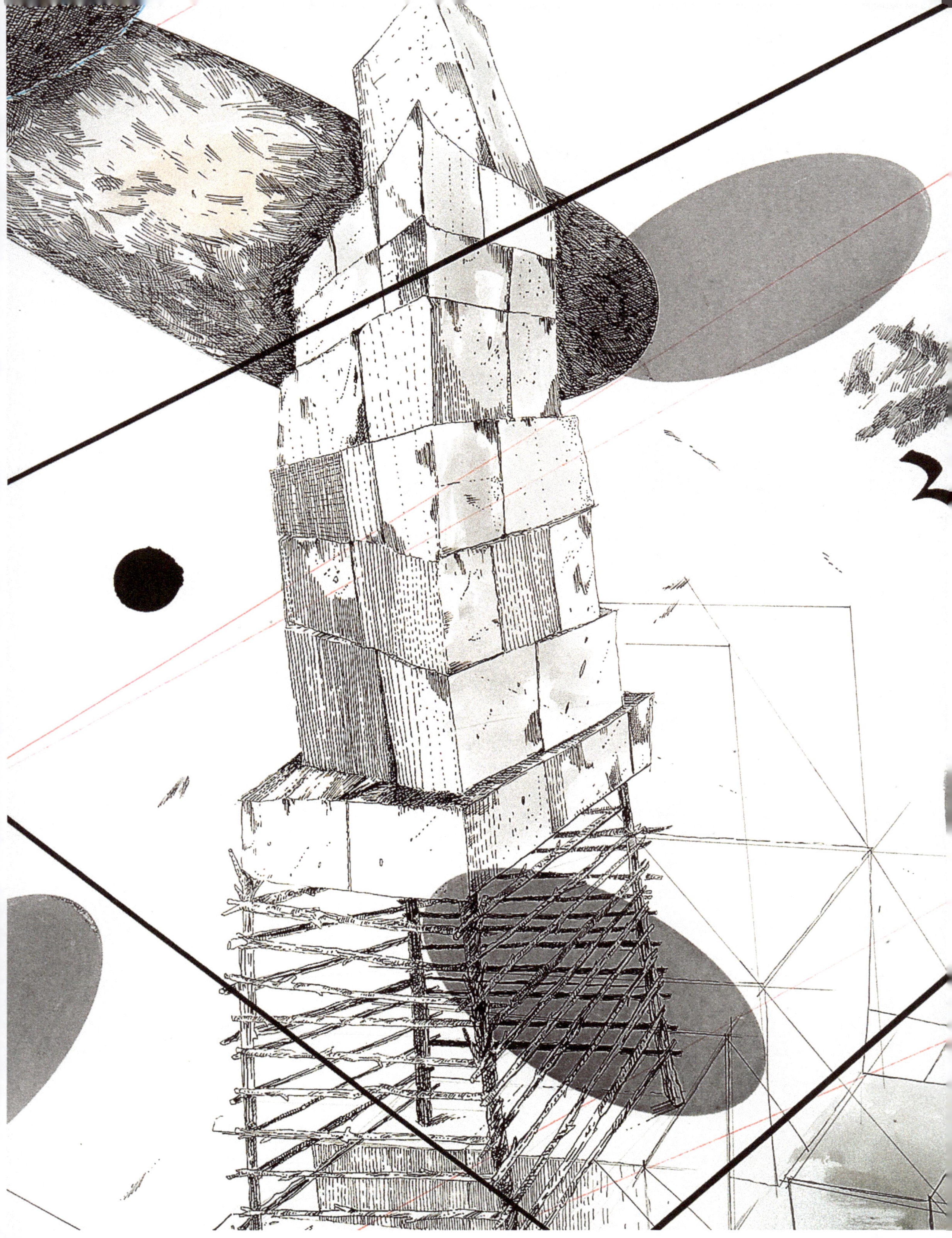

# Studio Art
## Introduction

Walking into Hugh Merrill's studio one has no where to sit. I choose the bicycle near the wall and rock the bike a bit back and forth while he patters about holding up various historical relics. A Spanish Mask, a folded and beaten up, beautiful print by his son, Emmett Merrill. A print of a false cover for Salman Rushdie's "The Satanic Verses" which Merrill admits to having never read. There are tables everywhere, with either pieces in process or mounds of pens, paints, nibs and brushes. There are drawers upon drawers of a life-time of original art pieces which he takes little account of, it's all about the new work to Merrill.

The back wall hangs his newest series, where he connects thin wood "canvases" of various sizes together with metal tackle. The large centerpiece has out-croppings, sort of growths emerging from its sides. This feels like a natural progression for Merrill's work he has always put the substrate of the artwork as a central aspect. In this series, he's glued dress pattern parcel paper to the wood and draws over the fine and distinctive brown of the clothing guides. His method of mark-making rules here as it does through so much of his history.

Merrill engages with images and ideas with a spirit of fluidity. Images emerge and disappear, their unraveling becomes a binding agent.  Objects, forms, and passages of drawing exist in a space that is variable and unfixed. The same objects appear in multiple contexts. The forms are in a continual state of motion and change. Their relationships are in a constant slow flux reflecting our own changing lives, times, and culture.

Merrill's complex prints and drawings communicate this deeper sense of knowing through an interaction between narrative, form, light, representation and abstraction. His interests are both intuitive and analytical, providing the works with tension, fluidity, and passage. There is no simple reading of the work provided to us by the artist, but hints abound of a more truthful and profound world of moving exchanges and transitory readings. He makes essay of ambiguity without ever leaving the seminal impact of the work on the mind's eye and the heart's ear.

*--Jeanette Powers*

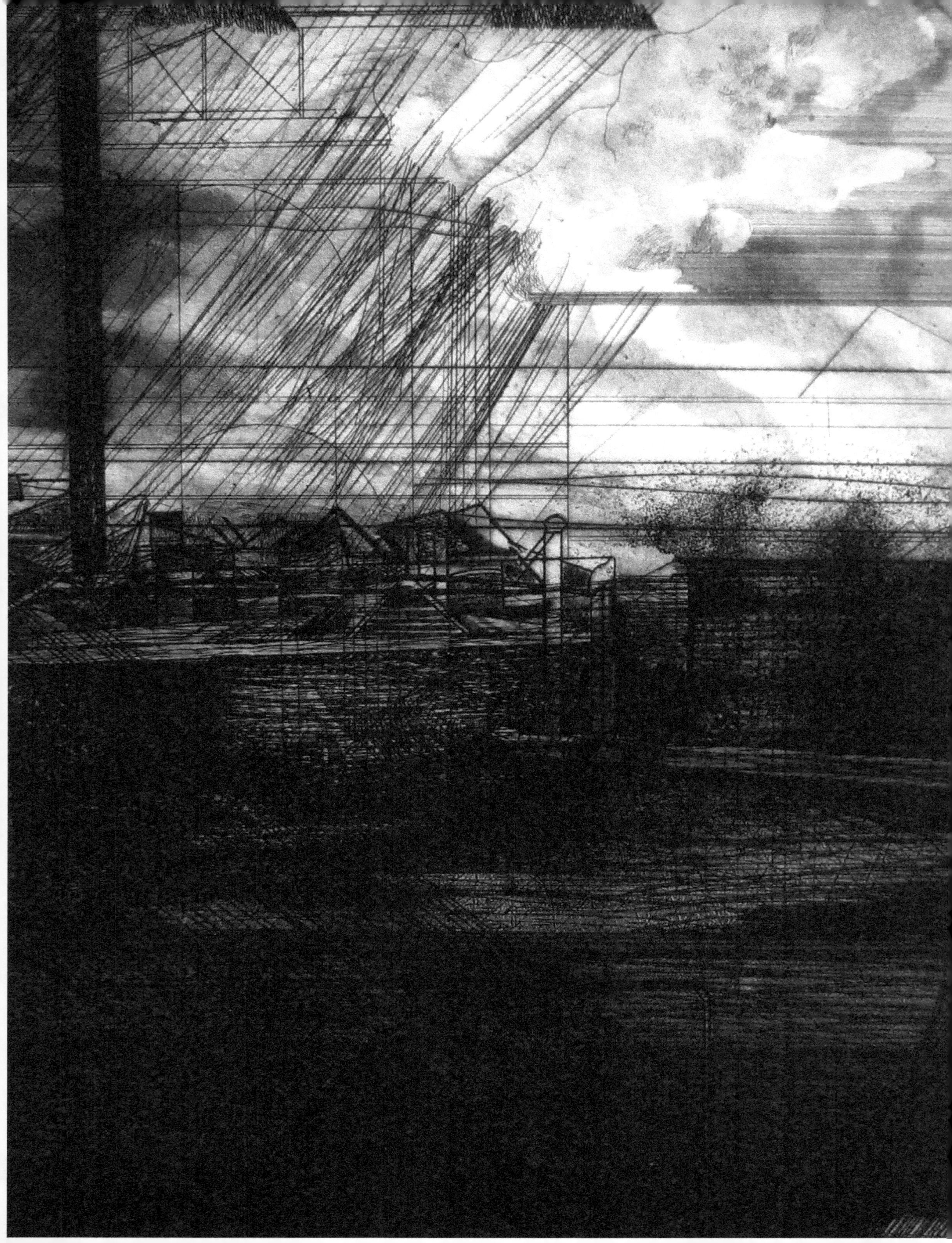

# **Etching**

Merrill says, "I do not believe that a creative journey is chosen by the individual but that the artist is chosen by the opportunity."

His southern background and inherent gregariousness didn't foreshadow becoming a printmaker. If anything, this natural storyteller is late to writing and poetry. But when he first started making etchings, the natural image-maker in him was inspired and activated and his natural, slightly disconnected manner of working caused printmaking to resonate with his intuition. As Merrill's work progressed, he found the pieces expressing his interior, subconscious voice. Through the relationship between the media and process he found a way to not only deepen his relationship with his art, but with his essential self: through recursively becoming, vibrant imagination, and an unthinking fearlessness. He describes this how the work evolved:

*"The work was outside of my control and I would be forced to respond to the material as it evolved independently of my influence."*



From Merrill's earliest engagements with studio practice, he was fascinated with the substrate. He found the etching plate and began explorations of its potential with mark-making, always with an eye towards challenging the academic infatuation with modernism and abstract expressionism.

He encounters the etching process and sees each moment in the plate's lifespan as a moment of art which has evolved into his sequential etching series. Merrill's early studio work, including the etching *Exedra and Baltimore Walker* (1969), is a quiet start to developing pictorial space of flowing time where object and subject become one and interchange in complex spatial and time relations. His work for decades has underlying themes of space, linear form, construction and deconstruction.

In 1970, he produced a series of landscape etchings and drawings seen from the inside of gigantic industrial areas looking out to an abandoned horizon. The images are reminiscent of America's growing Rust Belt, with its closing of steel factories in the 1970's.

In 1975, Merrill produced the series *Objects* which previews many of his ongoing concerns in the future work. *Object 1* cuts the industrial forms from their surroundings but retains quality of light, reflection and shadow. The shapes are cut from the visual plane and become elementary building blocks for a world that no longer exists. They have a combination of organic natural light on minimalist forms that are unfolding, patterned and flat yet projective and three dimensional.

This interest in the multiplication of the truth, flat shapes that turn to 3D forms and back have continued in his work for decades. Instability, change and transience remain a concern of his most recent drawings and paintings.

In the 1980's, Merrill focused almost entirely on prints, etchings, producing multiple series of sequential etchings, leading to his first museum exhibition at the Nelson-Atkins Museum of Art in Kansas City, Missouri: *The Lucky Dragon Suite*, 1986 (detailed in Chapter 3).

Merrill was not interested in the traditional use of the print matrix to produce editions but the sequential variation of an image by changing the matrix, the zinc plate, on a daily basis producing a series of related single images or monotypes. *The Lucky Dragon Suite* led to a continuation of the method of monotype image making as series of variations that would go on for over 5 years titled *The Facts of Fiction*. Merrill's commentary about the work was captured in an interview with artist Jim Leedy:

*"The destruction and distortion of the construct (plate) through the process of the acid attacking the metal is both the entropy that causes decay in all things and the reclamation of the natural process over the built environment."*

The process is one of ongoing construction and destruction informed by his early meetings with John Cage and Allen Ginsberg. Their Zen spiritual and philosophical interest relating to the creative process had a deep effect on Merrill. Merrill saw that as soon as an image is printed from the plate, the plate can then be reworked and changed. Leaving a ghost image of the previous workings, keeping underlying marks and broken bits of images from the prior state.

Another inspiration for many elements of Merrill's visual style is *Christ Crucified between the Two Thieves: Large Oblong Plate (The Three Crosses) State III*, produced by Rembrandt in 1653. This is an early example of a print produced in various states. Merrill's multiple state changes initiate the same type of philsophical questioning as beat poets, Zen masters and the Pope himself.

The plates are deeply etched and the edges are ripped lines of metal, the paper is lucky to survive the printing without ripping. The drawing, scraping away, grinding of the metal and redrawing the prints take on a ghostly greyness like a disturbing dream about issues important but not easily remembered. Each image slips and move before the viewer's eyes and the destination uncertain but frightening. Merrill says:

*"The slowness of printmaking begins with the mark, a physical gesture, drawn forcefully on the plate. The plate has to be placed in an acid bath where the length of time and the potency of the acid make the final determination as to the depth and tone of the drawn mark. Etching on a metal plate provides a durable, sculptural surface that can take a great deal of physical manipulation."*

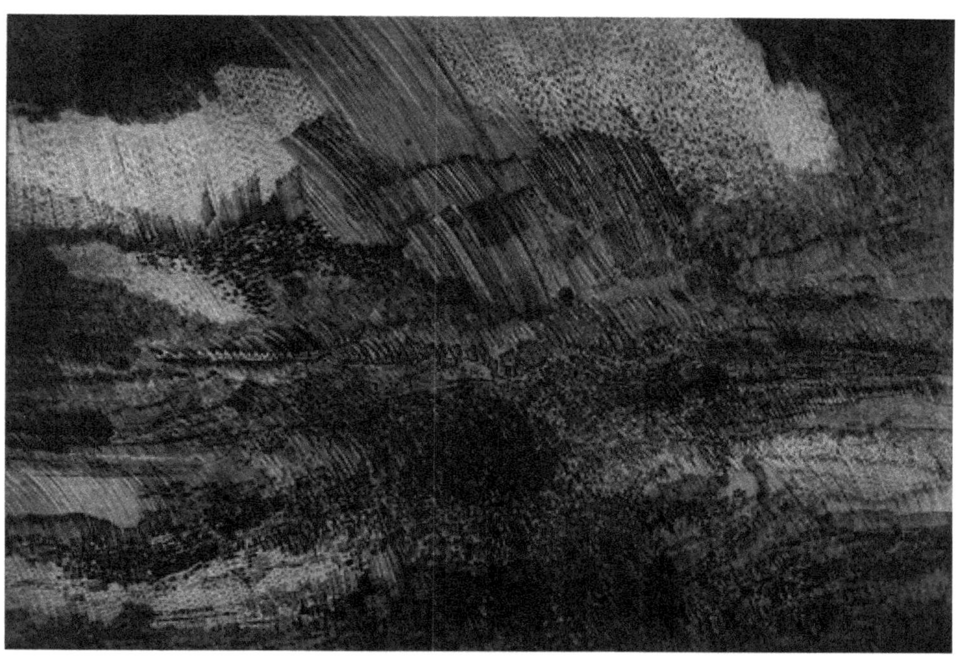

*Gabor Peterdi,* **Angry Sky***, 1959, etching, Rosenwald Collection, image courtesy National Gallery of Art, Washington, D.C.*

Monotypes with these extreme changes in the surface of the zinc plate are physical achievement. Hours of scraping, grinding, burnishing and drawing combine to create images outside of the rational self. It is as if Merrill wills the image into being rather than drawing it. The work is a physically exhausting experience for the maker and often for the viewer. One always sees the ghost of the past in the next image in the series, but then one is quickly drawn on to the next iteration of the sequence to the next stage as the eyes constantly move into the future while confronting the present and remnants of the past.

After 20 years of intense focus on etching, Merrill's work from the mid 1990's to the 2000's went through a number of quick and startling changes. His use of monotypes and sequence led to a reductionist strategy of image making and he broke out of this self-directed confinement with exhibitions in Chicago at the Print Works Gallery of relief monoprints. Then Merrill went on to produce mural-sized works exhibited at the Cranbrook Museum in Bloomfield Hills Michigan; The Davenport Museum of Art in Iowa; and the Works Festival in Edmonton, Alberta Canada.

He moved from printing large 4' x 8' sheets of birch plywood and plastic to cutting them into shapes and exhibiting the forms as the works of art. The matrix had become the art work and the printed image was pushed aside.

Merrill exhibited "*Life Cycles,*" a series featuring large cut forms of running, female figures being pursued by male heads at the Santa Barbara Contemporary Art Forum in California, curated by Ruth Weisberg in 1994. He was then invited to fill a ten-story glass pyramid the City Hall in Edmonton,

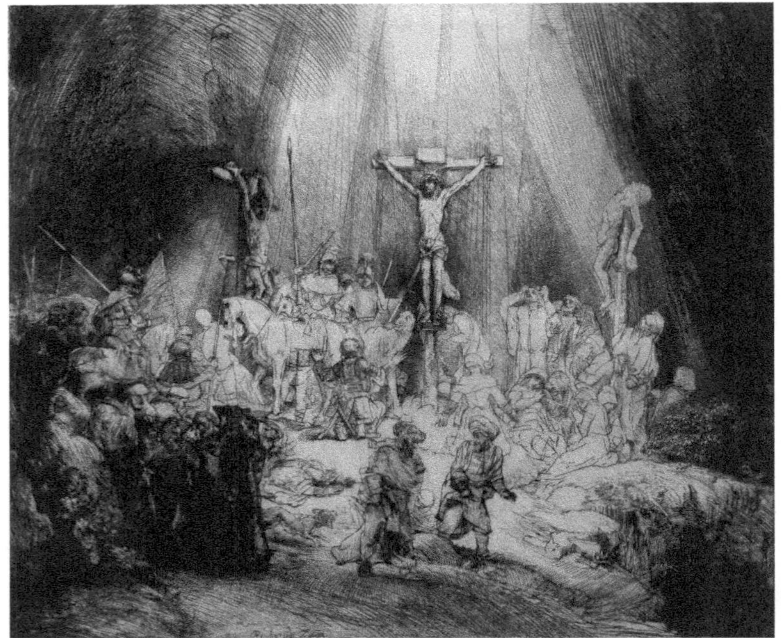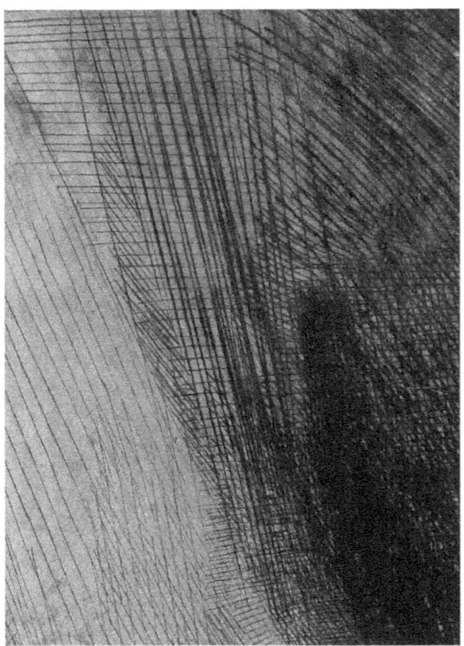

*Rembrandt Harmenszoon van Rijn,* **Christ Crucified between the Two Thieves:  Large Oblong Plate (The Three Crosses),** *1653, etching, State III, image courtesy Rijksmuseum, Amsterdam, The Netherlands.*

Alberta Canada with doubled armed running, eight-foot-tall female figures made of plastic and copper. The running figures spiraled up from the second to the 8th floor and were visible from both inside and out.

The installations merged easily with his dedication to community and public art projects. He became focused on the other, going beyond his own voice to give others a voice in their communities and in the art world. His development of the arts and social service agency Chameleon allowed him access to communities and funding to stage long term community arts actions.

There is a syllogism between Merrill's examination of the matrix object and his extensive working with the community in social practice: in both situations Merrill puts the emphasis on the element which binds, the experience. This is his great vision, creating art which is not merely an end unto itself, but a deeply engaging conversation with itself and the world of which its born. His examinations and celebrations of process are born from that naive curiosity which are the hallmark of his character.

Through mark-making, Merrill makes his mark.

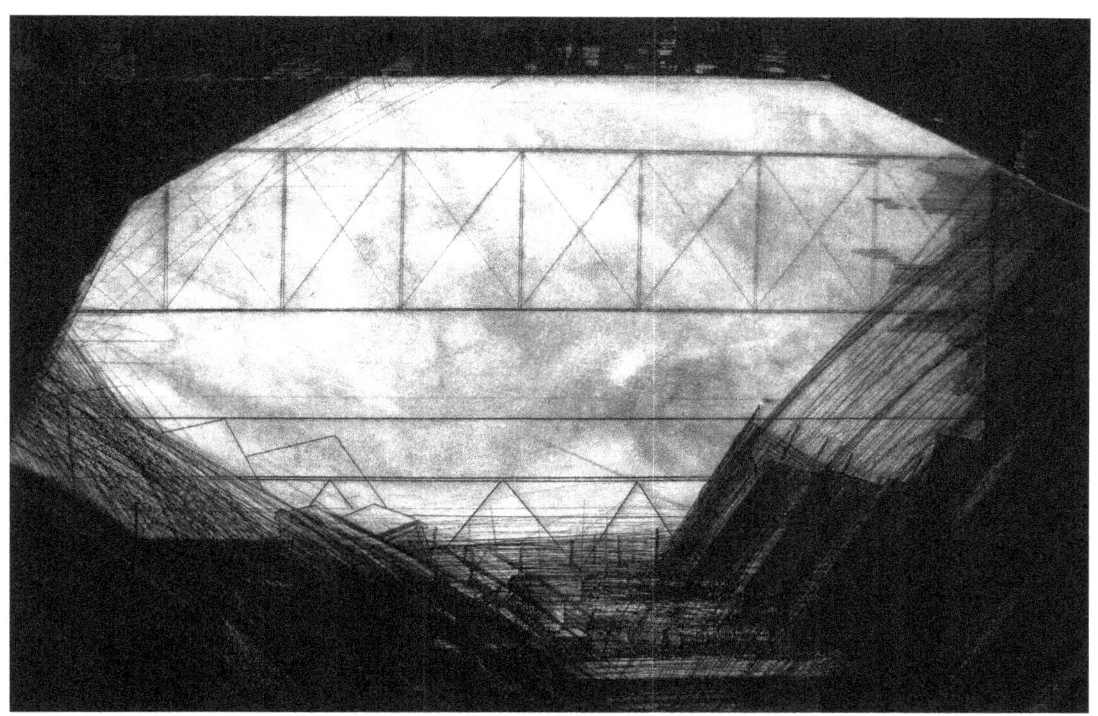

**Elm Street**, *from* **Western Garden Suite**, *1972-1985, etching, 18"x24", collection of the artist.*

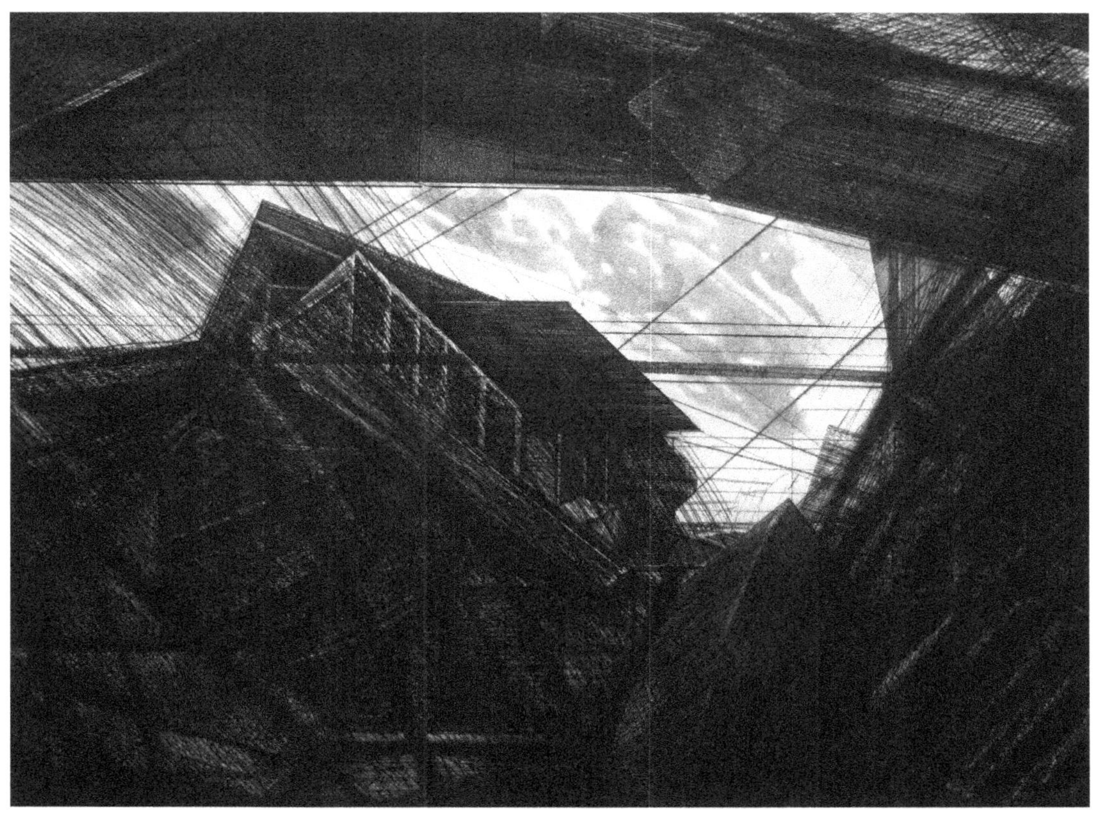

**Seminary Forest**, *from* **Western Garden Suite**,*1972-1985, etching, 18"x24", collection of the artist.*

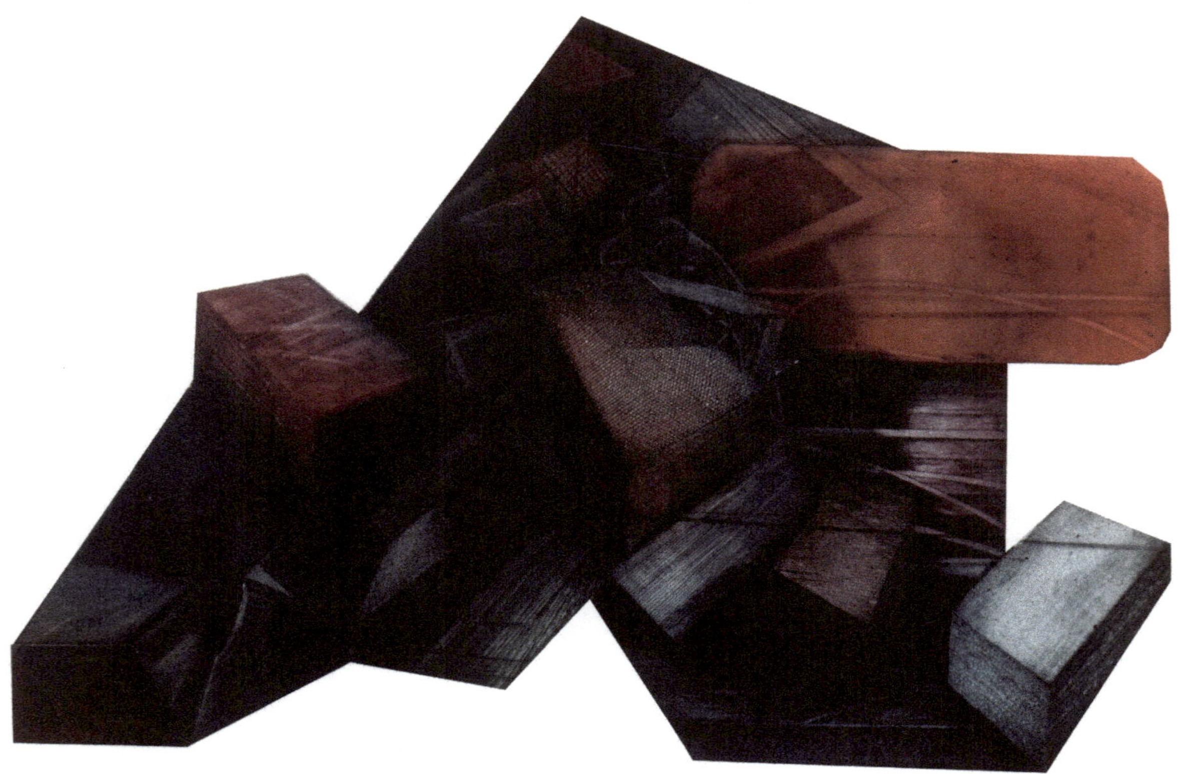

**Object 1**, *1975, etching, 18"x24", collection of the artist.*

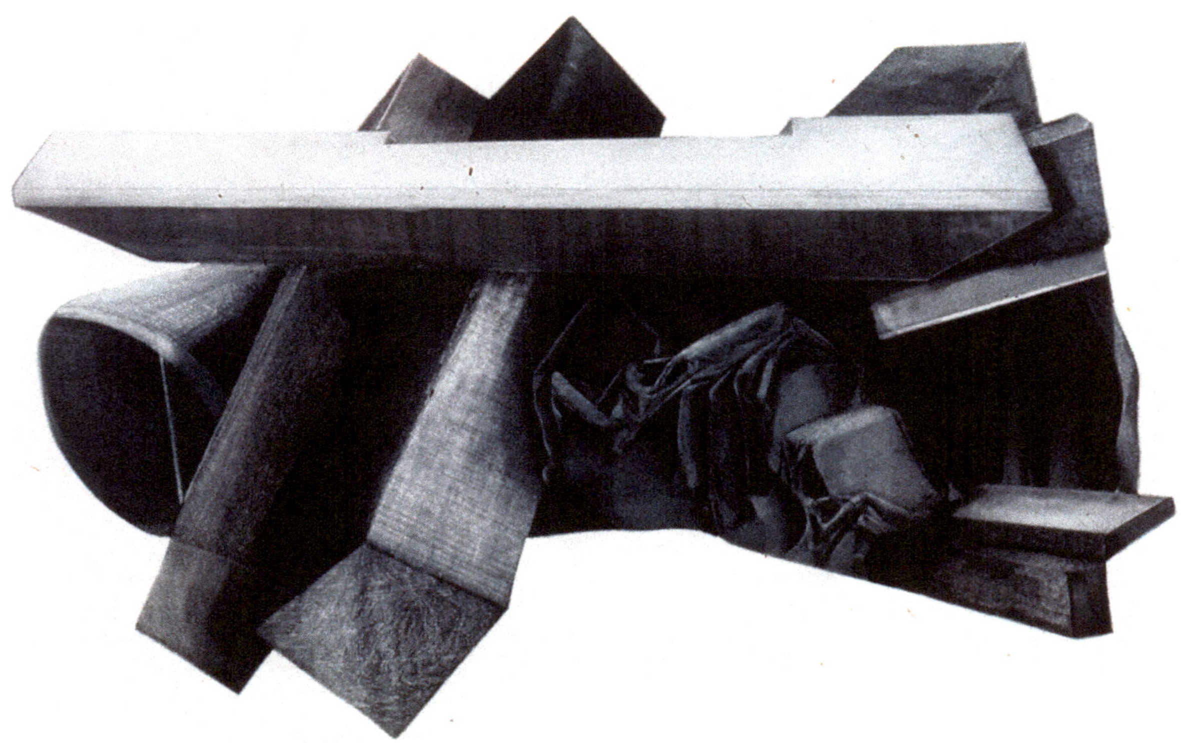

**Object 2**, *1975, etching, 18"x24", collection of the artist.*

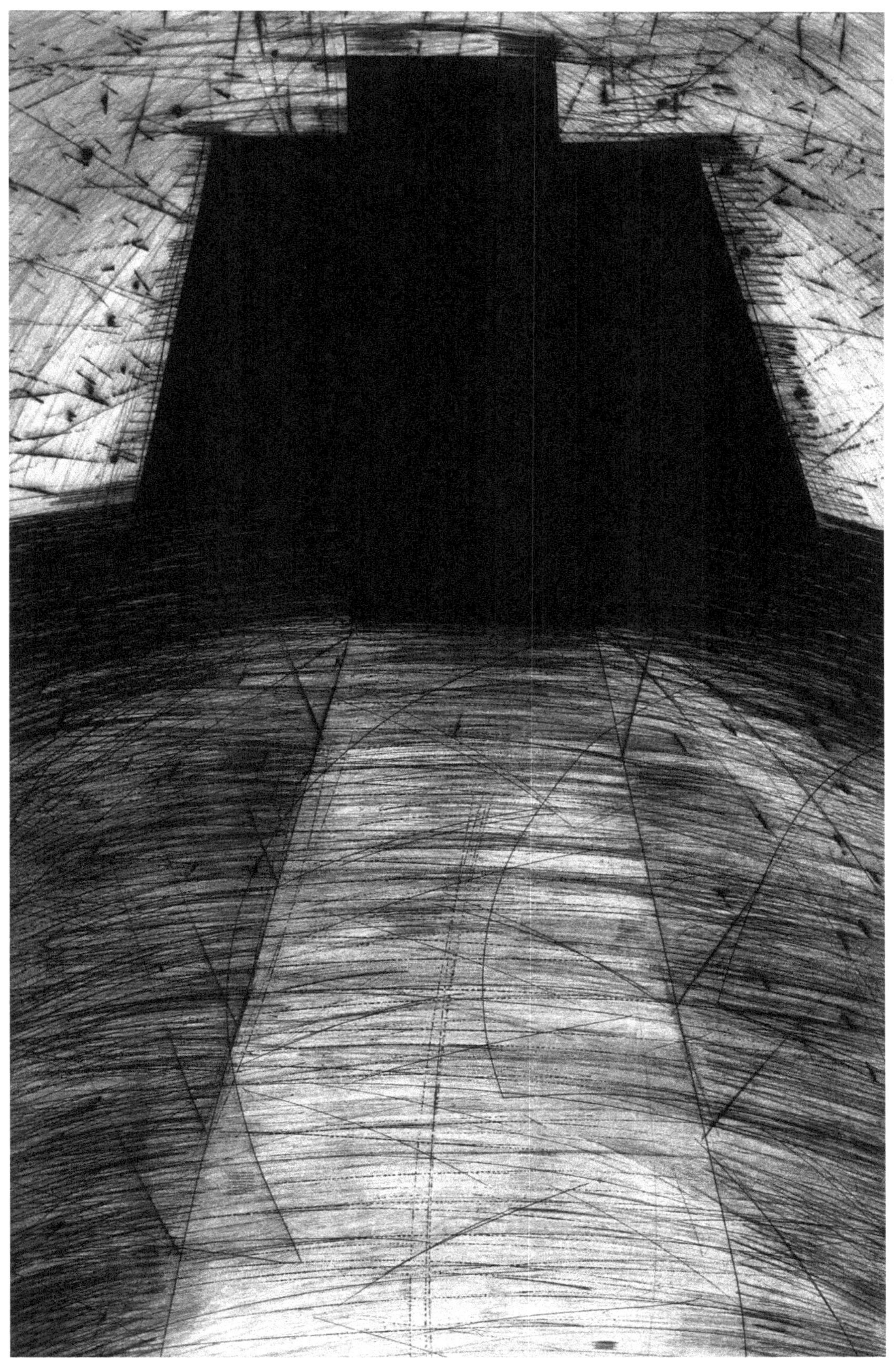

**Mall**, *1985, etching, 36"x24", collection of the artist.*

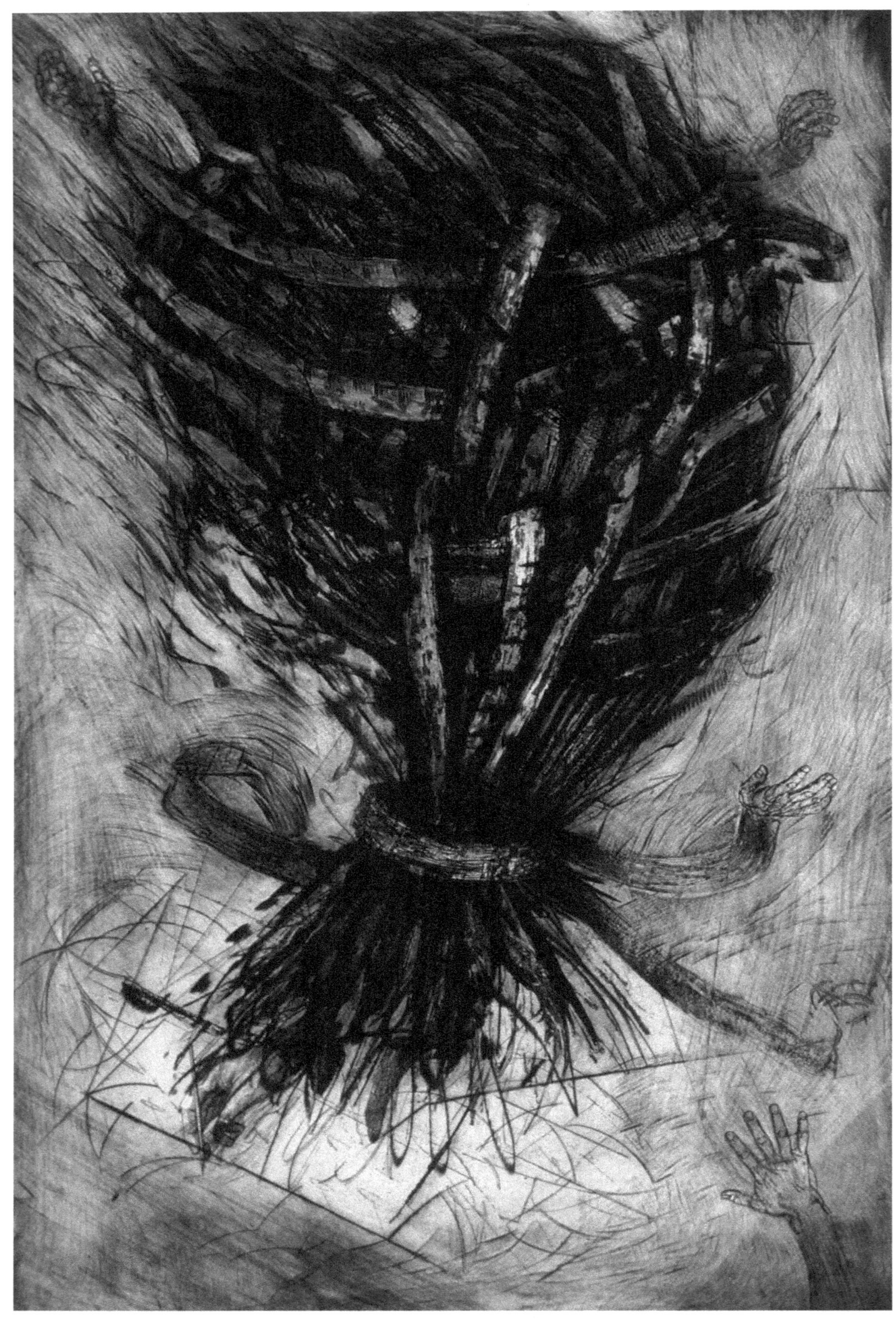

*From **Facts of Fictions Suite**, 1989-1996, sequential etching, 36"x24", collection of the artist.*

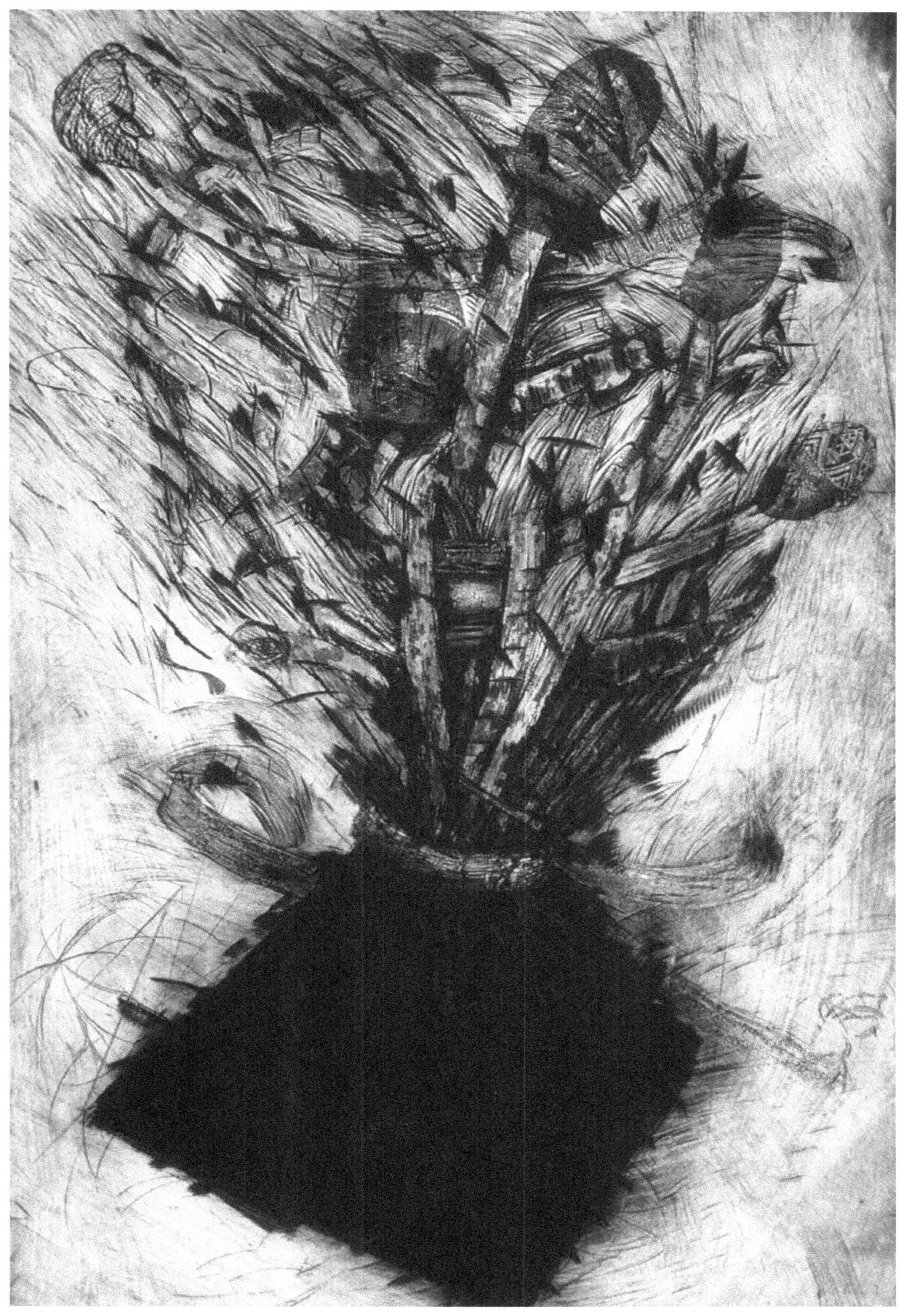

*From **Facts of Fictions Suite**, 1989-1996, sequential etching, 36"x24", collection of the artist.*

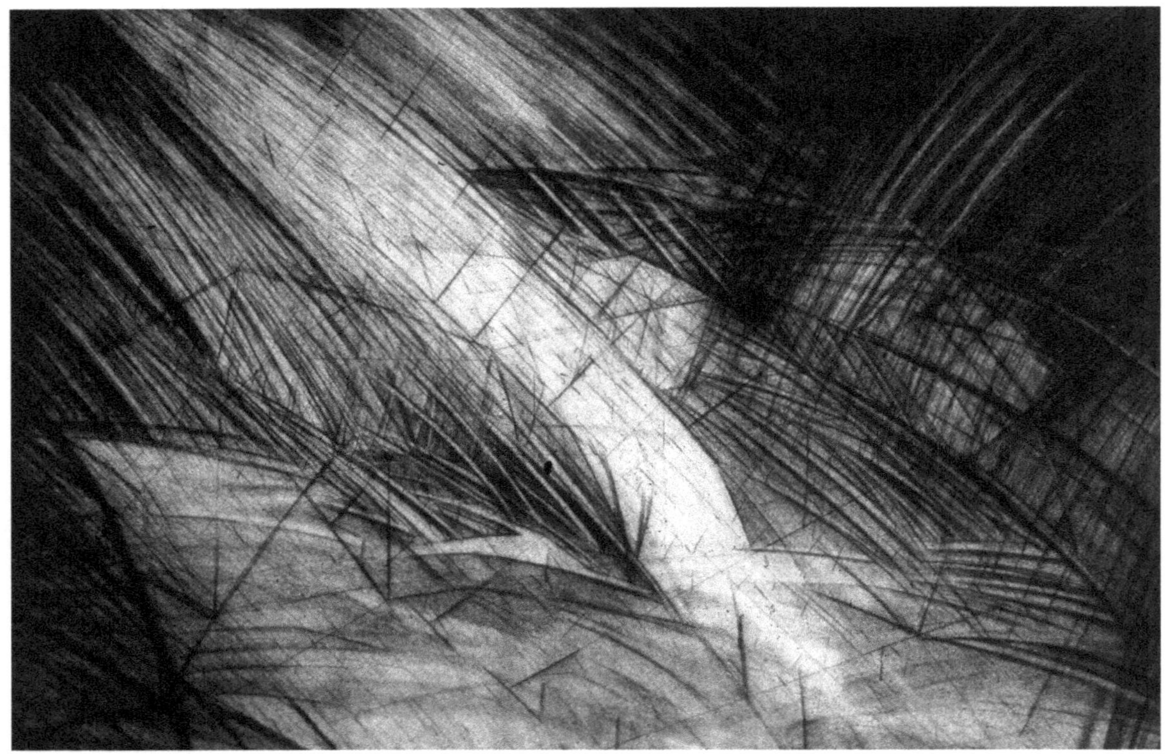

**Sacred**, *1985, etching, 18"x24", collection of the artist.*

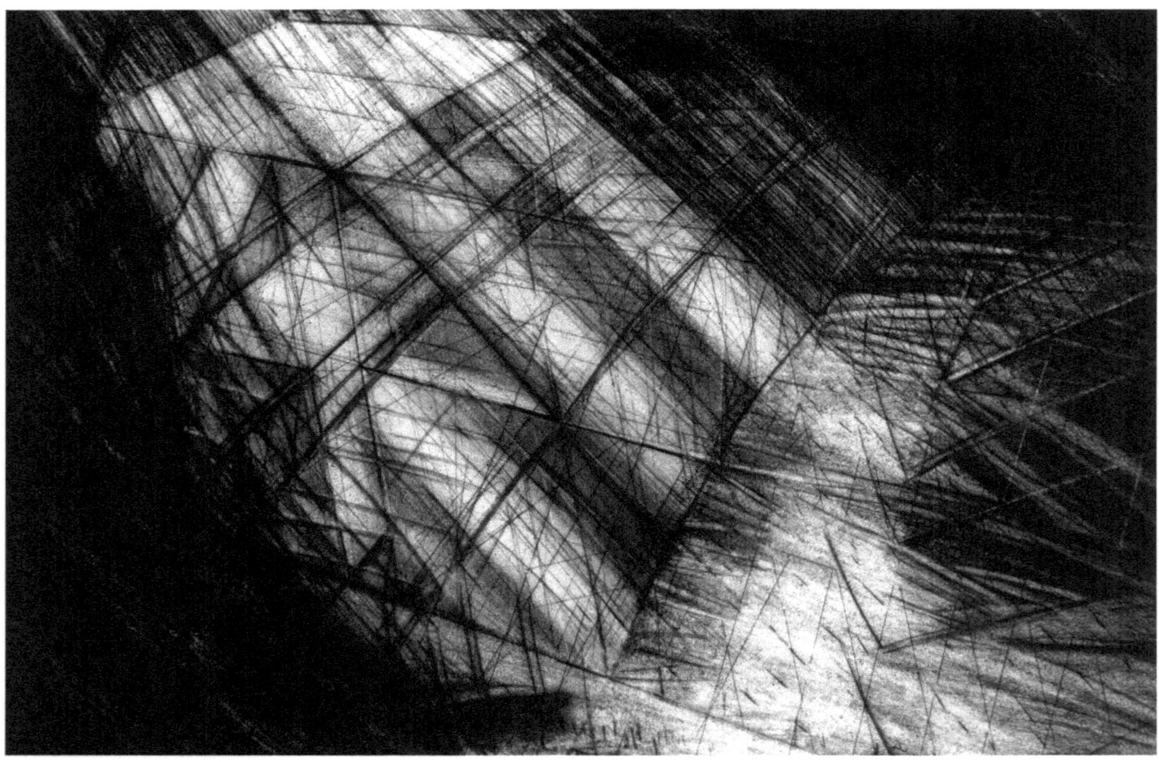

**Profane** *(detail), 1985, etching, 18"x24", collection of the artist.*

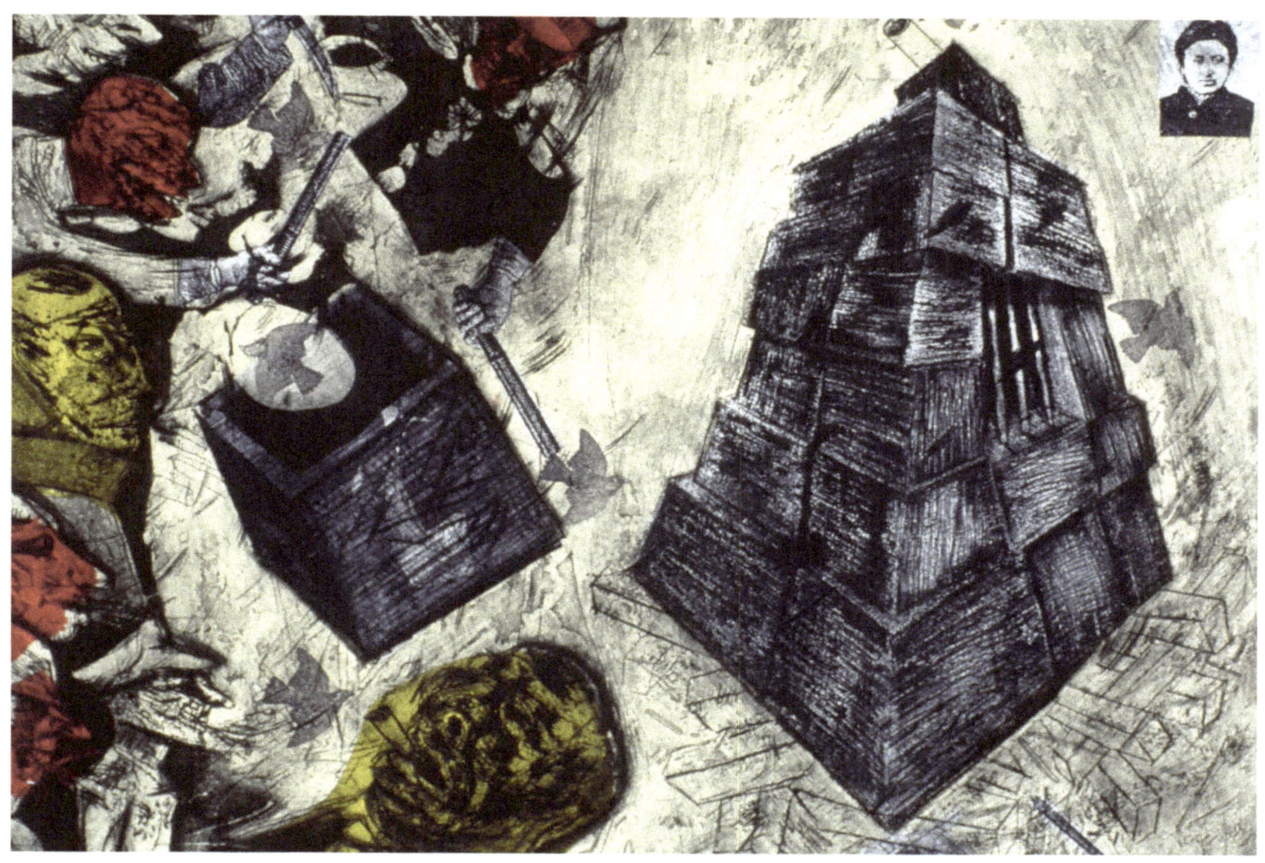

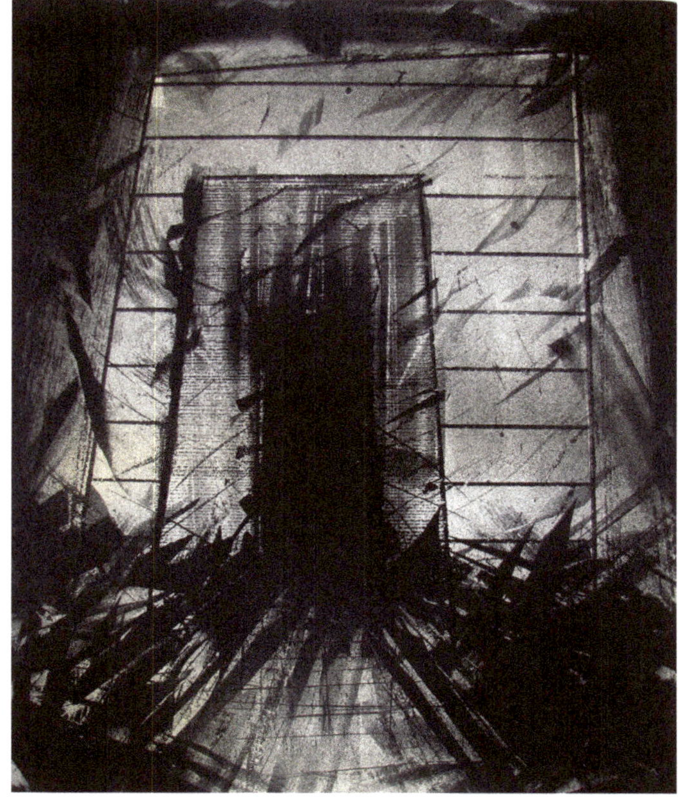

Top:  From **Rosa Luxemborg Suite**, 1992, sequential etching, 16"x20", collection of the artist.

Right: **Physician of Memory,** 1989, vitreograph, 20"x16", collection of the artist.

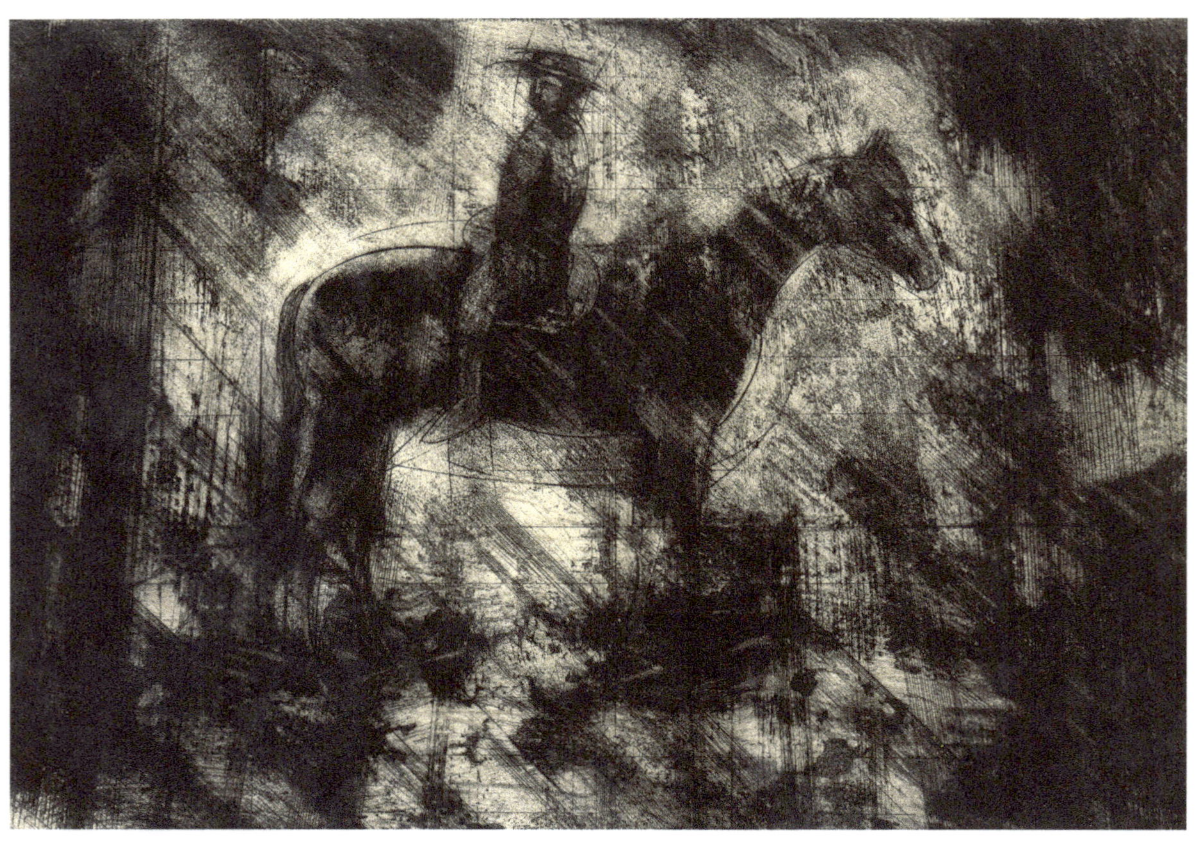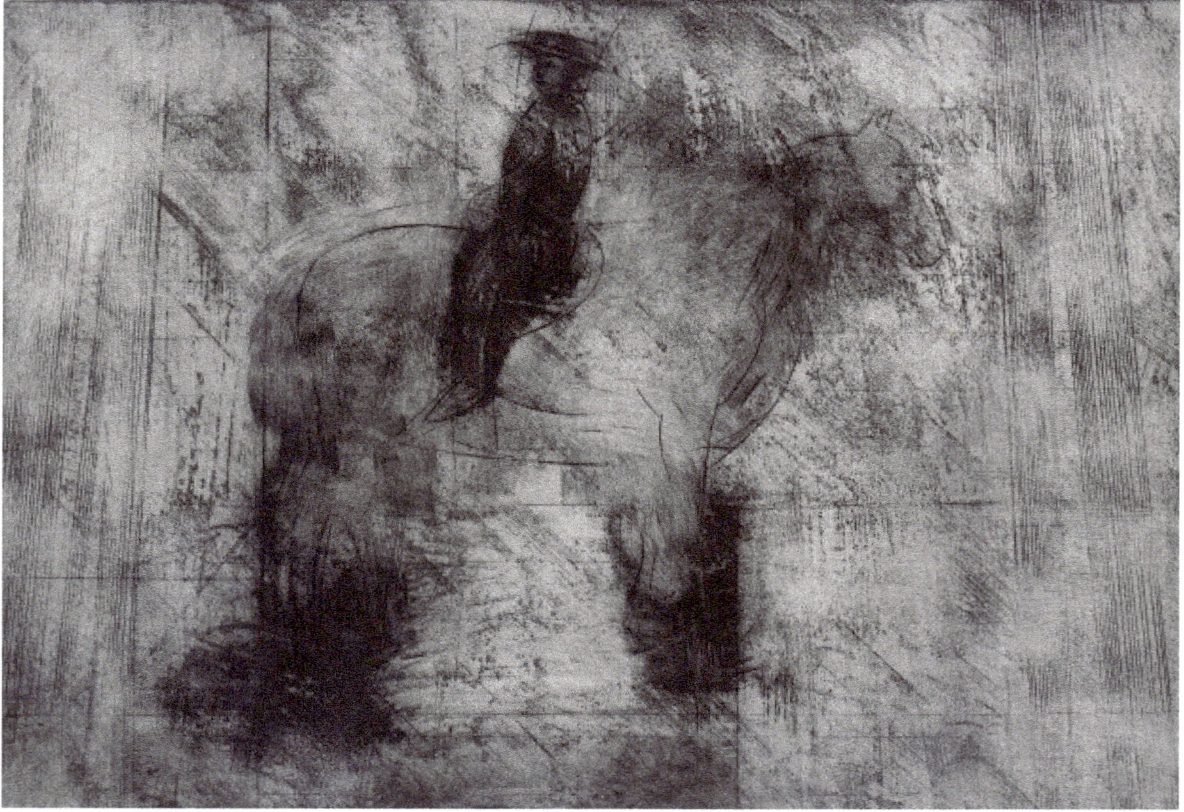

**General**, *stages 1 and 2, 2010, sequential etchings, 13"x18", collection of the artist.*

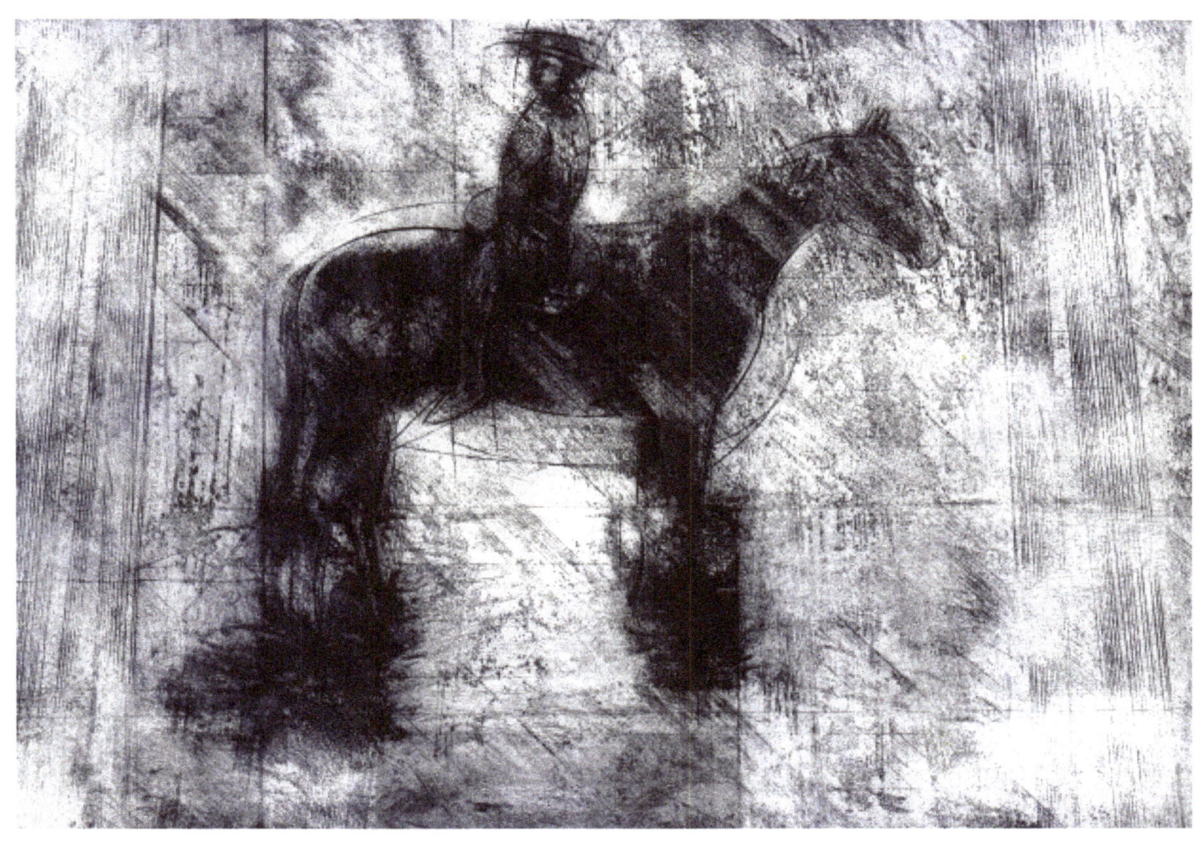

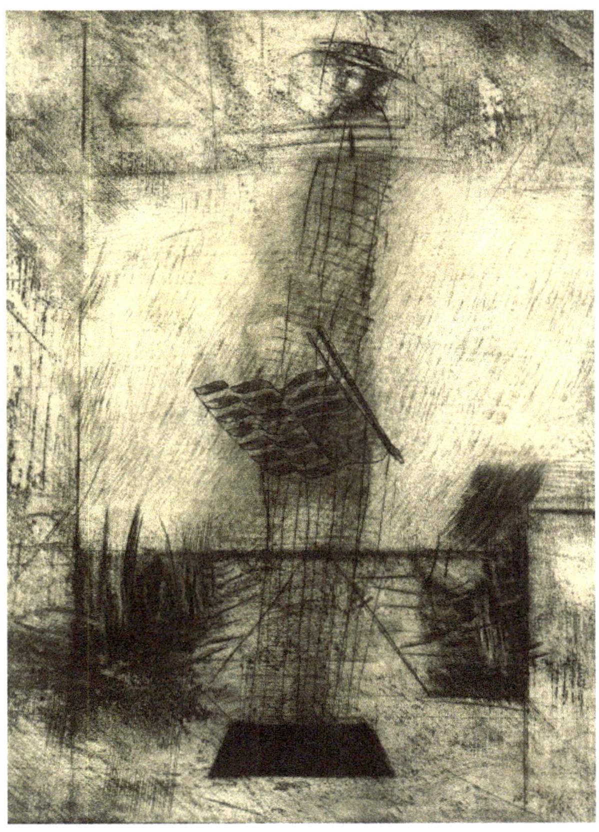

*Top:* **General**, *2010, sequential etching, 13"x15",*
*collection of the artist.*

*Right:* **General**, *2010, etching, 12"x9",*
*collection of the artist.*

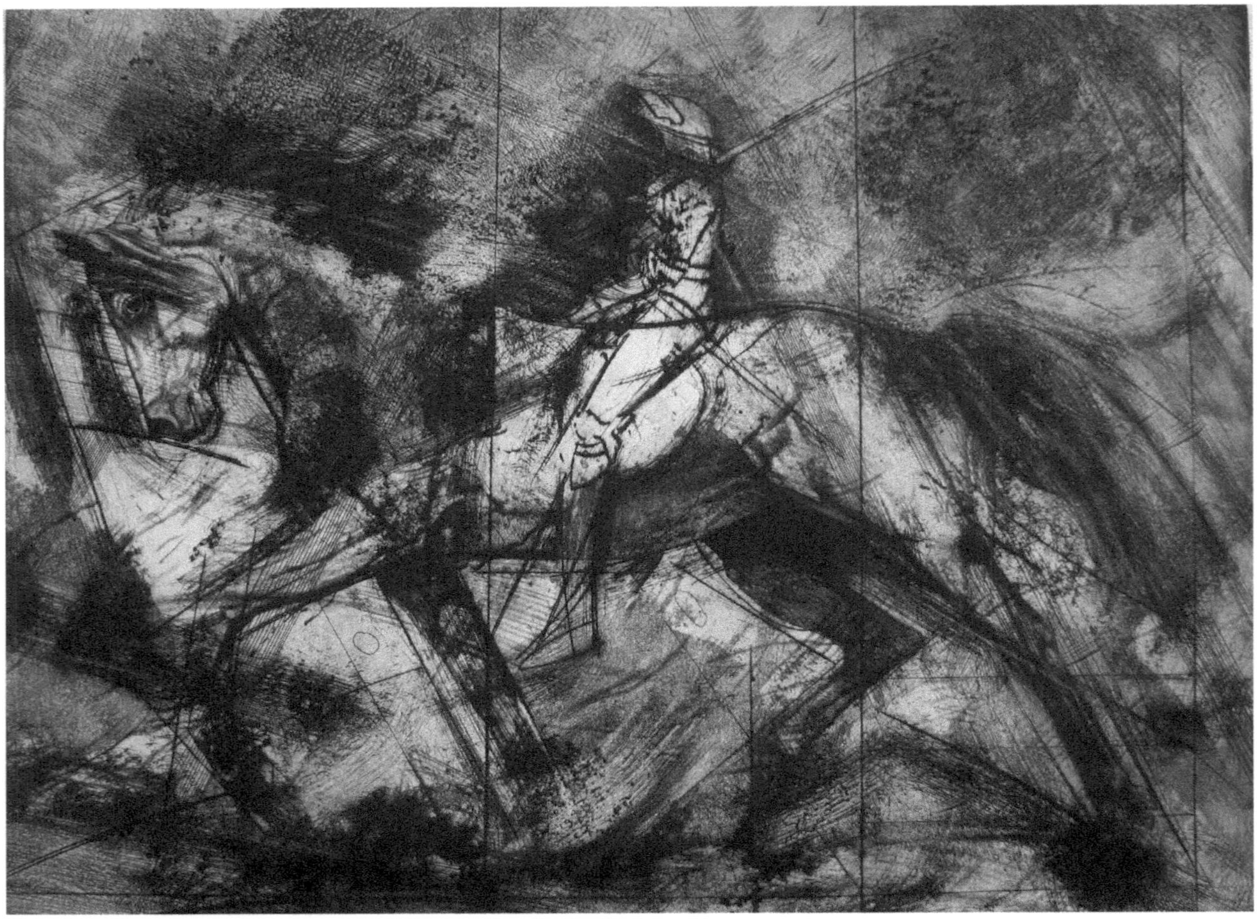

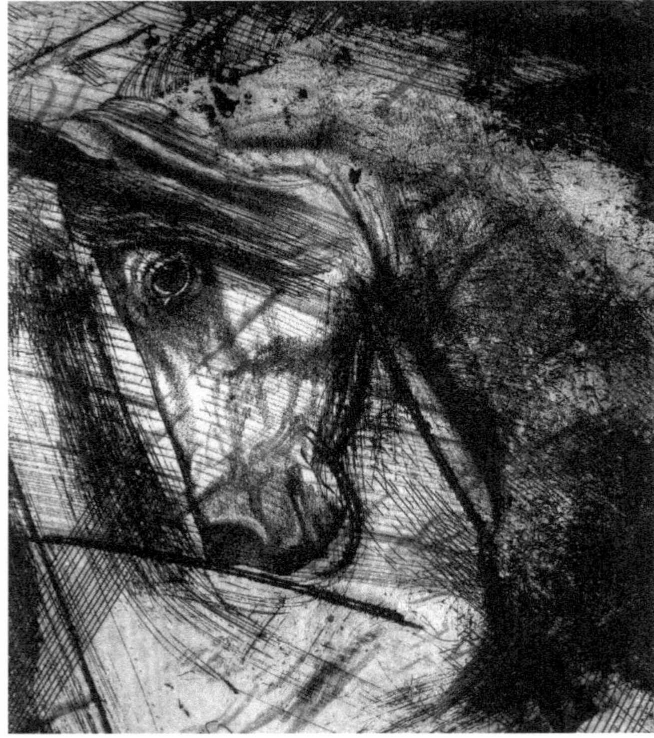

Top: **Warrior**, 2010, etching, collaboration with Leon Smith, 18"x24", Guanlan Original Printmaking Base, Shenzhen, China.

Left: detail.

Opposite Page:
**Memorial**, 2011, etching, 9"x12", collection of the artist.

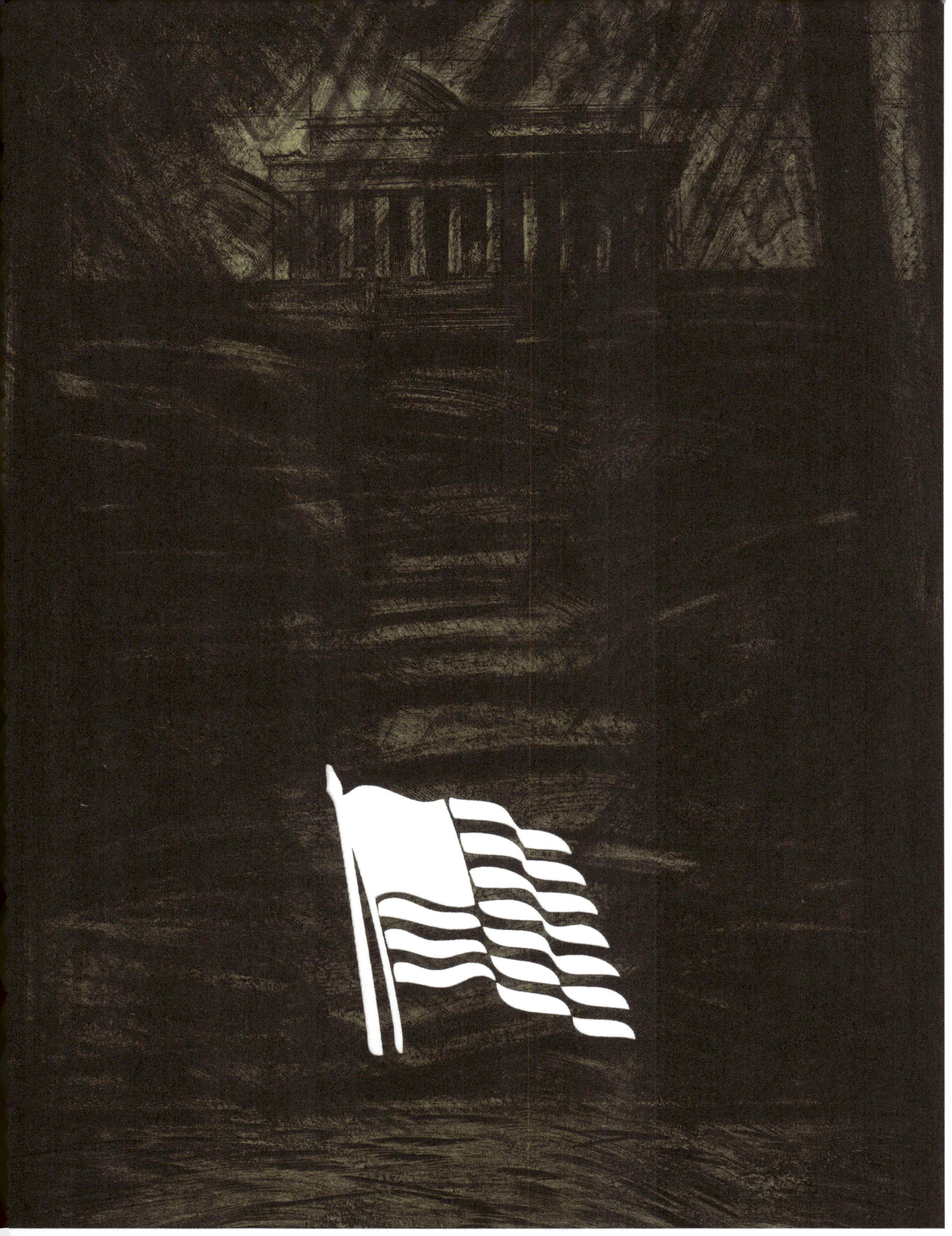

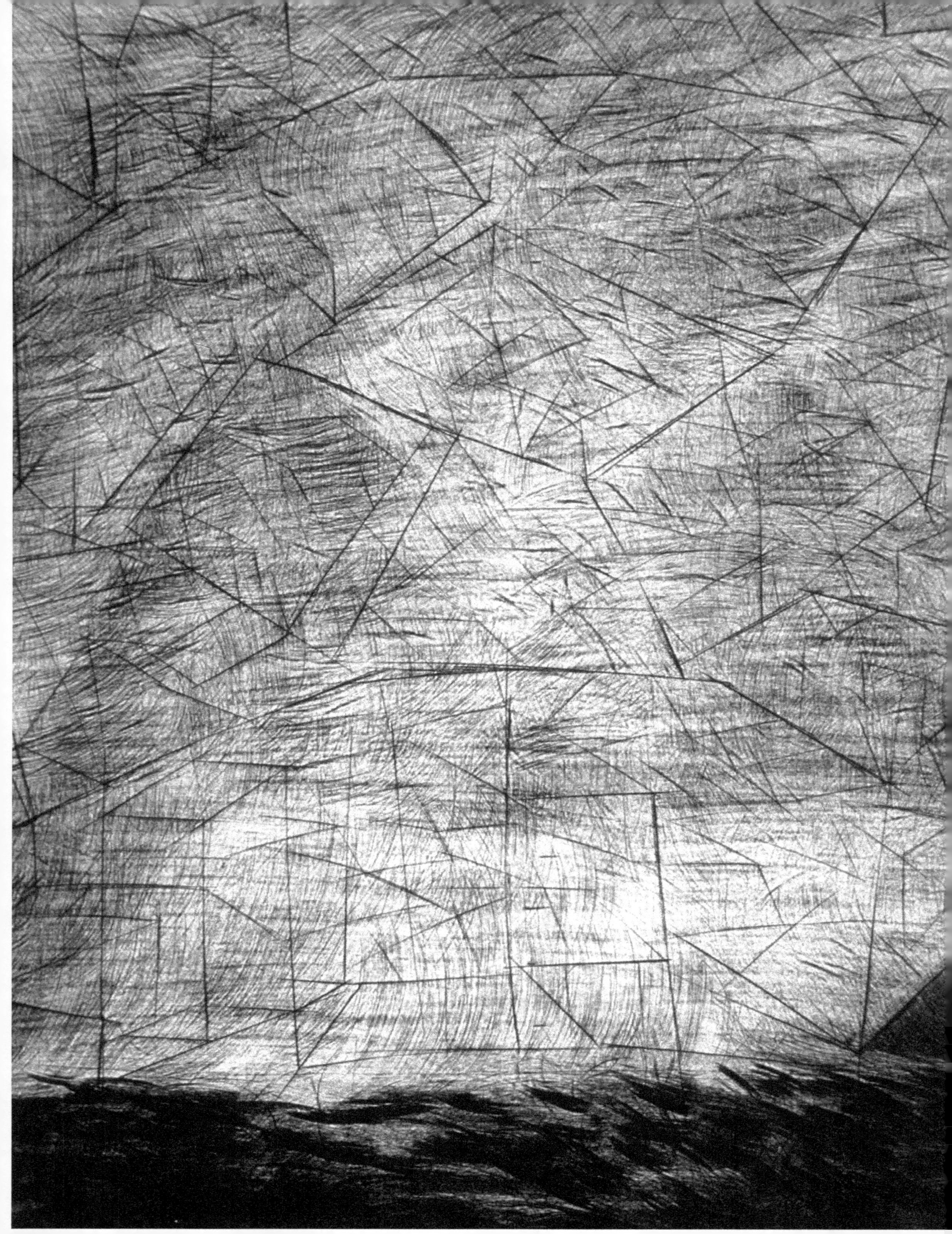

# Lucky Dragon Suite

In 1985, at the behest of George McKenna, Hugh Merrill's *Lucky Dragon* sequential etching suite was exhibited at the Nelson-Atkins Museum of Art in Kansas City, Missouri. McKenna, the curator of prints, drawings and photographs at the museum also chose to include the Western Garden suite of etchings and a series of Merrill's paintings in conjunction with the prints.

In 1954, the Lucky Dragon, a Japanese fishing vessel, was searching for new tuna fishing grounds when she cast her nets 80 miles off an island in the Pacific Ocean where an American hydrogen bomb test had occurred. The boat and crew were caught in a snowstorm of hot radioactive coral flakes. The story of the crew became one small event in the movement to ban the atmospheric testing of nuclear weapons. One of the crewmen died from radiation poisoning.

Merrill used this event as the subject for the *Lucky Dragon* suite of prints. Using an abstract visual language of forms, space, light, and sequential movement, he created an emotional tonality that took the audience beyond the facts of the event to a deeper understanding and insight. Merrill produced the *Lucky Dragon Suite* by altering a 24"x36" zinc etching plate. He pulled one print a day and then changed the plate, pulling a new impression the next day.

Only one impression of each state exists. The plate was worked for over 70 days, producing 70 unique impressions. The original 70 impressions were edited to the 36 images exhibited at the Nelson Atkins Museum in 1985.

Merrill discovered in the sequential process a mechanism for sustaining an investigation:

*"Each day, as I changed the plate, I became more deeply involved in the subject, the physical and emotional experience. The process of struggling each day to conclude an image records and documents my studio narrative. The studio narrative is the act of making and remaking and is always an act of discovery. It records both changes in the material and my interaction with the plate and the subject. In the end the plate became so thin that it could not longer sustain reworking."*

The prints were re-edited in 1994 into a series of 20 impressions that make up the final suite, which was purchased by Nick Jannes of Chicago in October of 1994. The Museum of Modern Art in New York acquired two of the original 36 images shown at the Nelson-Atkins Museum. The Daum Museum of Contemporary Art in Sedalia, Missouri, purchased the prints from Mr. Jannes in the fall of 2006. Merrill followed the *Lucky Dragon Suite* with over 10 years of exploring sequential etchings including the *Due Unto*, *Wallenberg*, *Rosa Luxemberg*, *Torso*, and *Facts of Fictions* series of prints.

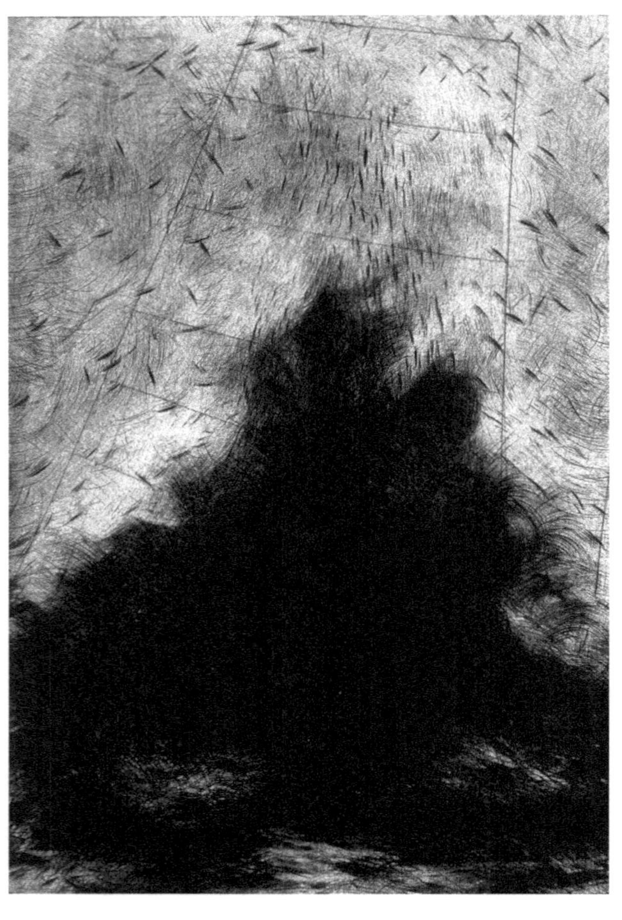 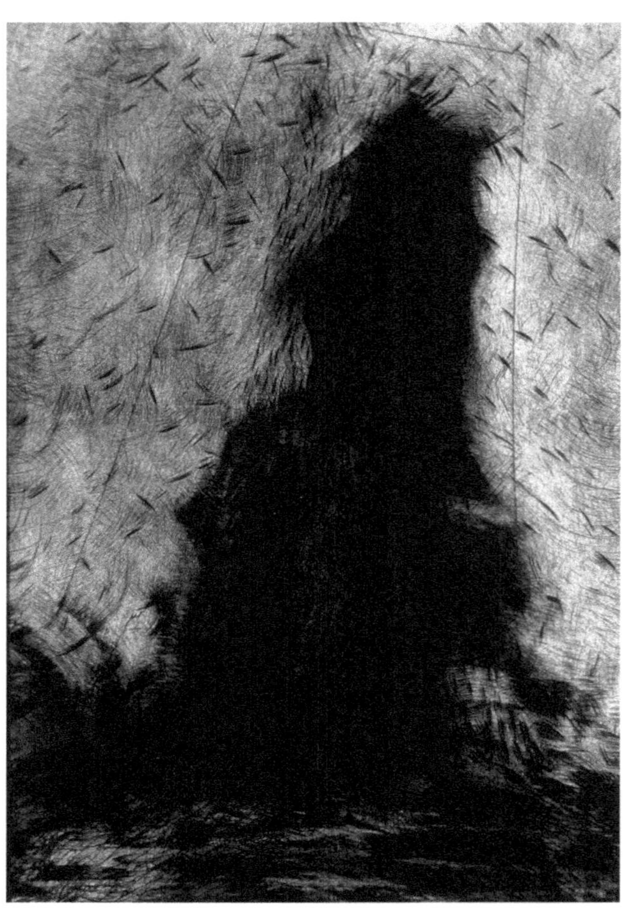

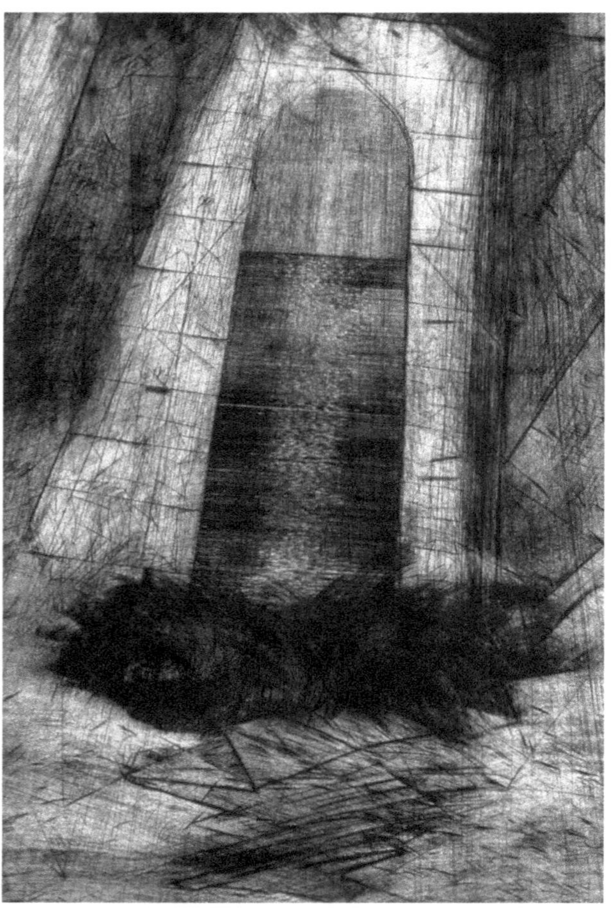 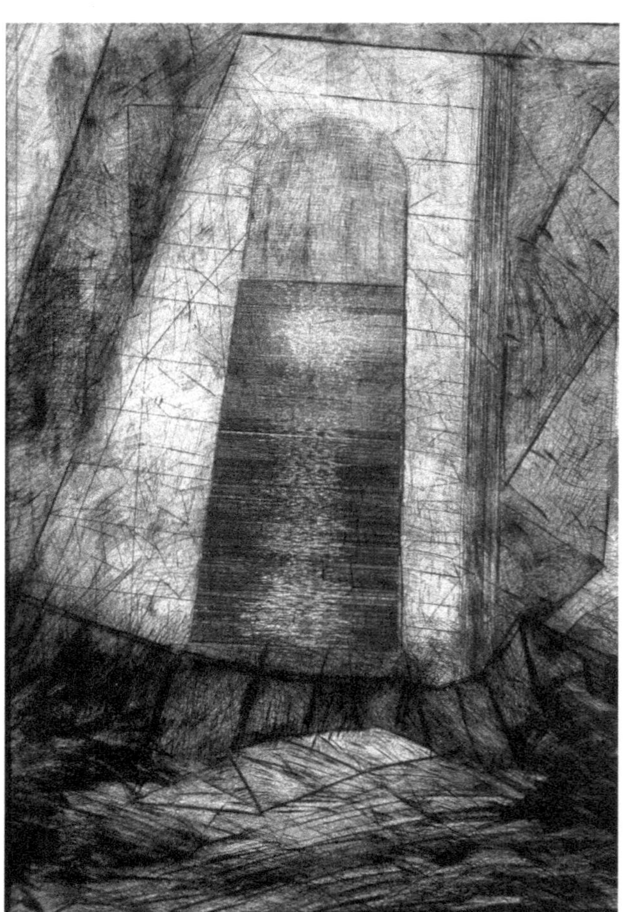

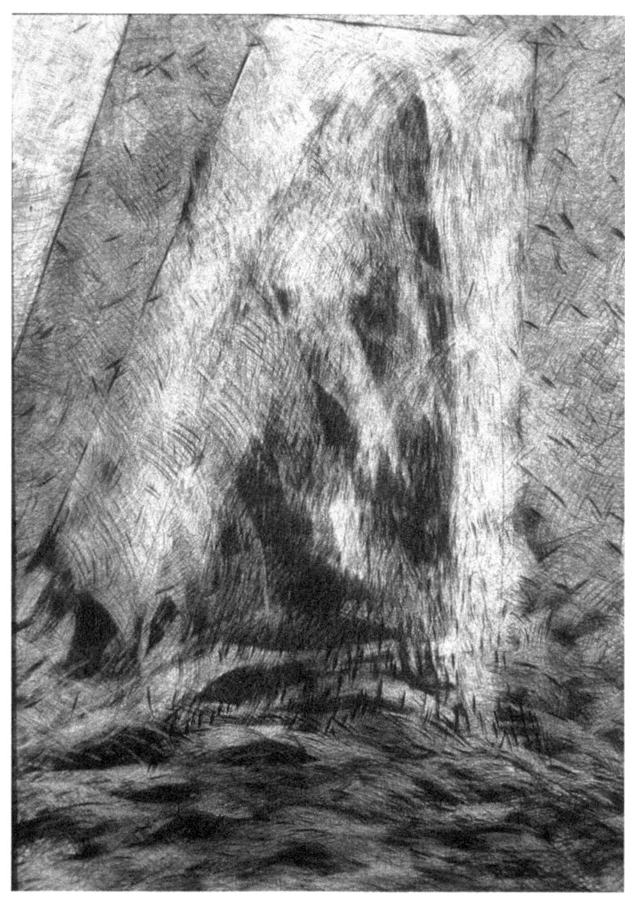
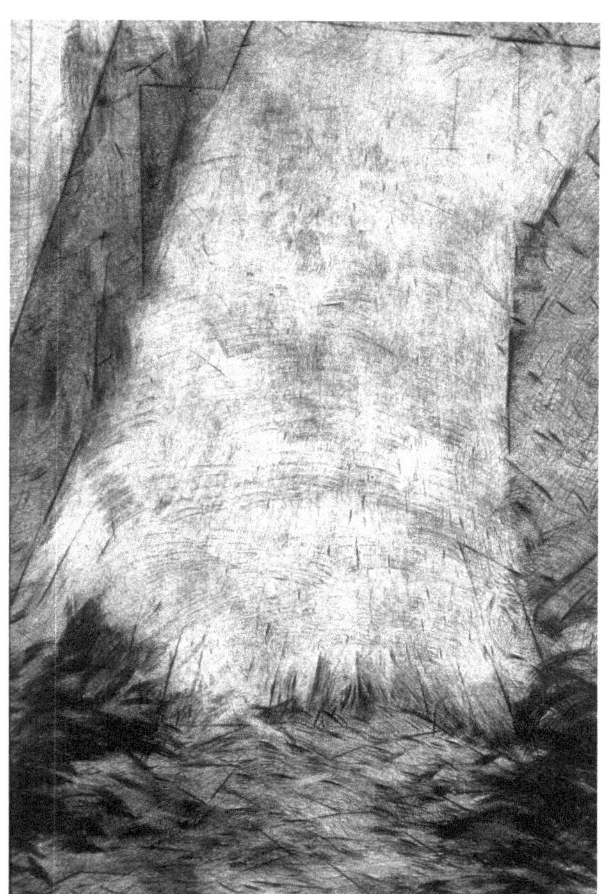
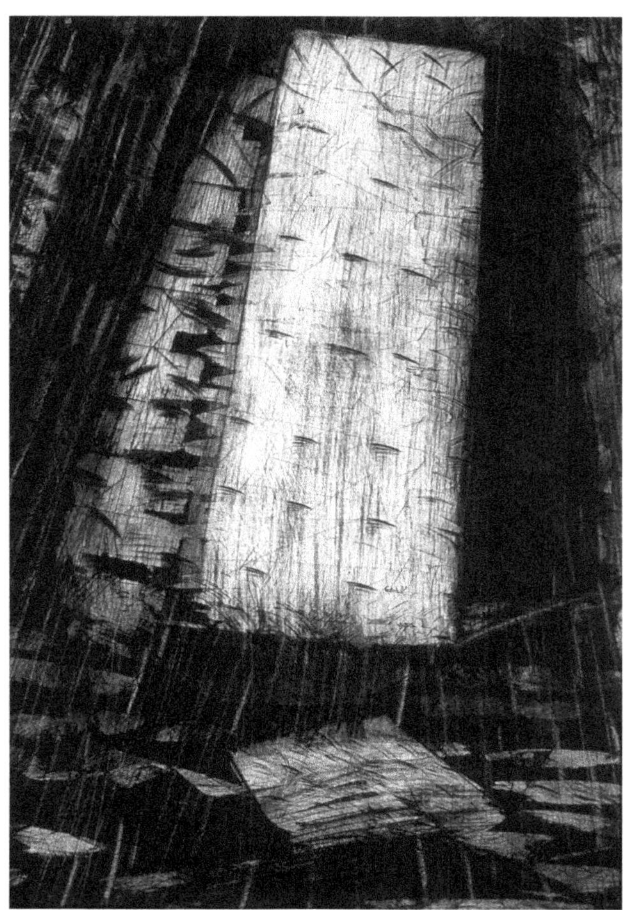
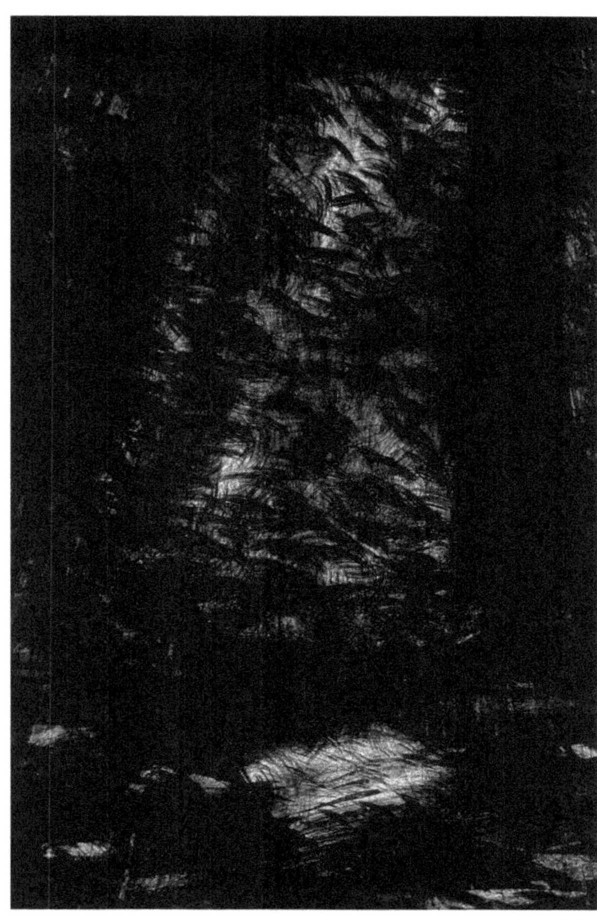

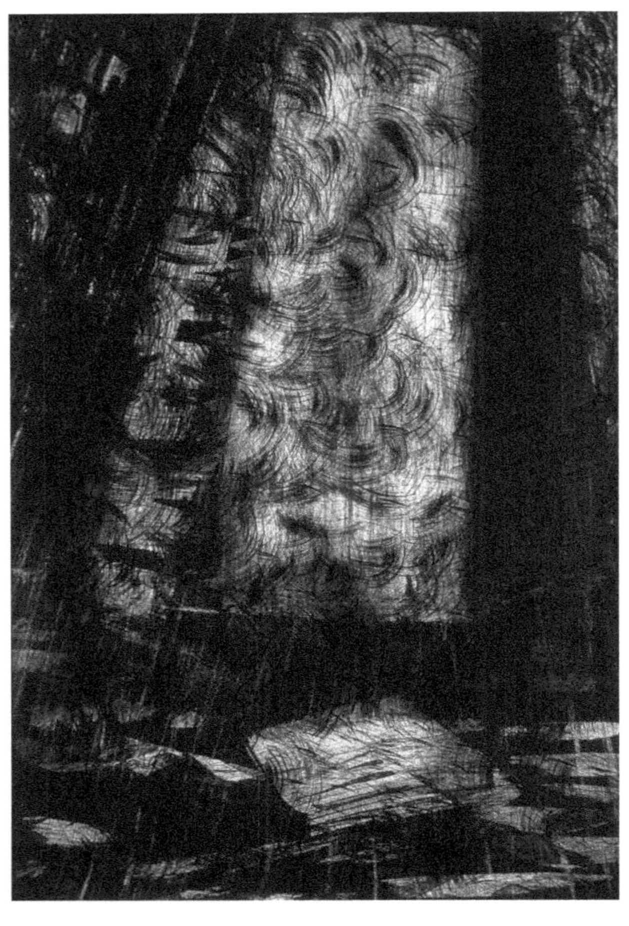
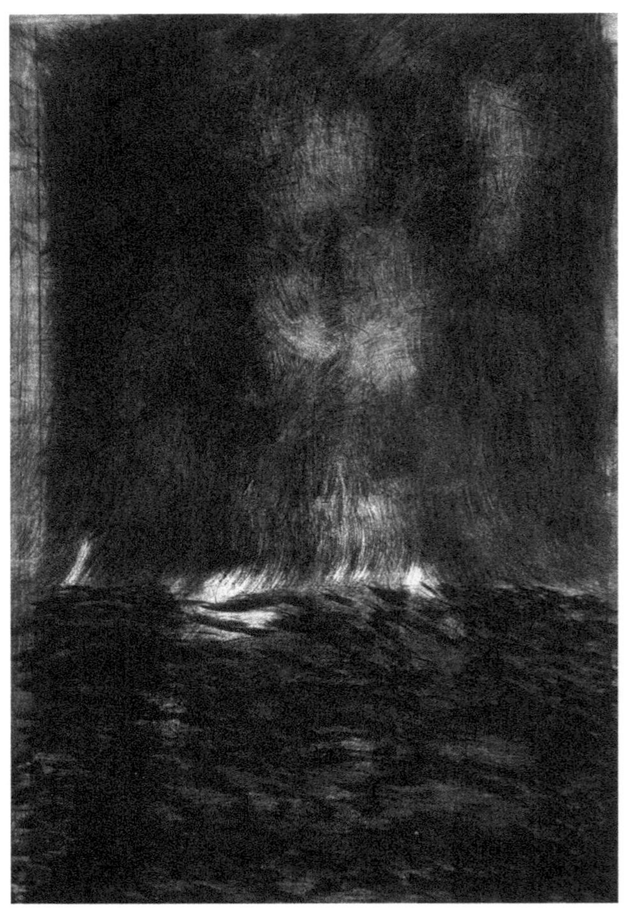
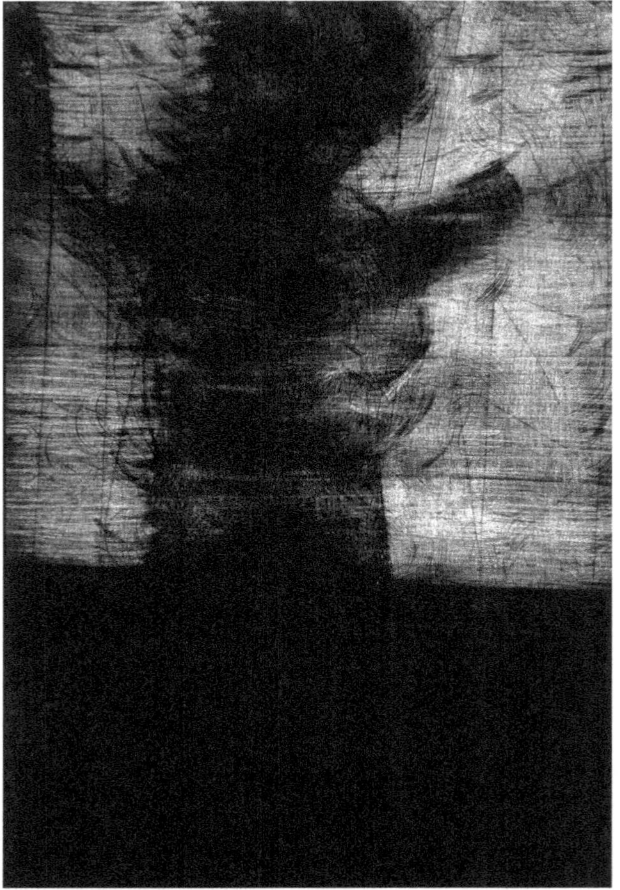
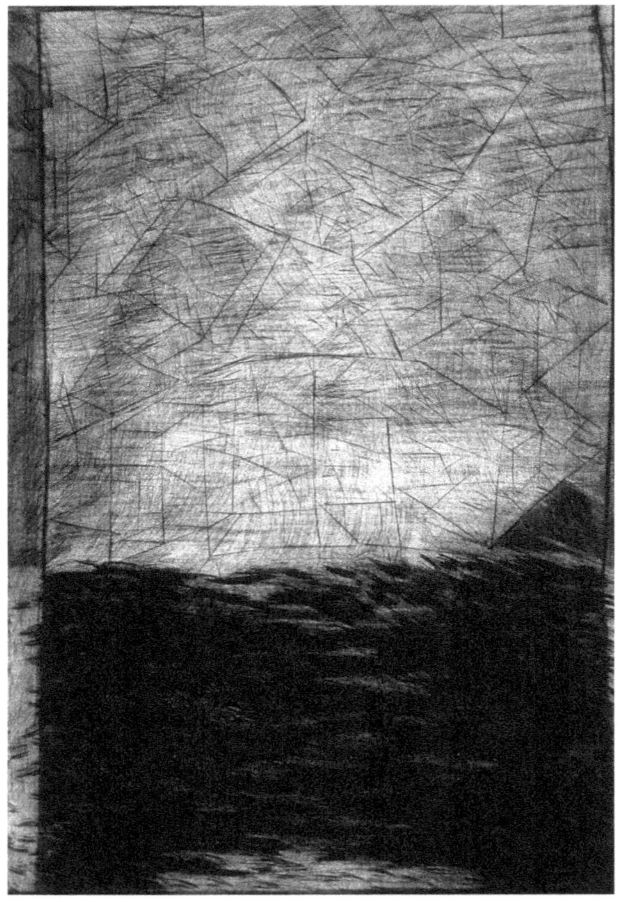

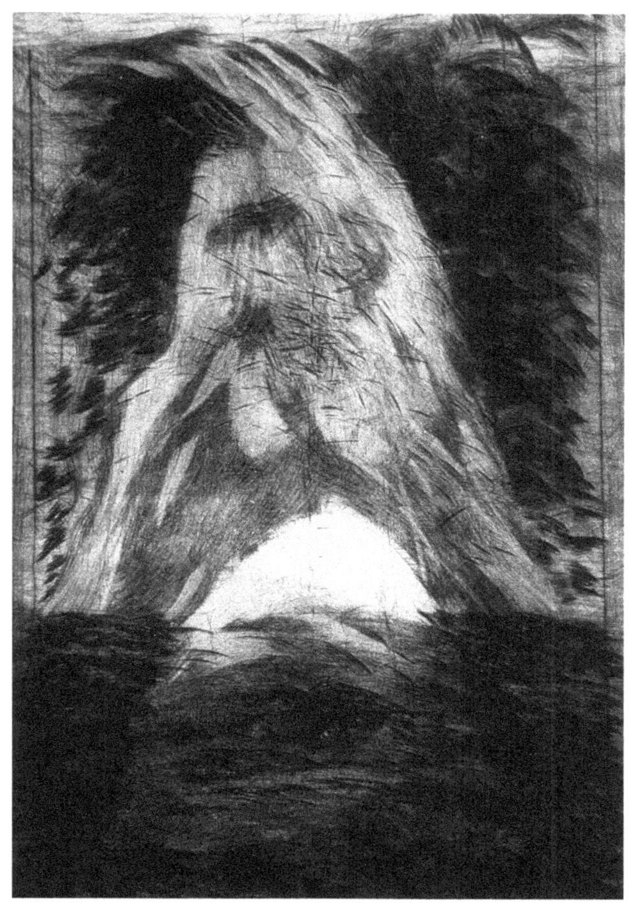

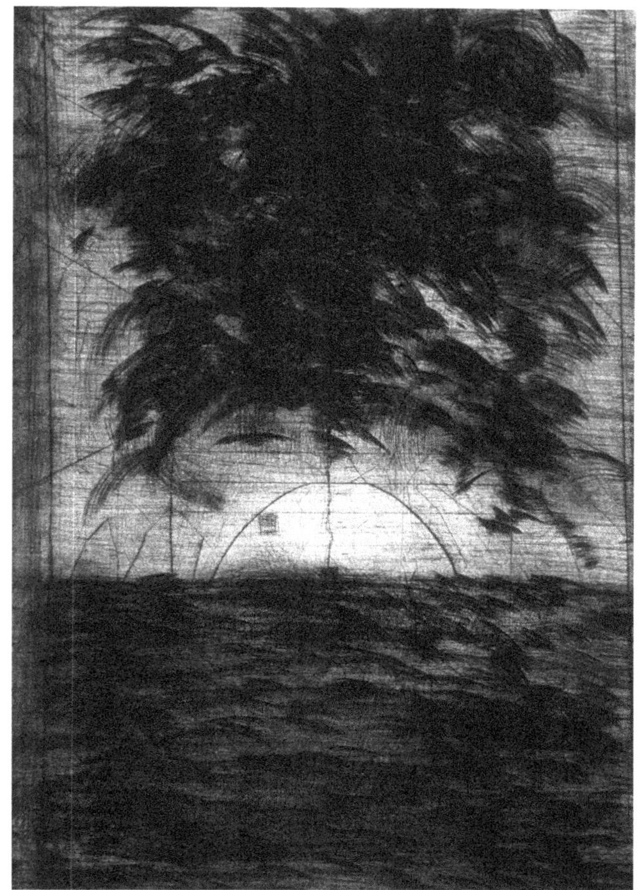

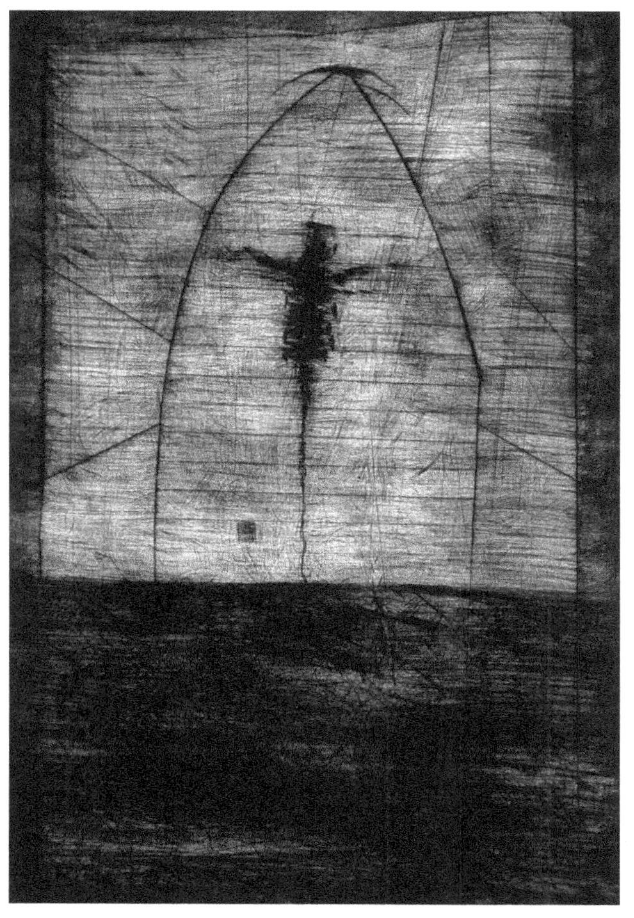

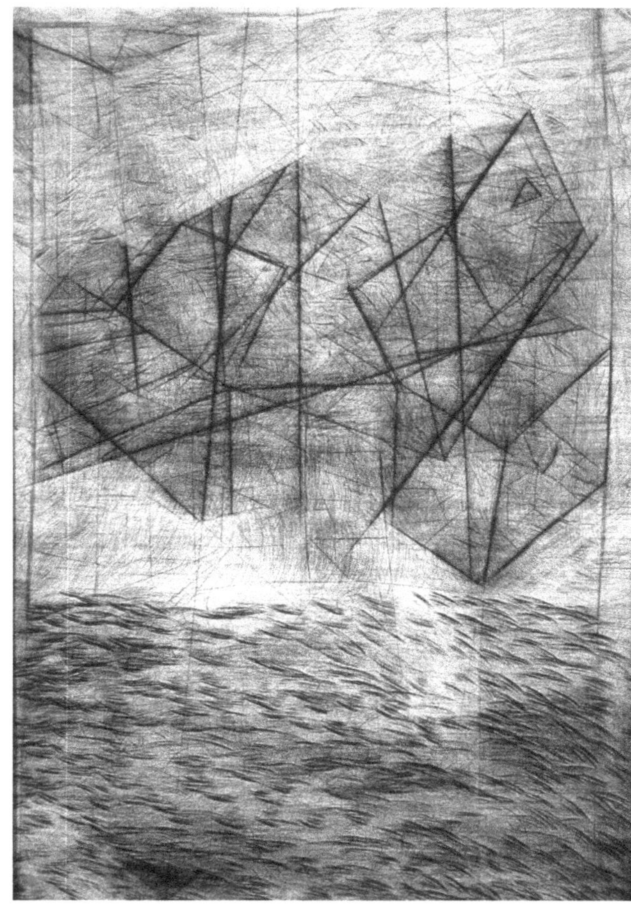

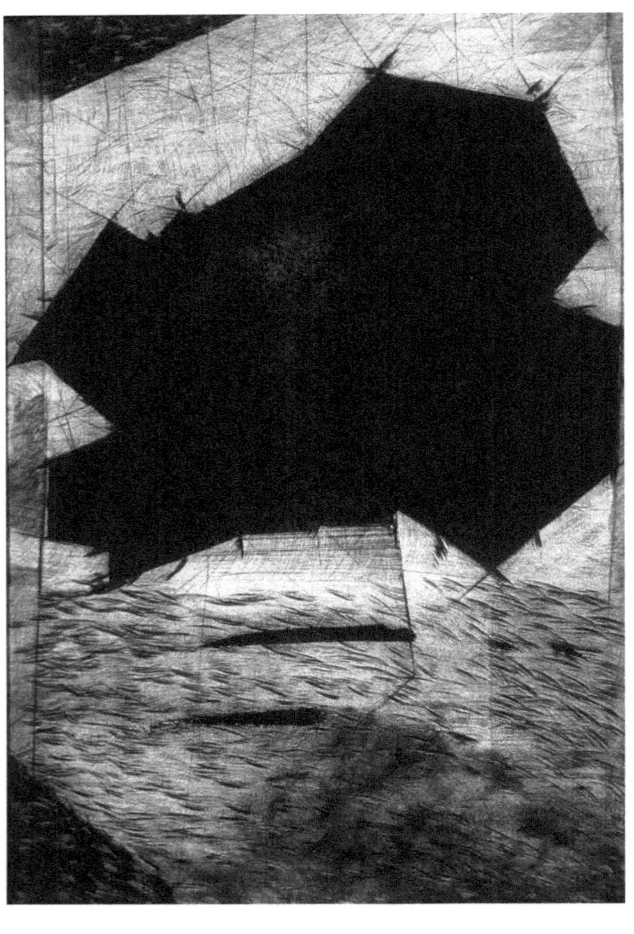
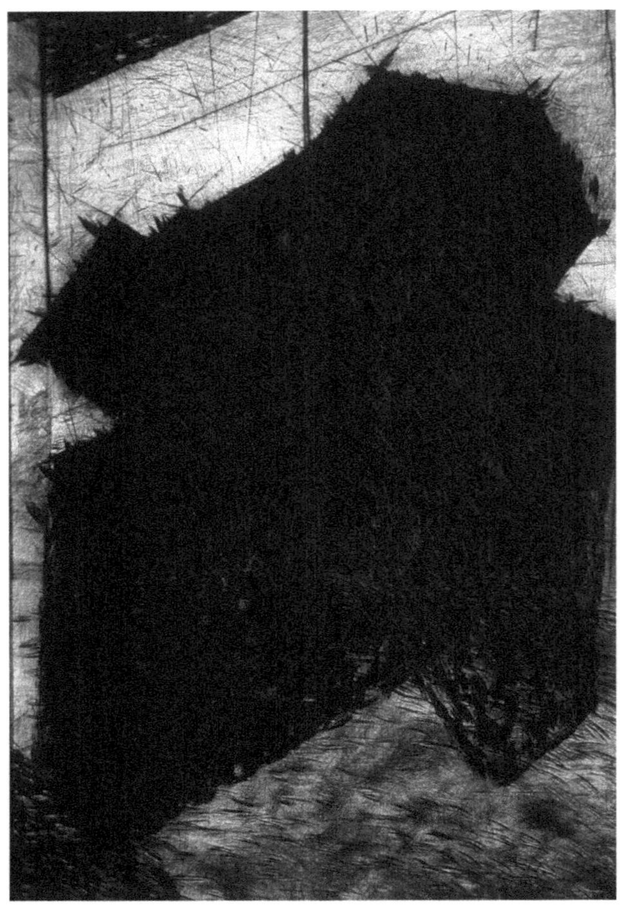
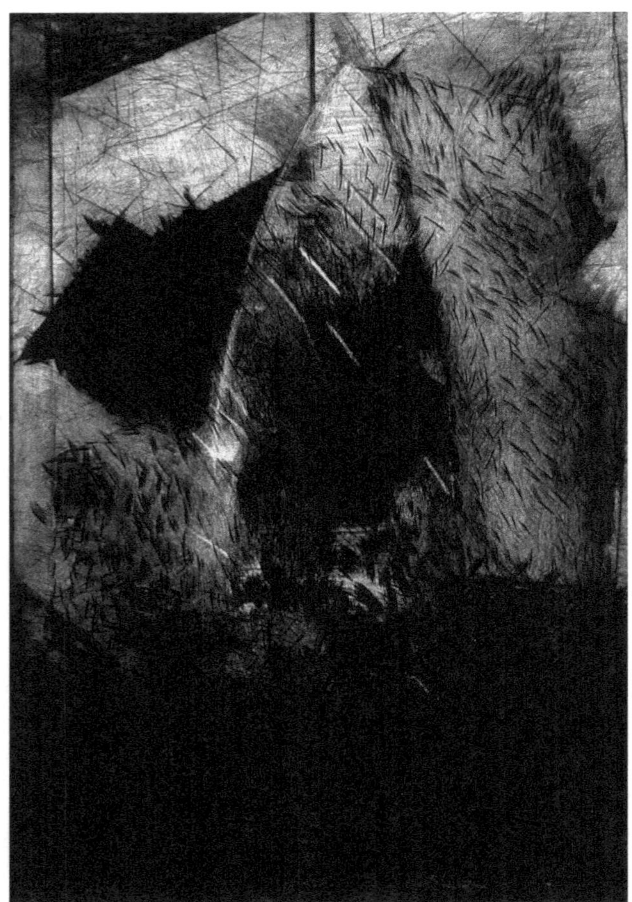
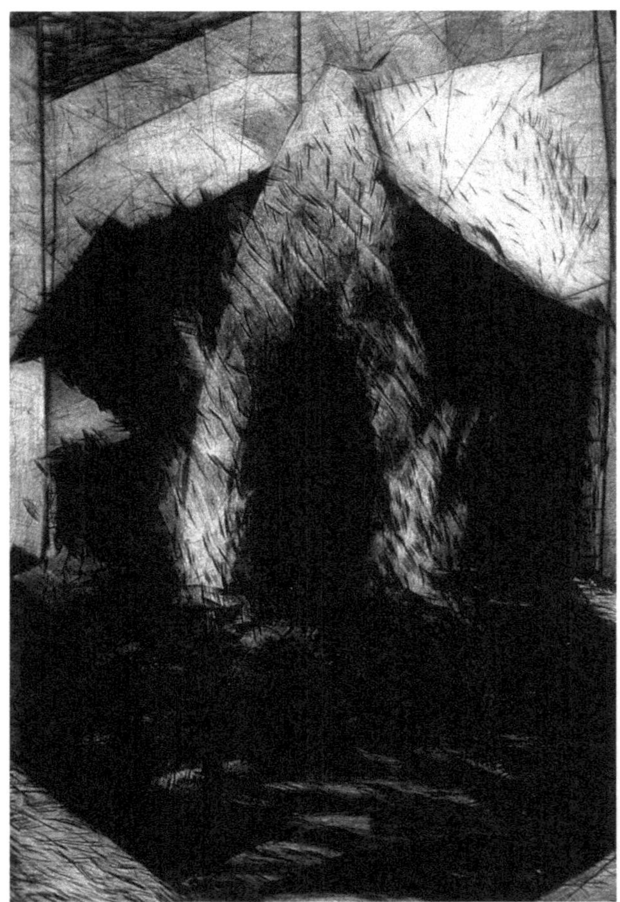

"Hugh Merrill's prints deal imaginatively with the confrontation between man-made construction and natural landscape. Merrill's approach to the dichotomy of our environment is appropriately twofold, contrasting the factual, visual data of the earthbound reality with an intuitively sensed romantic quality that transmutes natural and human surroundings alike into abstract forms that toll sonorously with the impact of their dynamic opposition. We perceive in his work the timeless unbounded spirit of the land invaded by the encroachment of utilitarian, architectonic forces bent on intrusive change and artificial order."

George McKenna, Curator of Prints
Nelson-Atkins Museum of Art, Kansas City Missouri

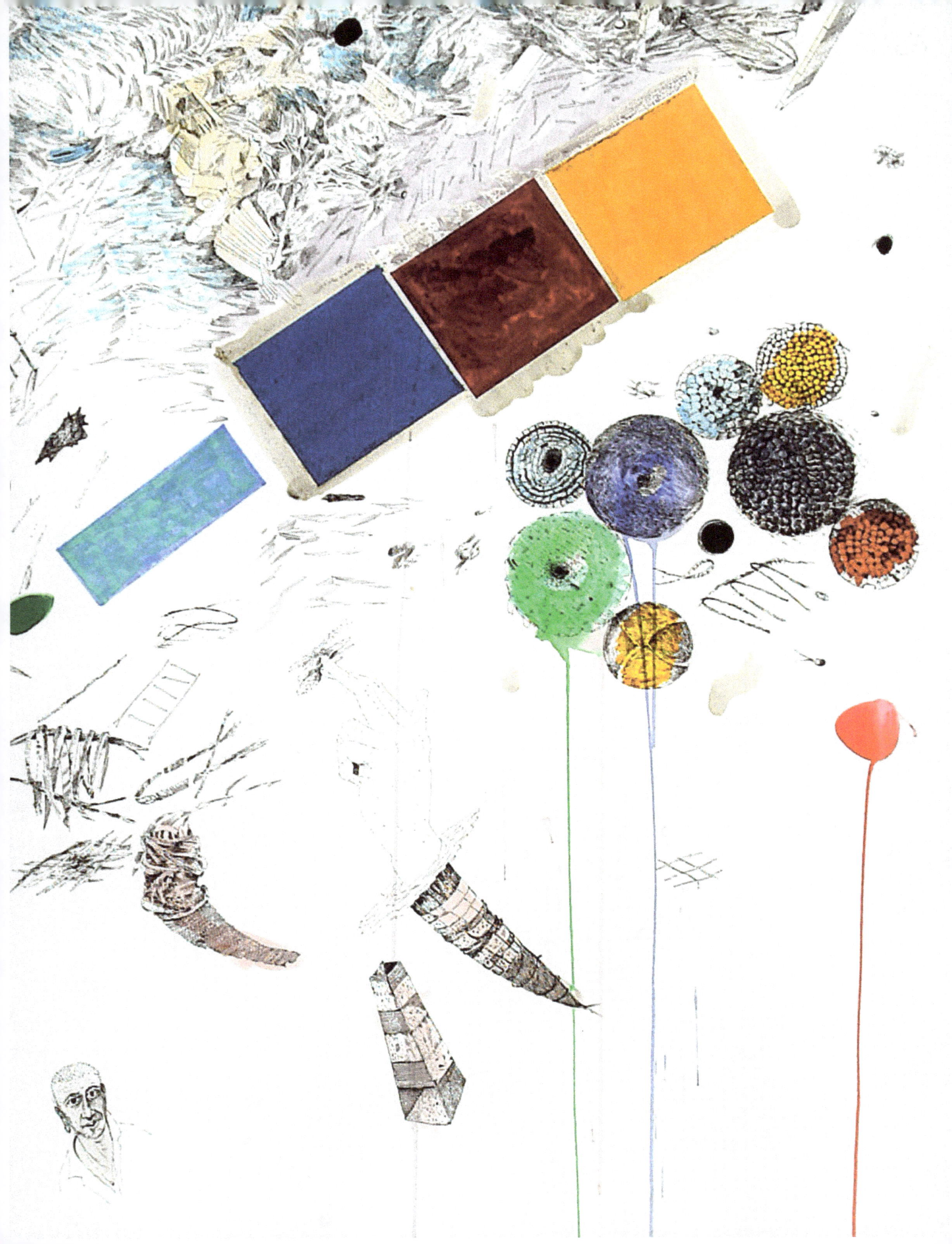

# Drawings, 2005-2011

Merrill's early drawings integrate systems of symbols and eager use of negative space. The marks take on a distinct intentionality which is somewhat uncharacteristic of his organic approach to etching. Discovering artist Julie Mehretu gave Merrill access to conceptualize integration of his social practice into the drawing realm. His work would include symbols and objects but would also direct the viewer to see the process of the idea through the layerings of the surface itself. Interaction with her densely layered pieces liberated the ambiguity and sub-conscious directed methodology to begin earnest explorations into the world of pure drawing.

*"While I think of the paintings as originating here—being very grounded in this world and based on the cities, monuments, systems, and infrastructures that we have built—I do like to think of them as being narrative maps without a specific place or location. I am interested in ways to picture and map our relationships and interactions within this constructed world. I think of the paintings as narrative pictorial vistas of memorial experience, weaving in and out of daily func-tioning, resistance, and understanding."*

--Julie Mehretu

Similar to Mehretu, Merrill's drawings are directly interested in social commentaries, integrating architectural abstractions with disconnected cultural symbolisms. Both artists exhibit high energy, large scale artworks which invite a sense of curiosity and connection with viewers. Merrill displays the shared symbolisms of his local communities; crosses, globes, shooting stars, concentric rings, pyramids. These emblems become the recursive element of the story, estab-lishing sequences of moments in the ritual of contemplation.

Julie Mehretu's *Empirical Construction, Istanbul* (2003) is a dreaming city, what the artist might draw with their eyes closed, the piece is an exploration of the soul of Turkey. The flag lines and fires intersect the light beams and street corners and each mark fits with its neighbors and the viewer is traveling warp speed through the heart of downtown. It's the ephemeral of the society that both artists are drawing about.

Merrill and Mehretu work with non-objective elements and create sequences of genetic recombinatorix with the archetypal symbols of cultures. Both artists on some level reject objects, they are

*Opposite Page:* **Dreams of the Wicked Hunter** *(detail), 2005, mixed media, 72"x36", private collection.*

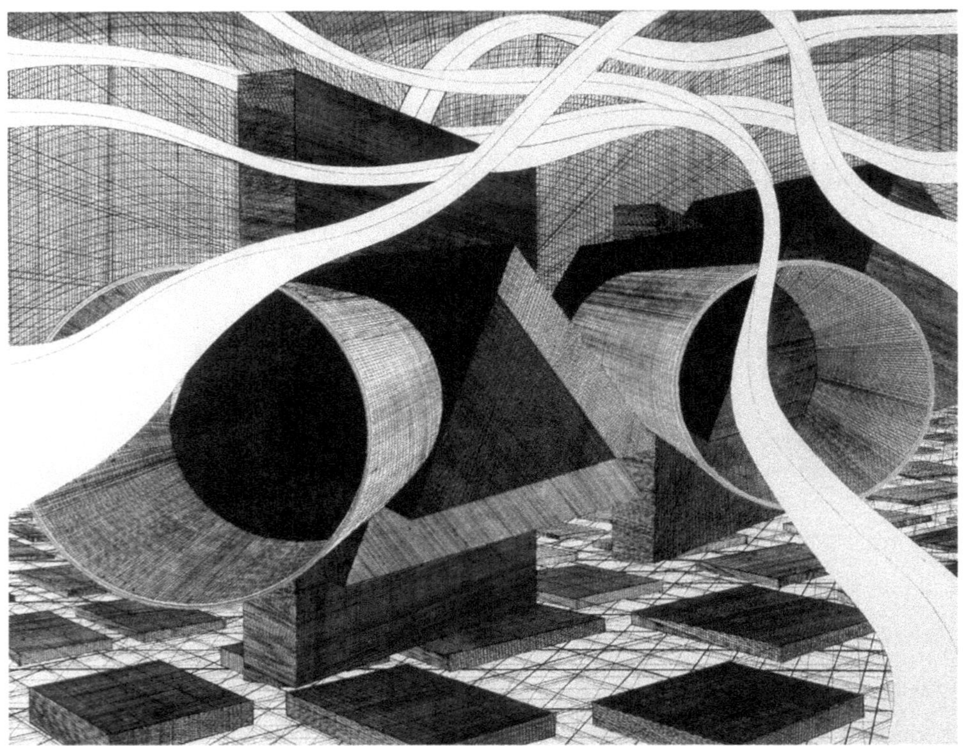

*Al Held,* **MN Black***, 2003, etching, 30.5"x36.75", Art © Al Held Foundation/Licensed by VAGA, New York, NY.*

not drawing still-lives, they are drawing kinetic-lives.

At the outset of Merrill's investigations, as an undergraduate at the Maryland Institute College of Art, he encountered instructor Fairfield Porter. This formalist painter was also renowned for his expressive and detailed writing style. These elements were intriguing to Merrill and their work together became formative to the artist.

Porter was a contemporary of Clement Greenberg and Jackson Pollack, but fearlessly went against the prevailing winds of the art elite of the day. Porter was deliberate, even labored, set on immersive assays into the mundane of middle class Americana and Merrill shared this abiding interest in the surrounding community. Merrill took many lessons from Porter's ideas and was perhaps the first visual and verbal artist Merrill encountered. Merrill recalls a particular kinship when recounting Porter's idea that *"feelings cannot be divorced from ideas in art."*

This essential early impression becomes an underlying theme in Merrill's work: the physical action of art creation is the actual art itself, there is no distinction between the needs of the artist and the needs of the community, the images of the culture are the language of the sub-conscious-collective.

For Merrill, any separation of art from world is a false start and potential damages both the understanding of the work and the viewer's impression of the marks. This equanimity removes the artist from the pedestal and elevates the community to

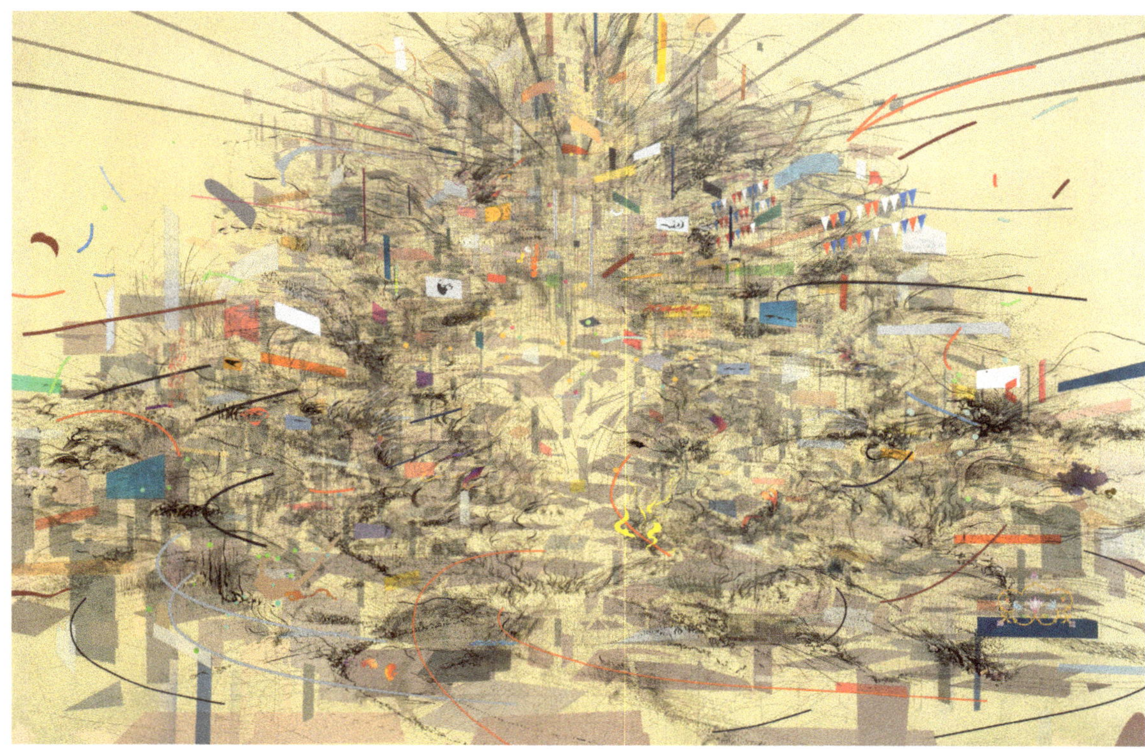

*Julie Mehretu (b. 1970) ©,* **Empirical Construction, Istanbul**, *2003, ink and synthetic polymer paint on canvas, 10'x 15',*
*The Museum of Modern Art, New York, NY, USA.*

the museum.

Merrill moved on into the graduate program at Yale University where he was able to study with Al Held, an artist known for his bold, bright geometries and investigations of repetition. Again Merrill found connection with outsiders to the modern thrust of art movements.

In Held, Merrill found a cohort in distrusting theory and a curiosity in the emerging fields of chaos theory and fractals. Both men sensed that this science was seeing deeper and there was no denying the elevated and gorgeous complexity of non-linear dynamics. Fields which study recursion and examine how self-similarity occurs at all scales. This was the very stuff Merrill and Held were sniffing after.

Merrill waxes philosophical about the meaning to the method of mark-making, he says:

*"To understand a drawing, you just read the lines. It's not a language you learned, but it's a language you know."*

He winks that trickster glint and the implication is that the meanings of the marks are greater than their shape or their subject. He passes the concept to the viewer and invites the reaction of understanding. When the viewer reacts, the drawing suddenly has more to imbue. The marks are a map, a system of symbols which invoke deep memories, both personal and cultural.

Merrill's investigations of wells, castle towers, islands and mountains is the apex series to illustrate the confluence of these important artists in Merrill's development. Merrill takes the context of Mehretu's layerings and sense of being the voice of something bigger than the self, Porter's deep emotional well in conjunction with color, Held's geometric acumen of developing brilliantly connected spaces and unifies it with his own love of surface and substrate to create what becomes distinctly Merrill to the core: an obsession with the repeating mark.

*--Jeanette Powers*

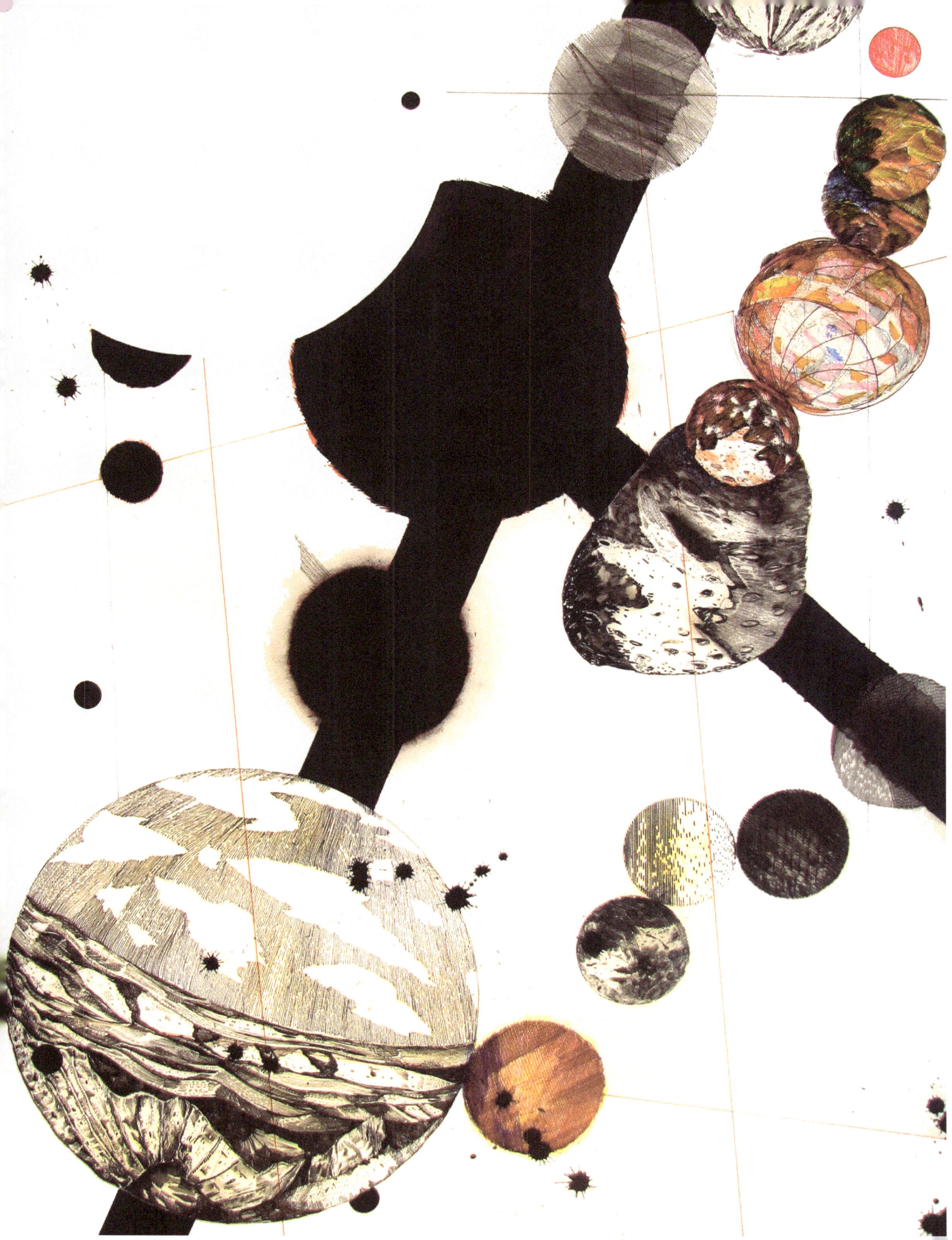

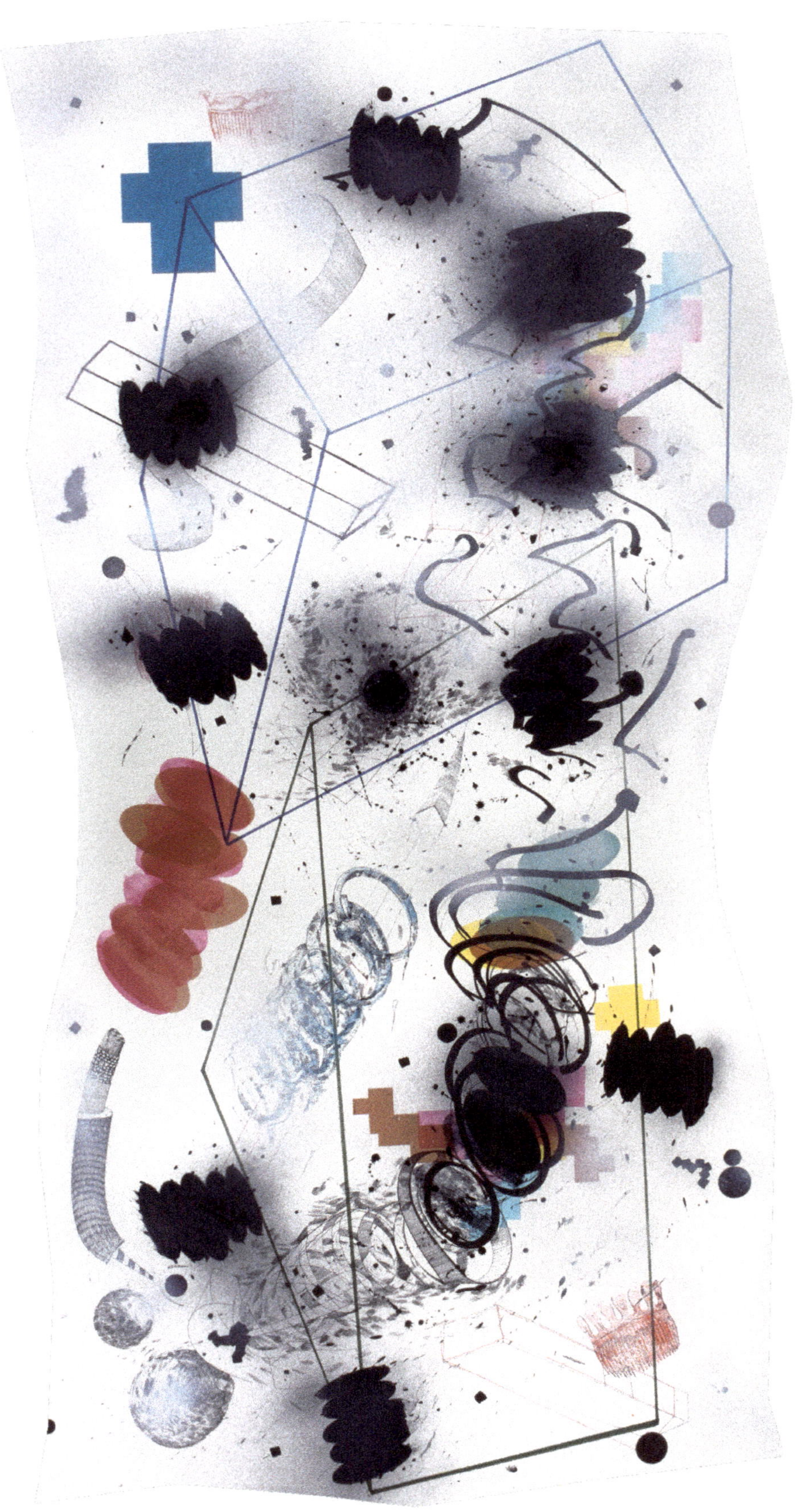

**Death of Luxuria**, *2008, mixed media drawing, 40"x65", collection of Leedy-Voulkos Art Center, Kansas City, Missouri.*

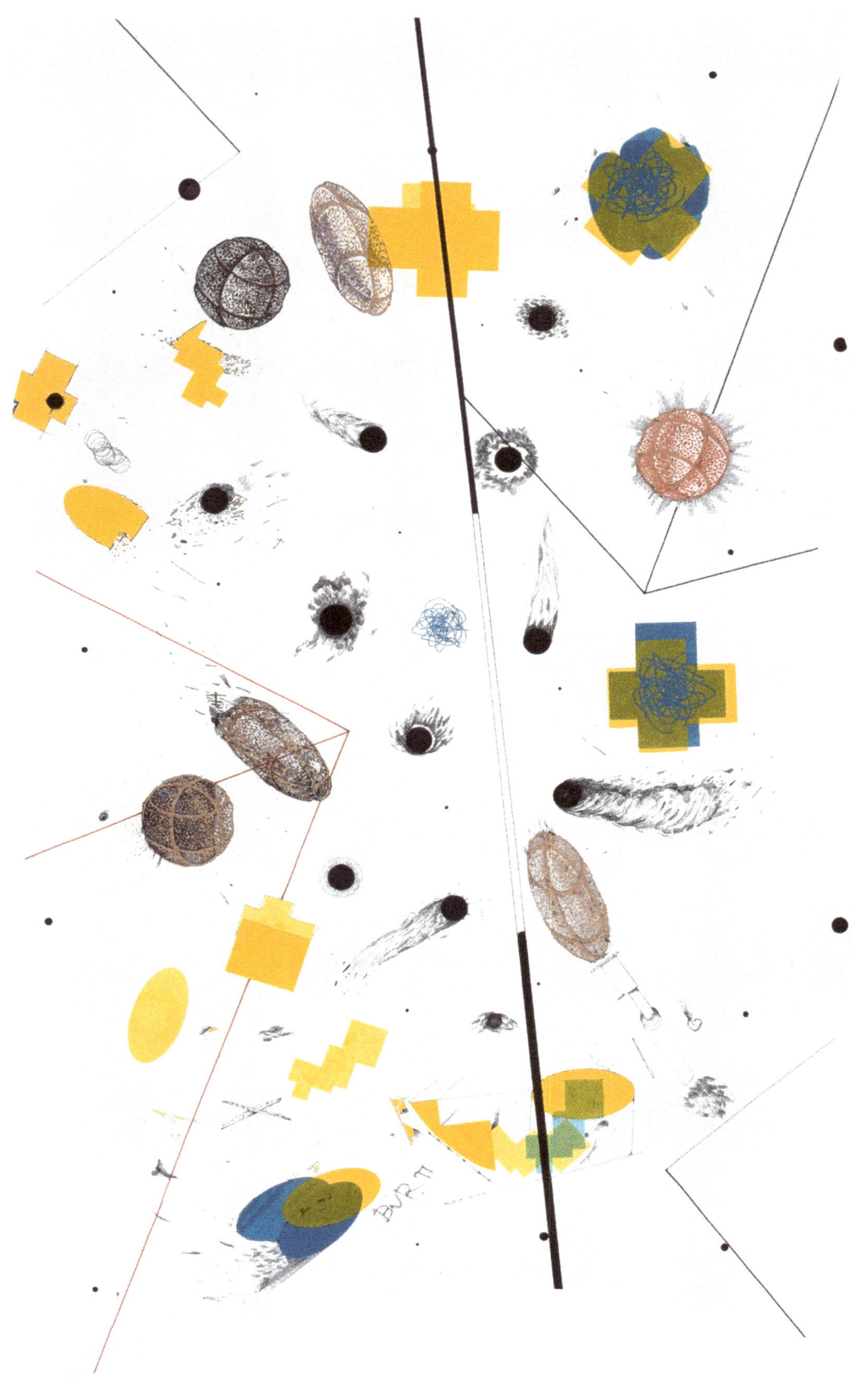

**Rap Brown Dreaming**, *2007, mixed media drawing, 40"x65", Collection of Jim and Molly Leedy, Kansas City, Missouri.*

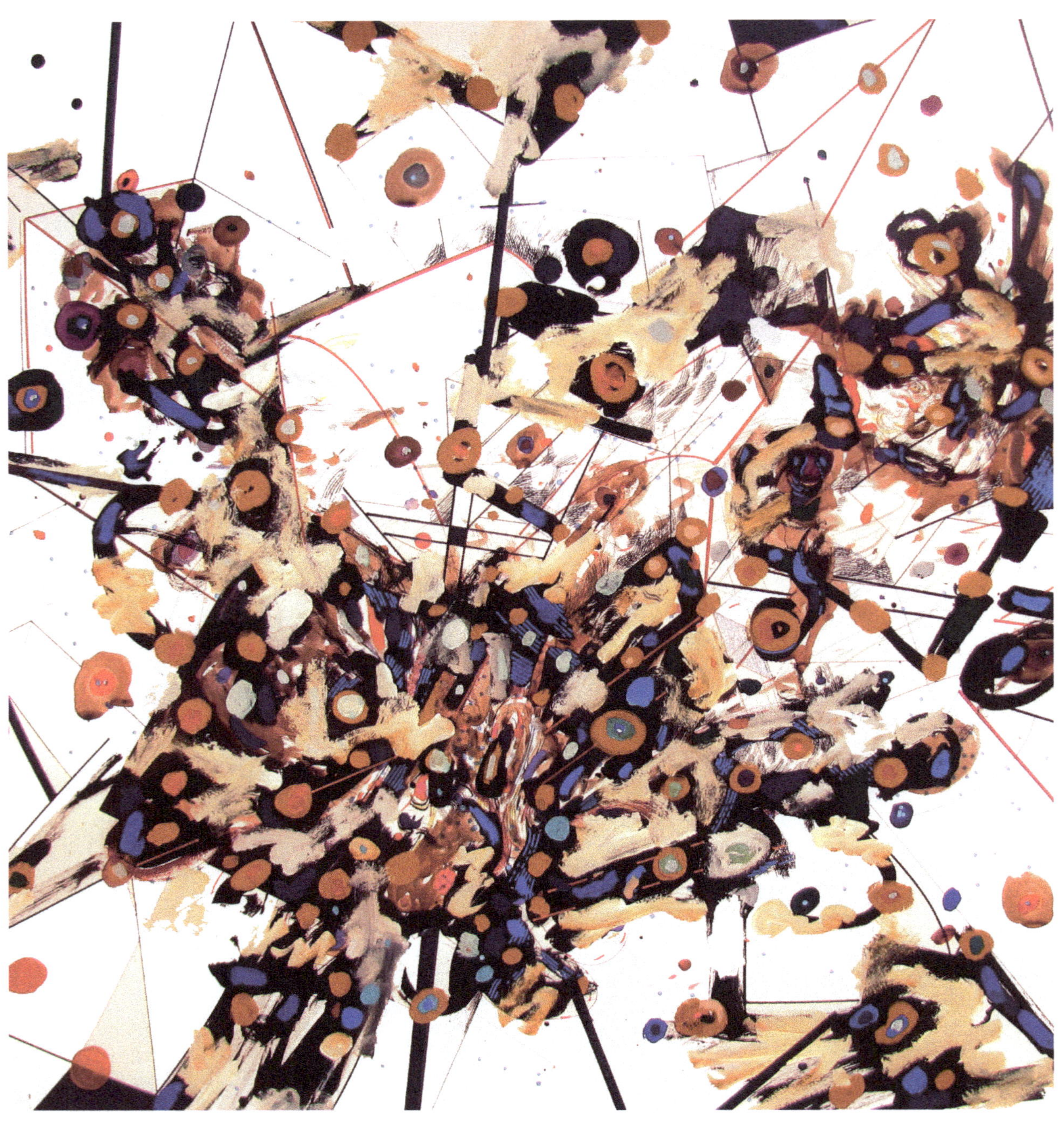

**Stations**, *2011, mixed media drawing, 49"x35", collection of the artist.*

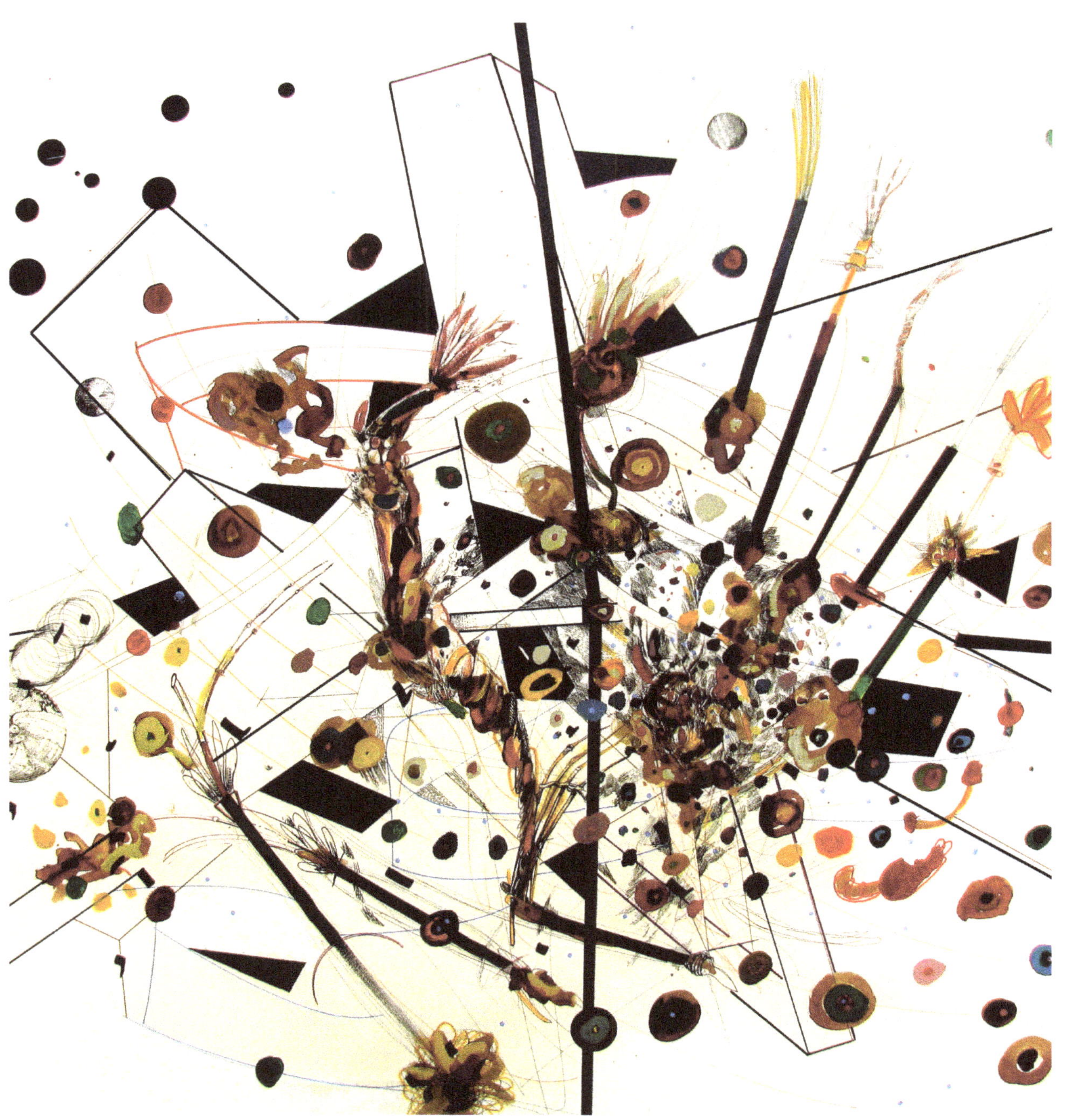

**Glow Worm Hunting**, *2011, mixed media drawing, 38"x44", collection of the artist.*

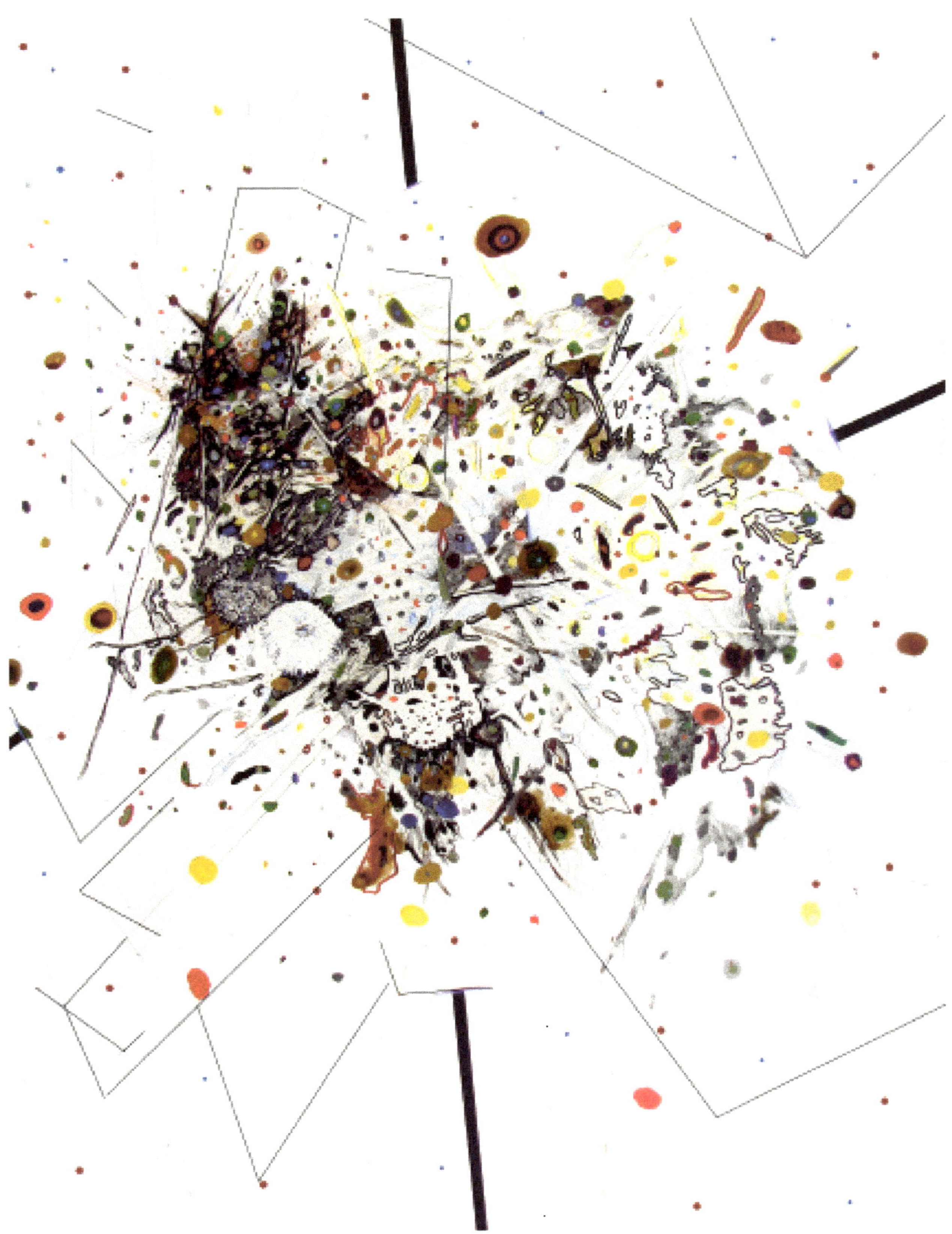

**Fox's Assistant**, *2011, mixed media drawing, 40"x44", collection of the artist.*

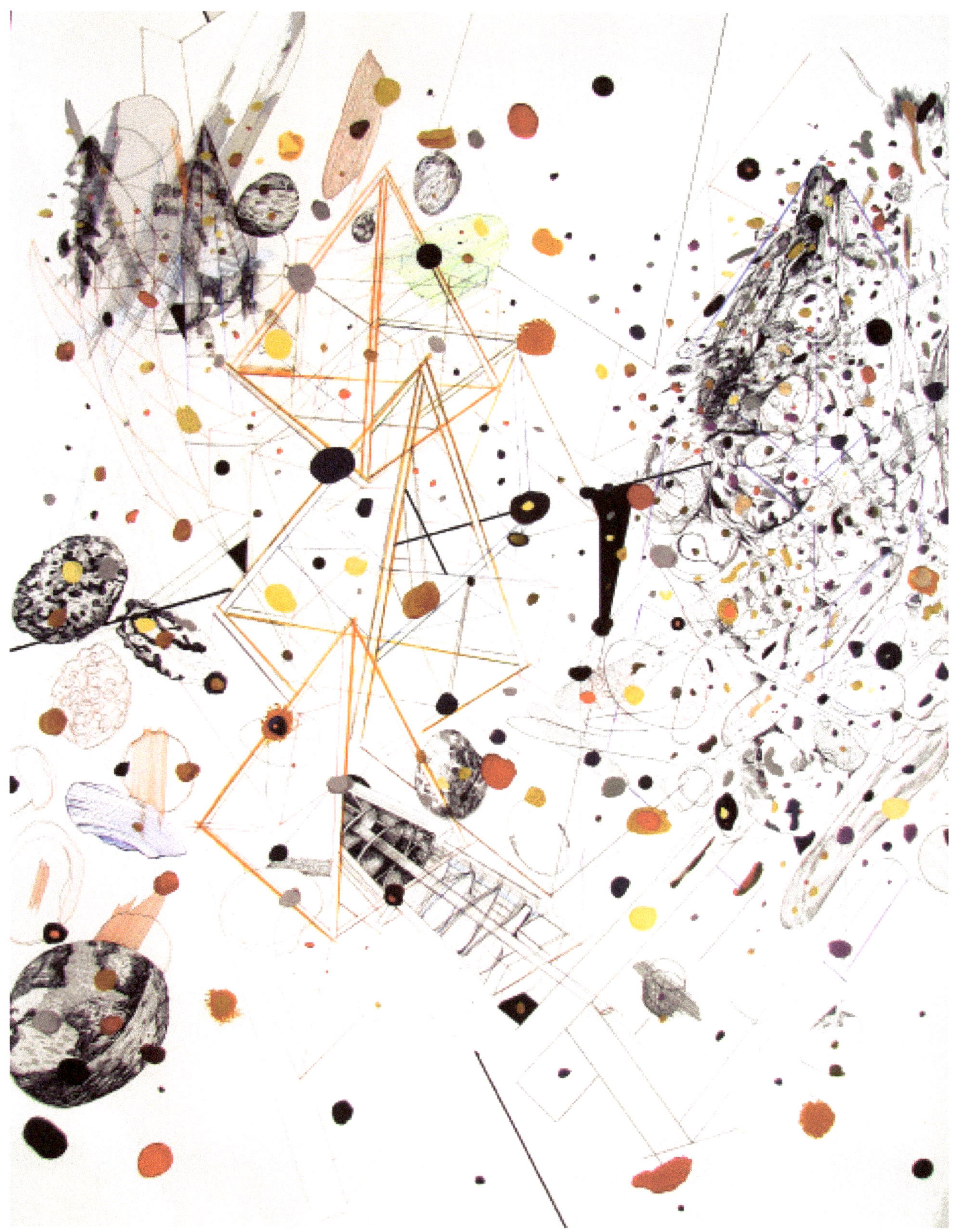

**Watchtower**, *2011, mixed media drawing, 40"x44", collection of the artist.*

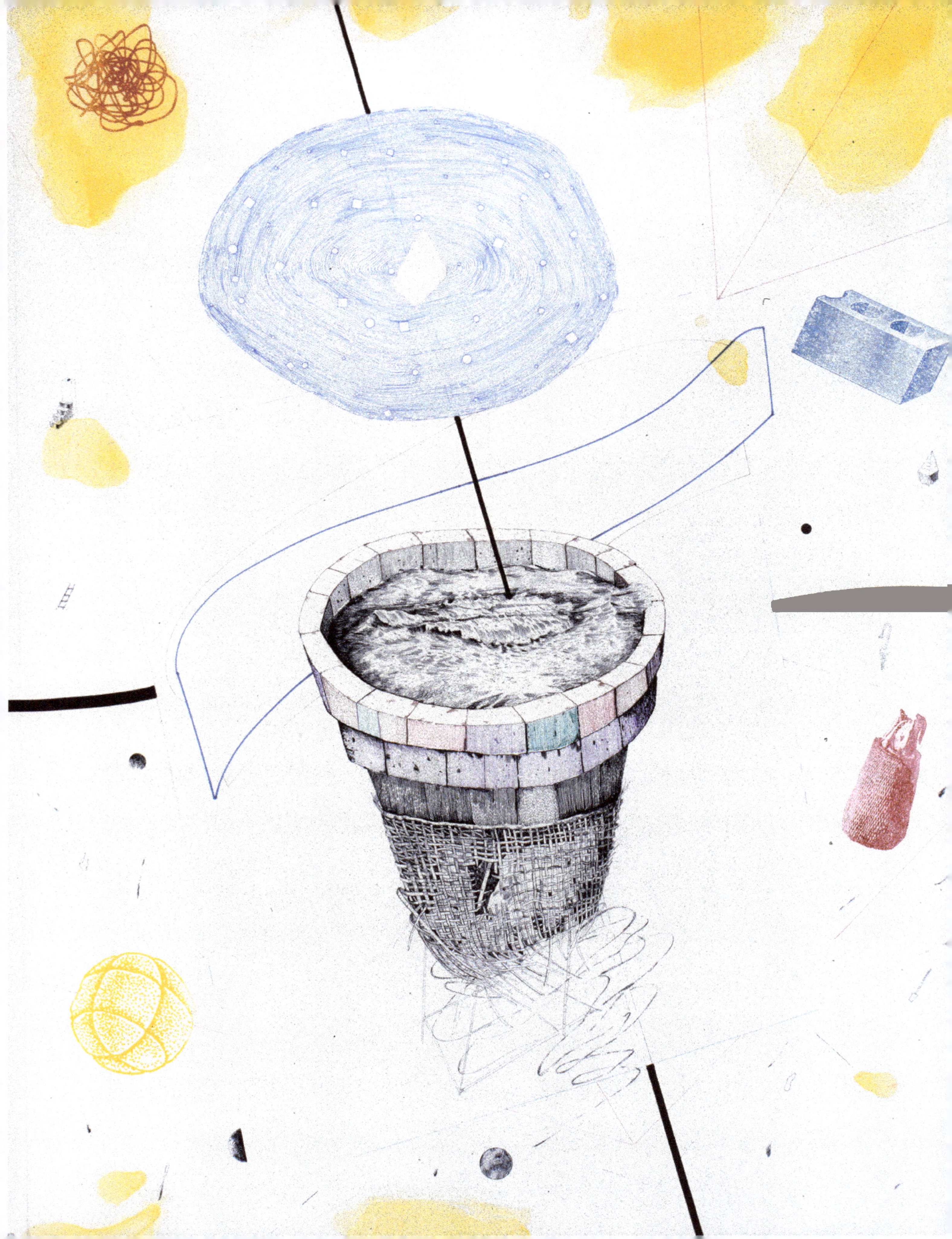

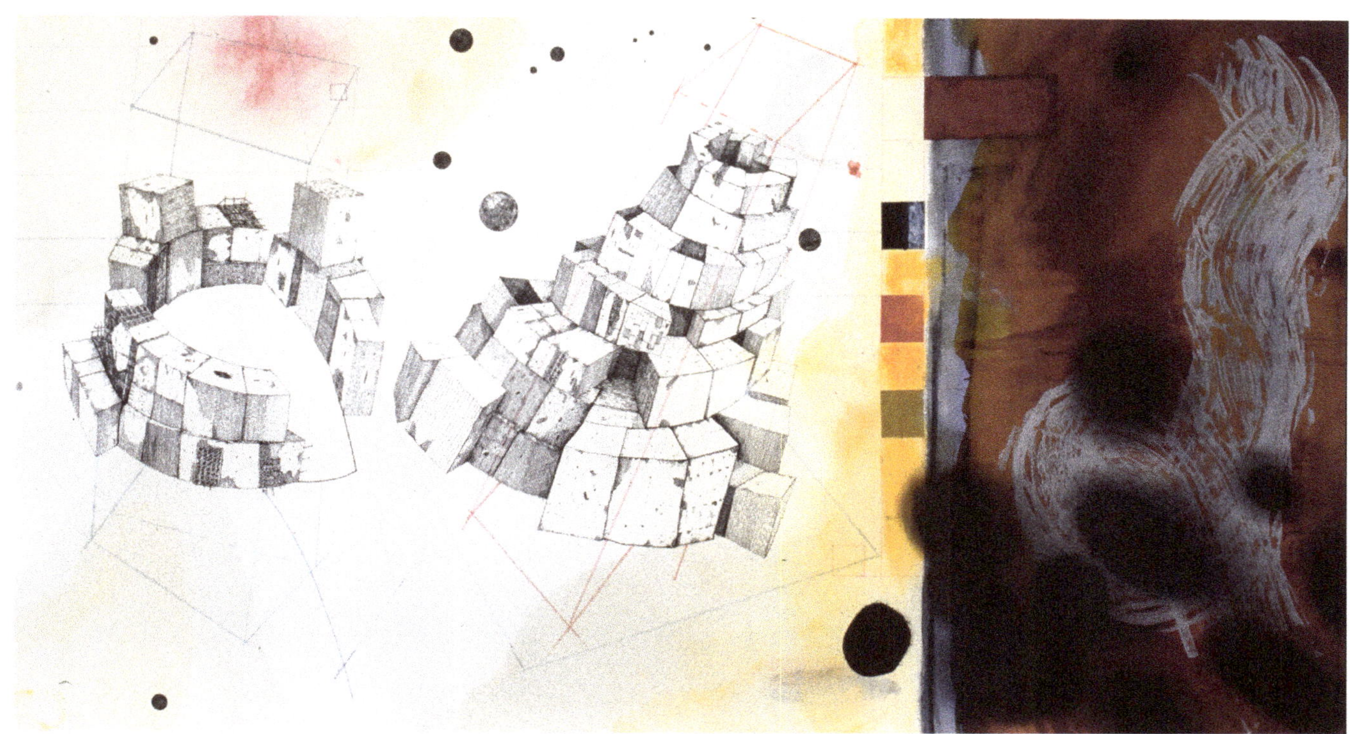

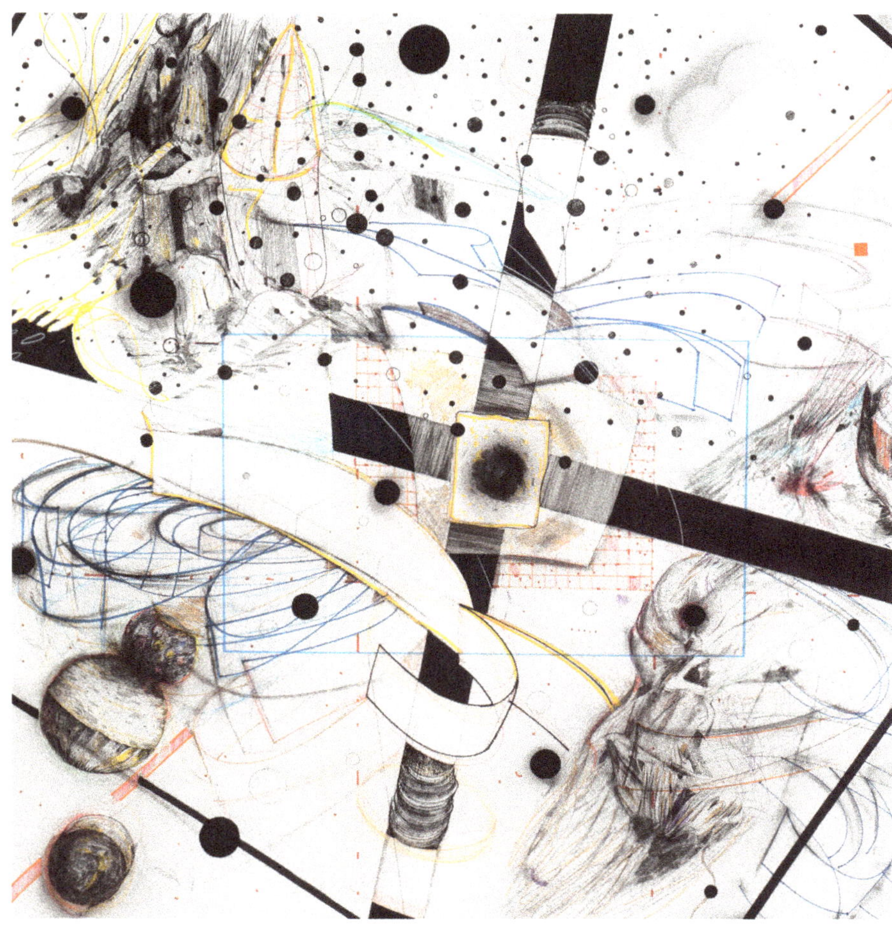

*Top:* **Drunken Tiger,** *2008, mixed media drawing, 42"x42", private collection.*

*Right:* **Flow**, *2008, mixed media drawing, 38"x40", private collection.*

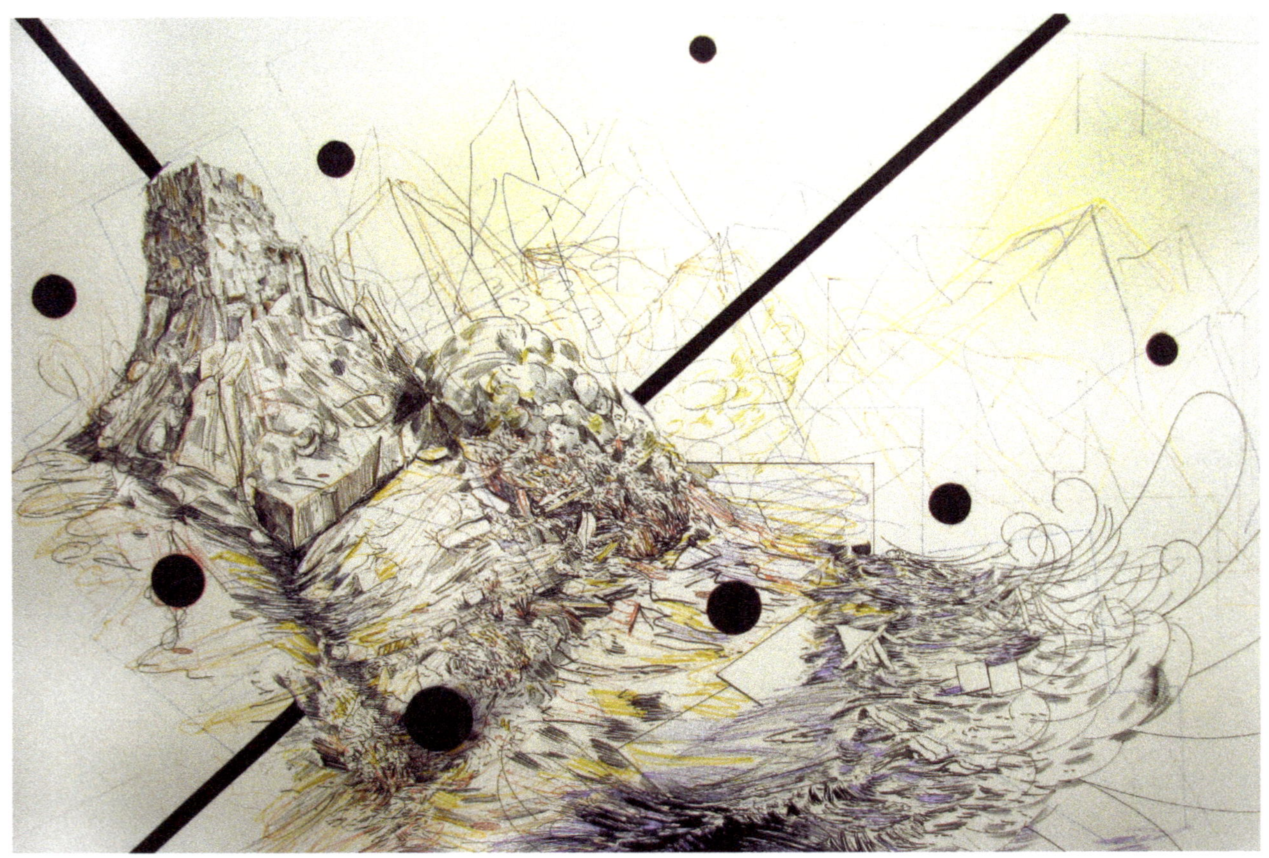

**Island 2**, *2008, mixed media drawing, 32"x42", collection of Luz and Antonio Racela*

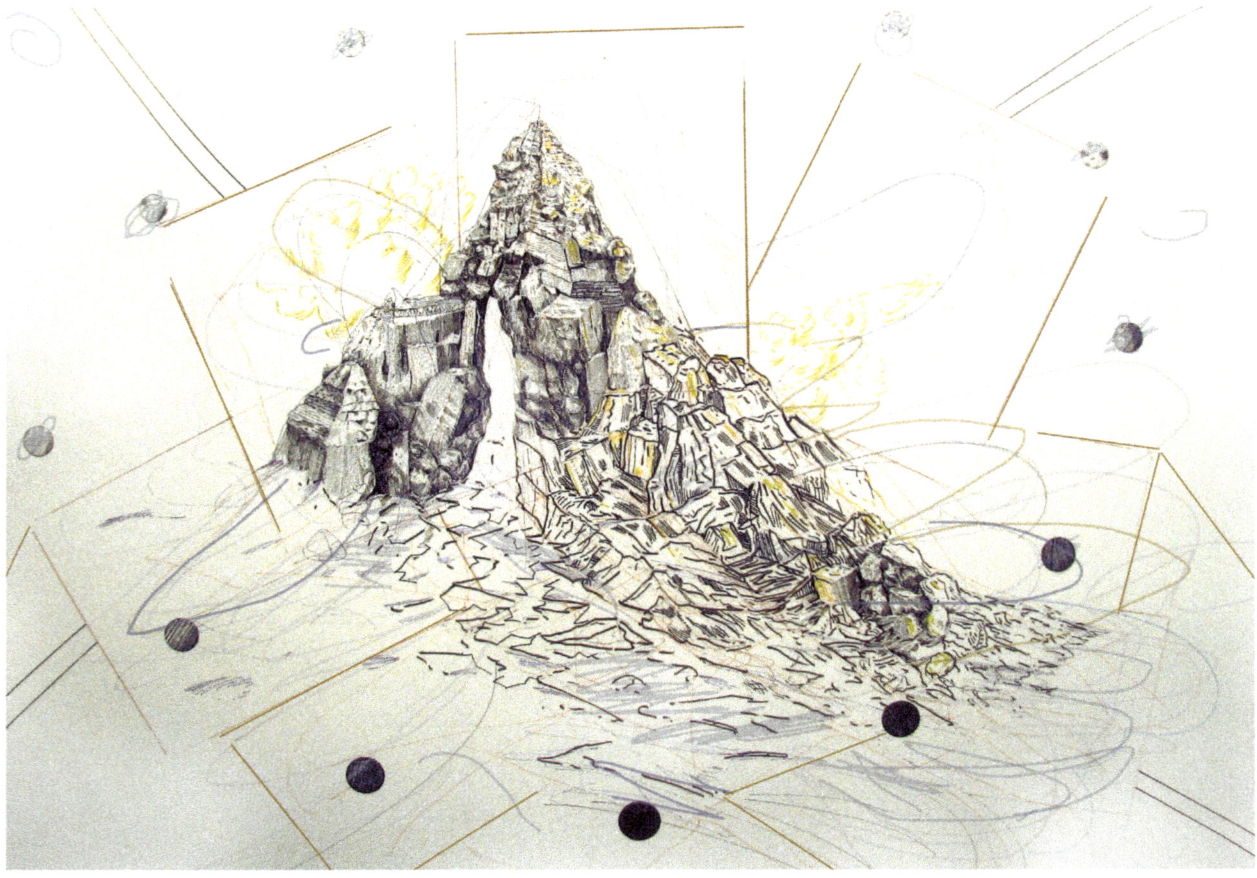

    **Island 4**, *2008, mixed media drawing, 32"x42", collection of the Kemper Museum of Contemporary Art, KCMO.*

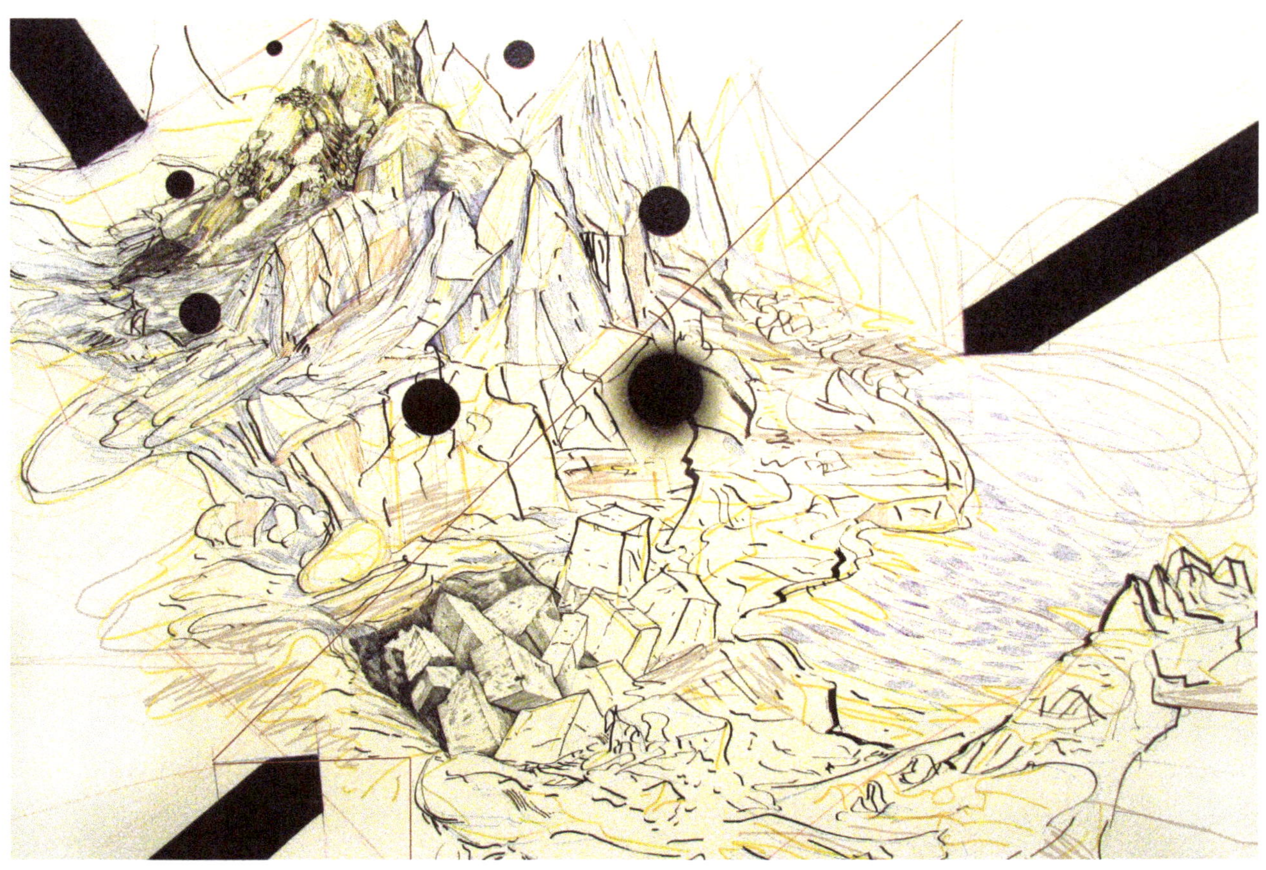

**Mountain 3**, *2008, mixed media drawing, 32"x42", collection of Luz and Antonio Racela.*

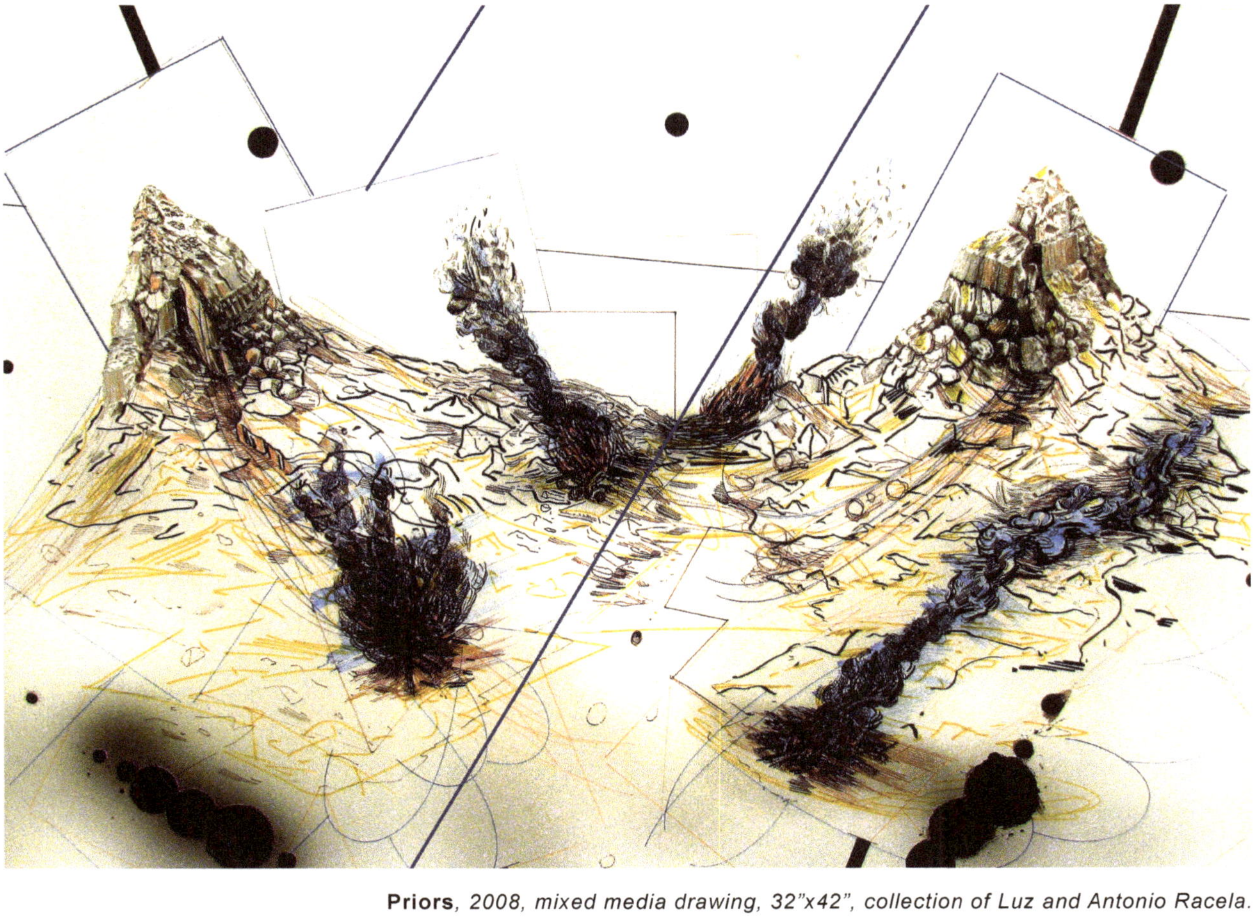

**Priors**, *2008, mixed media drawing, 32"x42", collection of Luz and Antonio Racela.*

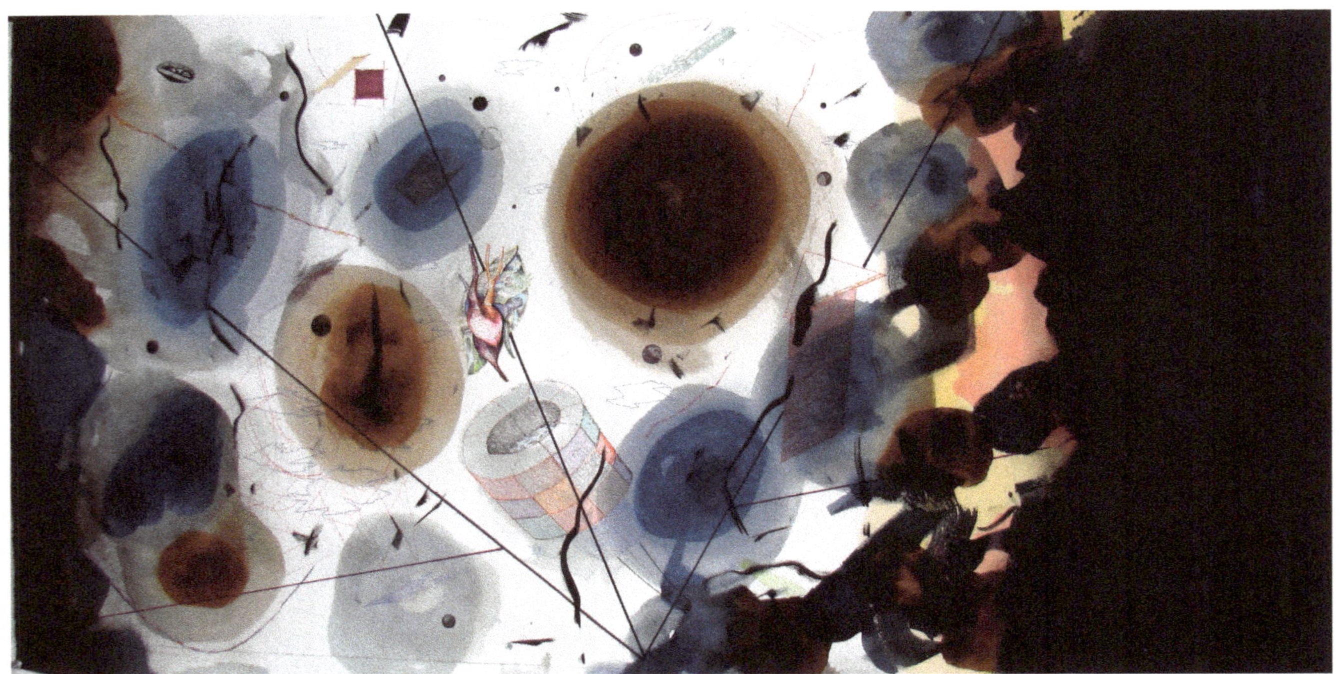

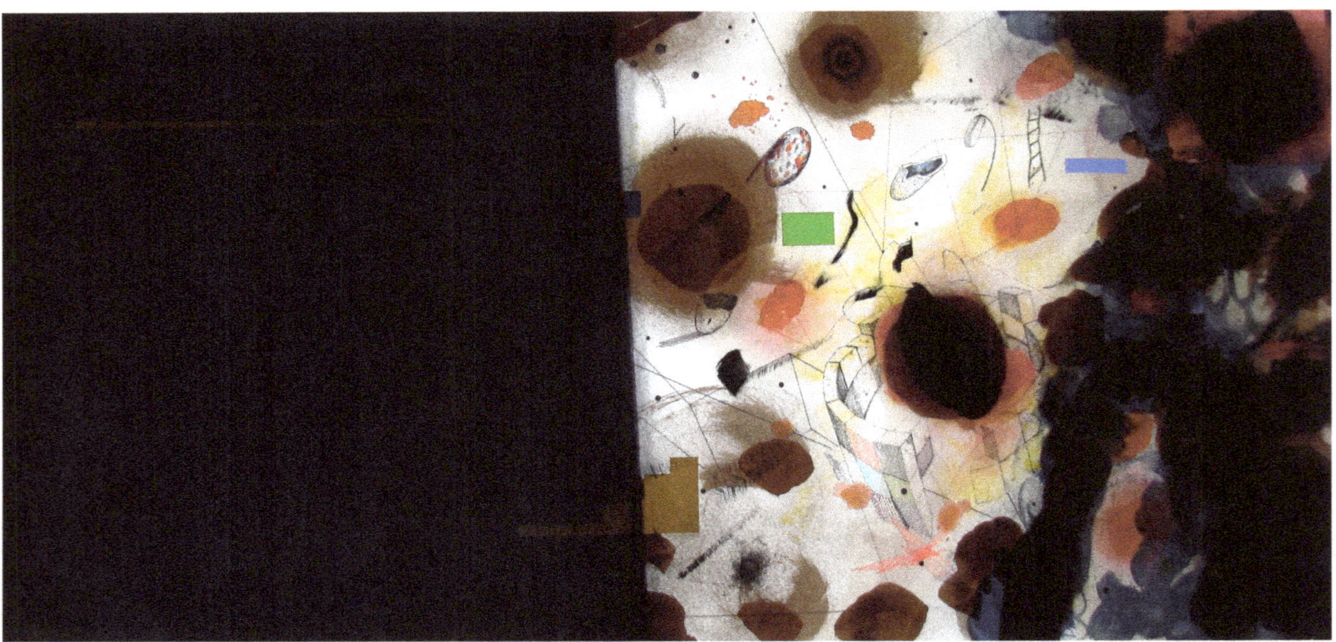

*Top:* **Bankers Cinch**, *2009, mixed media drawing, 24"x42", private collection.*

*Bottom:* **Elements of the Landscape**, *2009, mixed media drawing, 24"x42", private collection.*

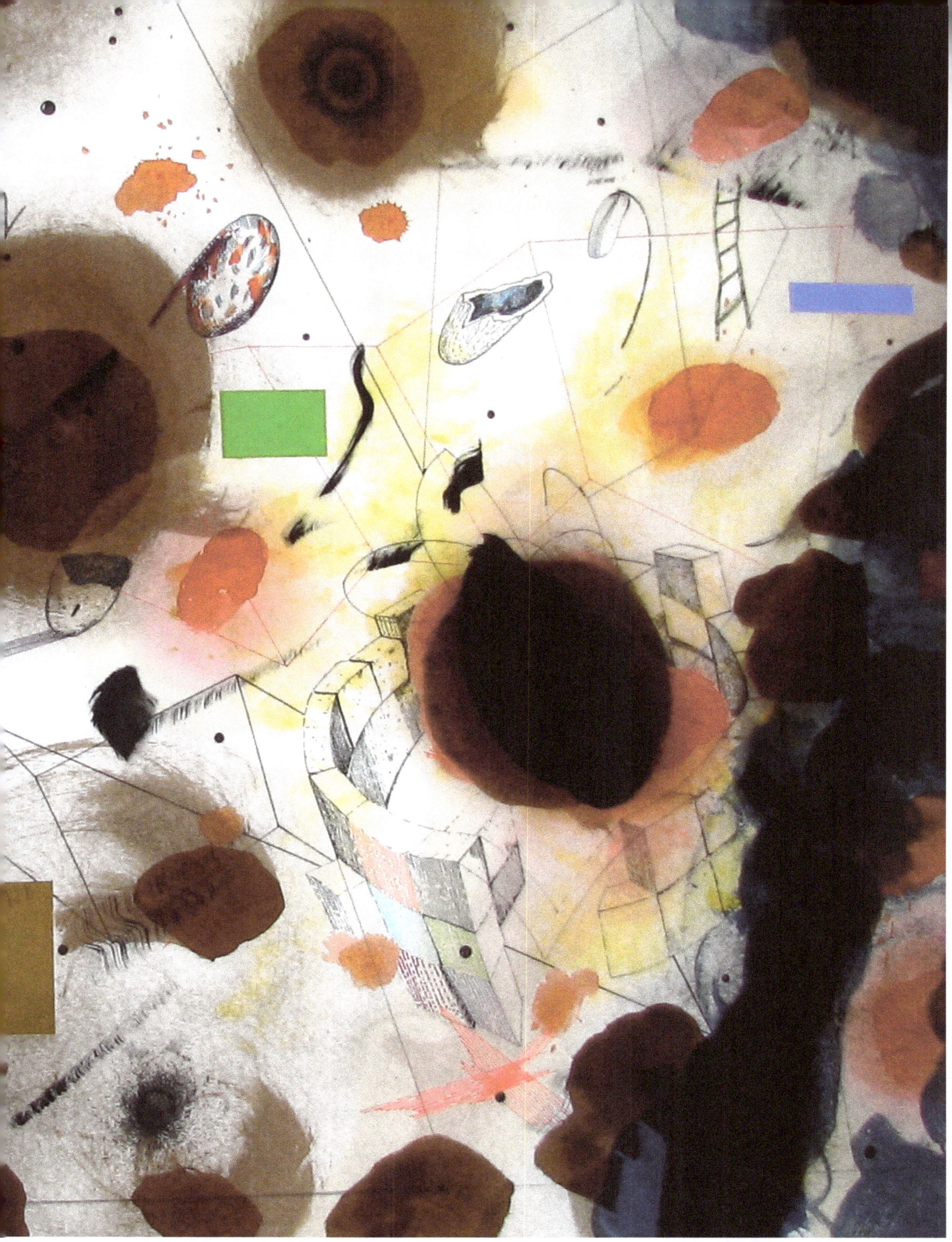

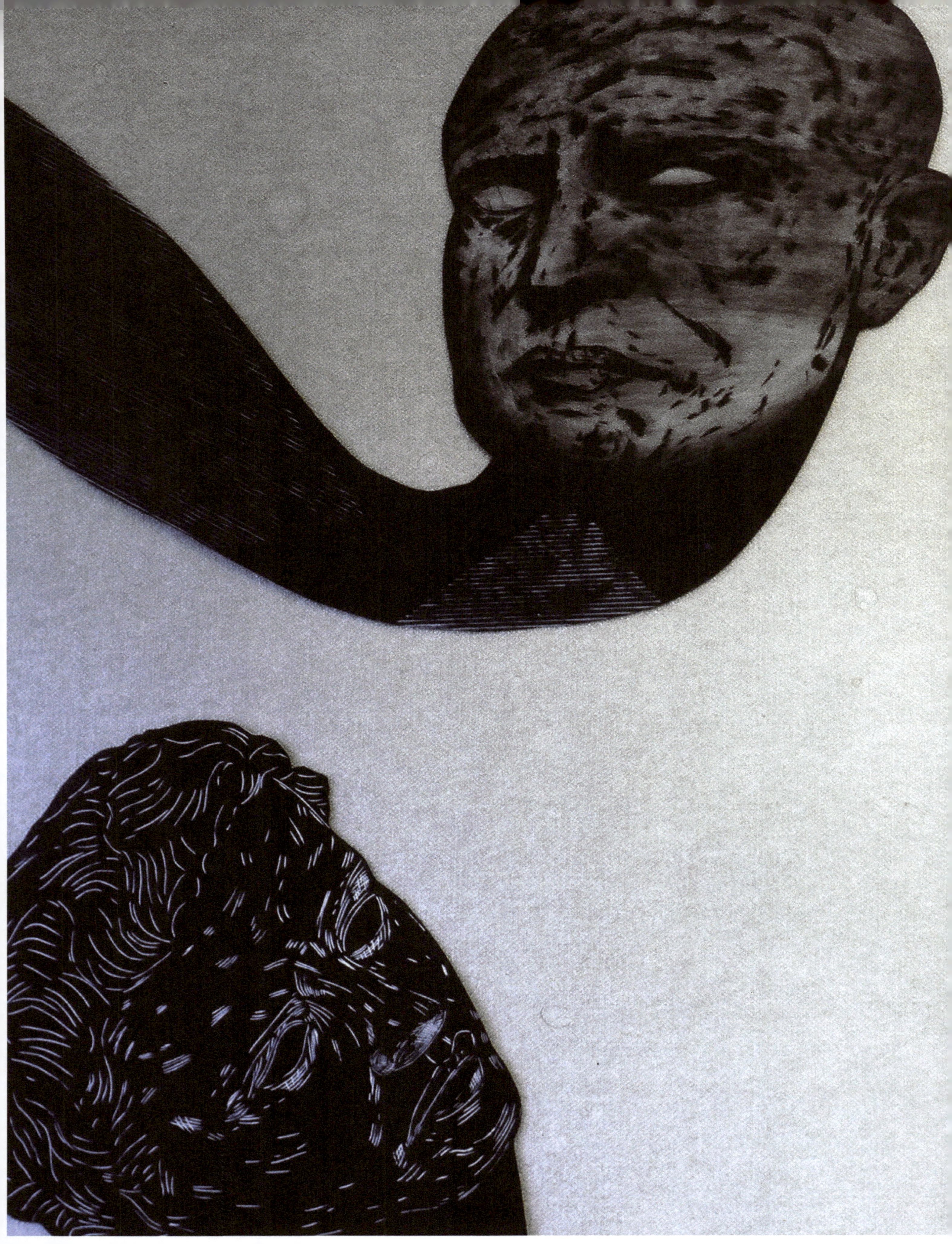

# Relief/Installation

Hugh Merrill is known for bold moves, and so it was no surprise when in the 90's, after two decades of hyper-focus on black and white etching, he began creating deeply engaging installation art pieces and the studio practice of relief printing. Merrill speaks to this transition:

*"The ceramics artist, Jim Leedy, had a major influence on my studio work. He encouraged me to expand my investigations and go beyond etching, not to give up etching but to explore other creative avenues.*

*Leedy's work is significantly based in ceramics; it is his core media and is the process and medium to which he always returns. Yet he has not let himself be confined or limited by the discipline.*

*His work ranges from performance to sculpture, from installation to painting, to drawings and prints. He makes the work he needs to make to express his diverse vision. He helped me expand my studio vision, beginning with large relief prints, which led to installations."*



In 1989, Merrill's woodcuts and monotypes were exhibited at the Printworks Gallery in Chicago, Illinois, leading to a commission from the Davenport Museum of Art in Davenport, Iowa. A 12'x20' wood-block print coated in bees wax and titled *Dead Serious* was produced for this exhibition. Merrill saw the show as an opportunity to modernize the understanding of the historical tradition of wood-cuts.

*Life Cycles*, a relief installation, was created by cutting, engraving, and painting images of oversized male heads and corresponding running female figures positioned together. Their open hands, disembodied fists, and abstract shapes suggest Indian baskets from the plastic substrate. The artist says:

*"Each installation was unique and dictated by the architecture of their location. Fans and lighting were employed to create moving shadows to animate and explore the various spaces. The installations relied on the tension and narrative created by the male and female images and their constantly changing and moving shadows."*

Merrill quips about this installation piece, "you know why the women have two sets of arms? They have to because the world expects them to do all the work." Merrill exhibited *Life Cycles* first at the Santa Barbara Contemporary Arts Forum in Santa Barbara, California in 1994.

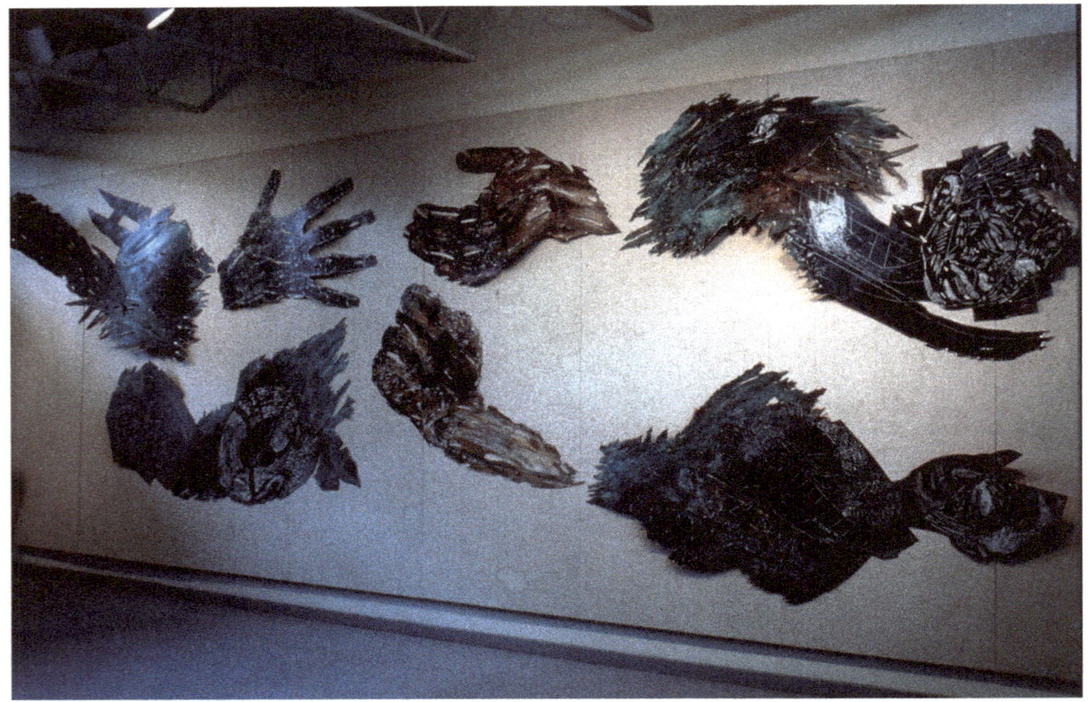

**Runner**, *1990's, installation, Indianapolis Contemporary Arts Guild, Indianapolis, Indiana.*

Later that year, Merrill filled a ten-story glass pyramid at the Edmonton, Alberta, Canada City Hall in collaboration with their Works Festival. The pieces were then installed at various venues including: Stephen F. Austin University in Nacogdoches, Texas; Harris Community College in Houston, Texas; and the Indianapolis Contemporary Arts Guild in Indianapolis, Indiana.

Merrill continues creating installation works and also commits himself to helping emerging and self-taught artists to create multi-sensory performance art/installation exhibitions, especially in the context of engaging communities. His ongoing work with red-lined city districts, including Troost Fest in Kansas City and his ongoing emphasis on zine creation for his students are emblematic examples of how Merrill empowers each person he encounters with the idea of their self-worth.

Each ongoing project serves as ample inspiration and motivation for new series.

*--Jeanette Powers*

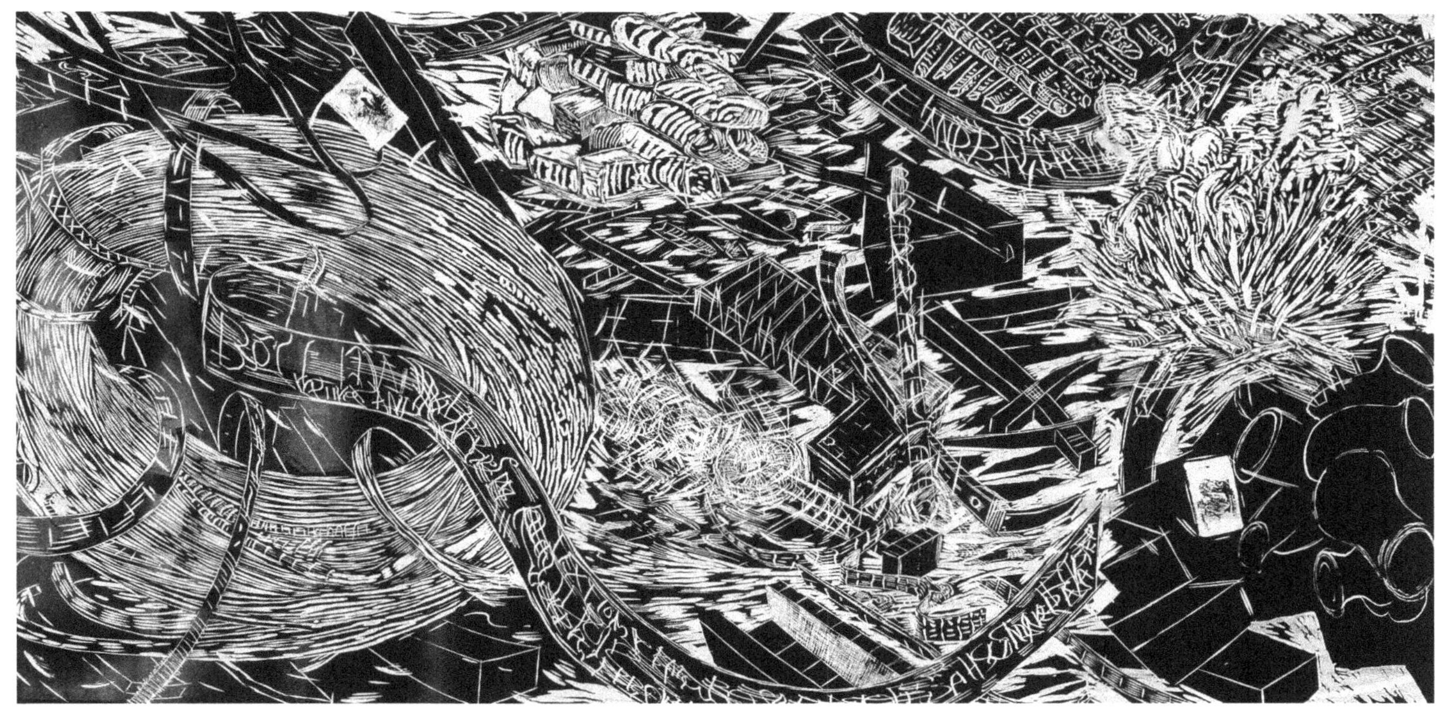

**Dead Serious**, *1989, relief print, 4'x8', Davenport Museum of Contemporary Art, Davenport, Iowa.*

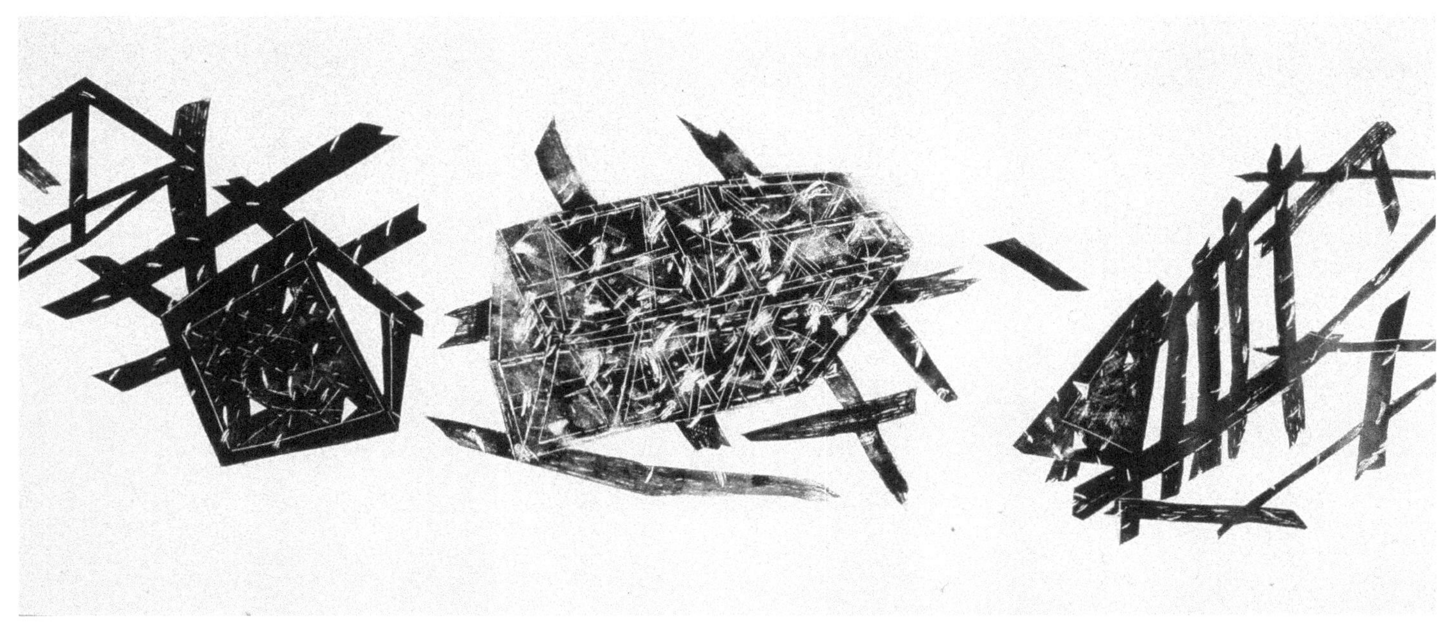

**Smith's Bridge**, *1989, relief print, 5'x20', collection of the artist.*

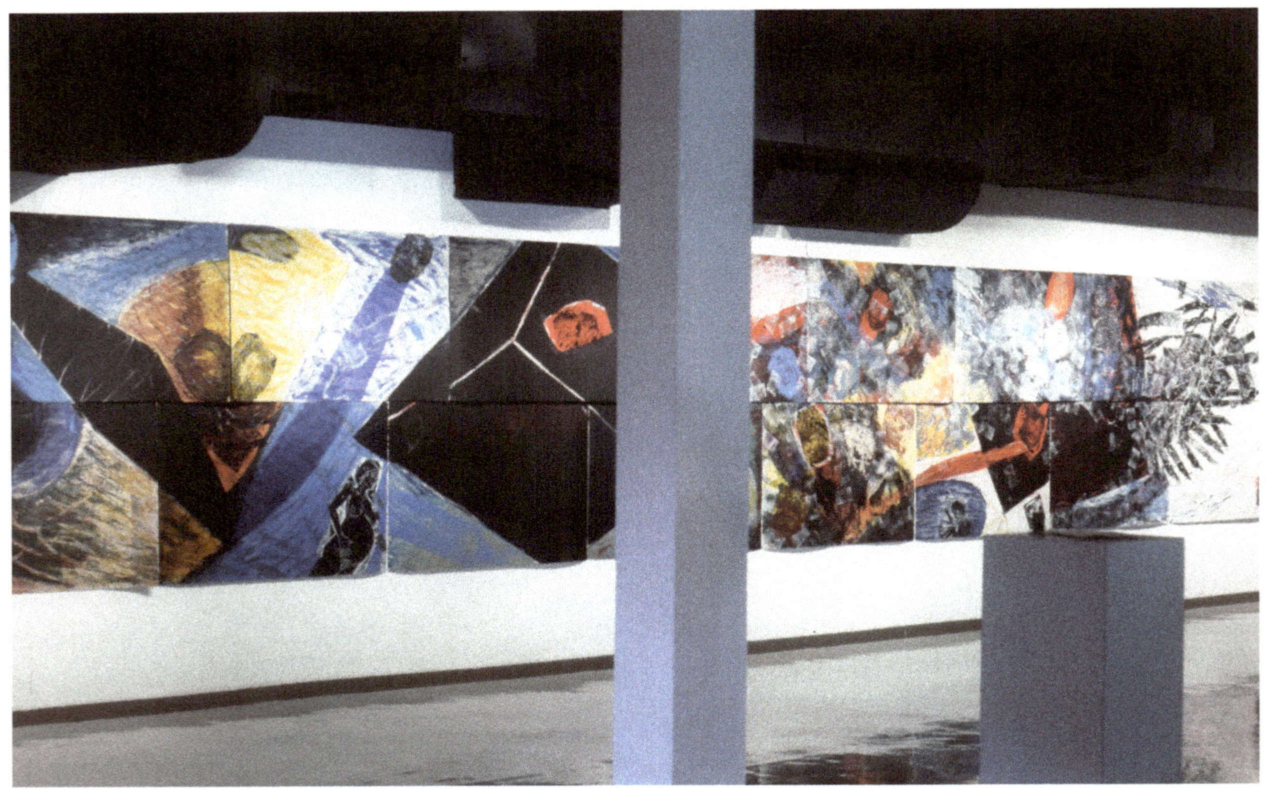

**Birth**, *1995, monoprint installation, 48"x20', University of Alberta, Edmonton, Alberta, Canada.*

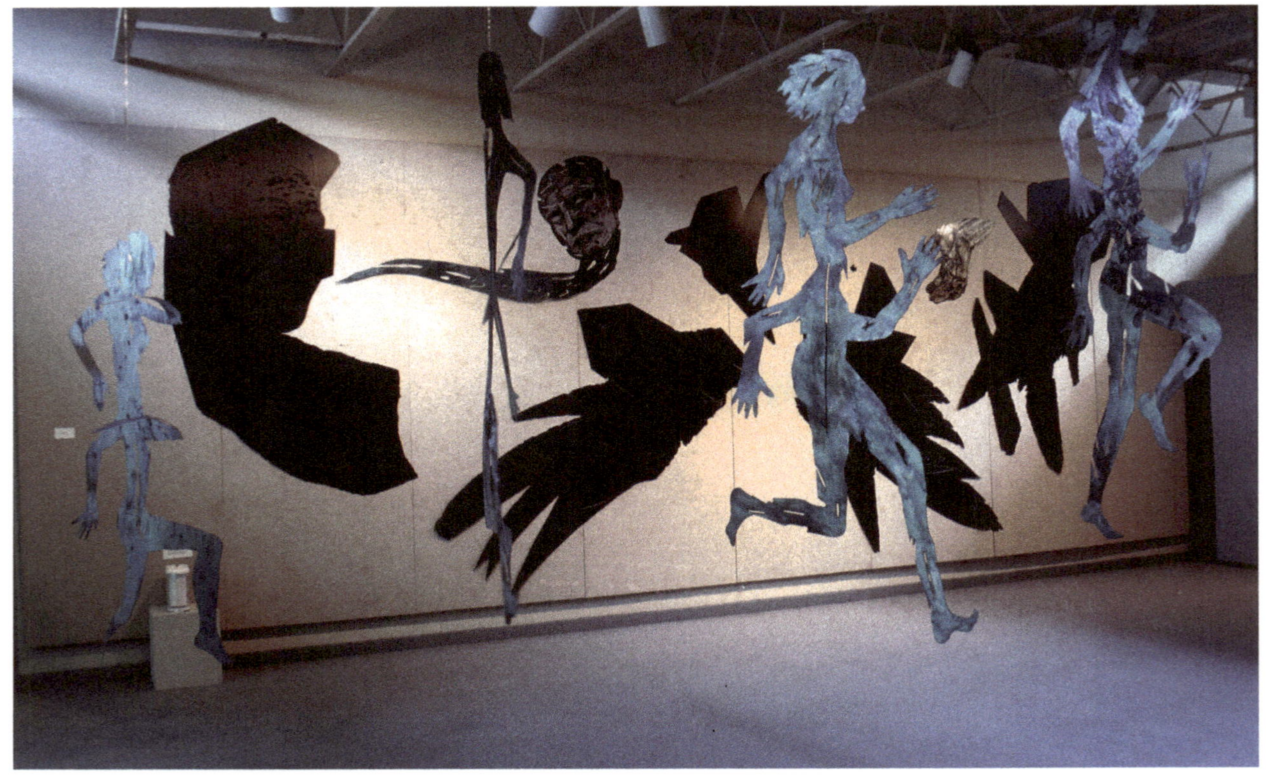

**Little Lives**, *1995, installation, Community Christian Church, Kansas City, Missouri.*

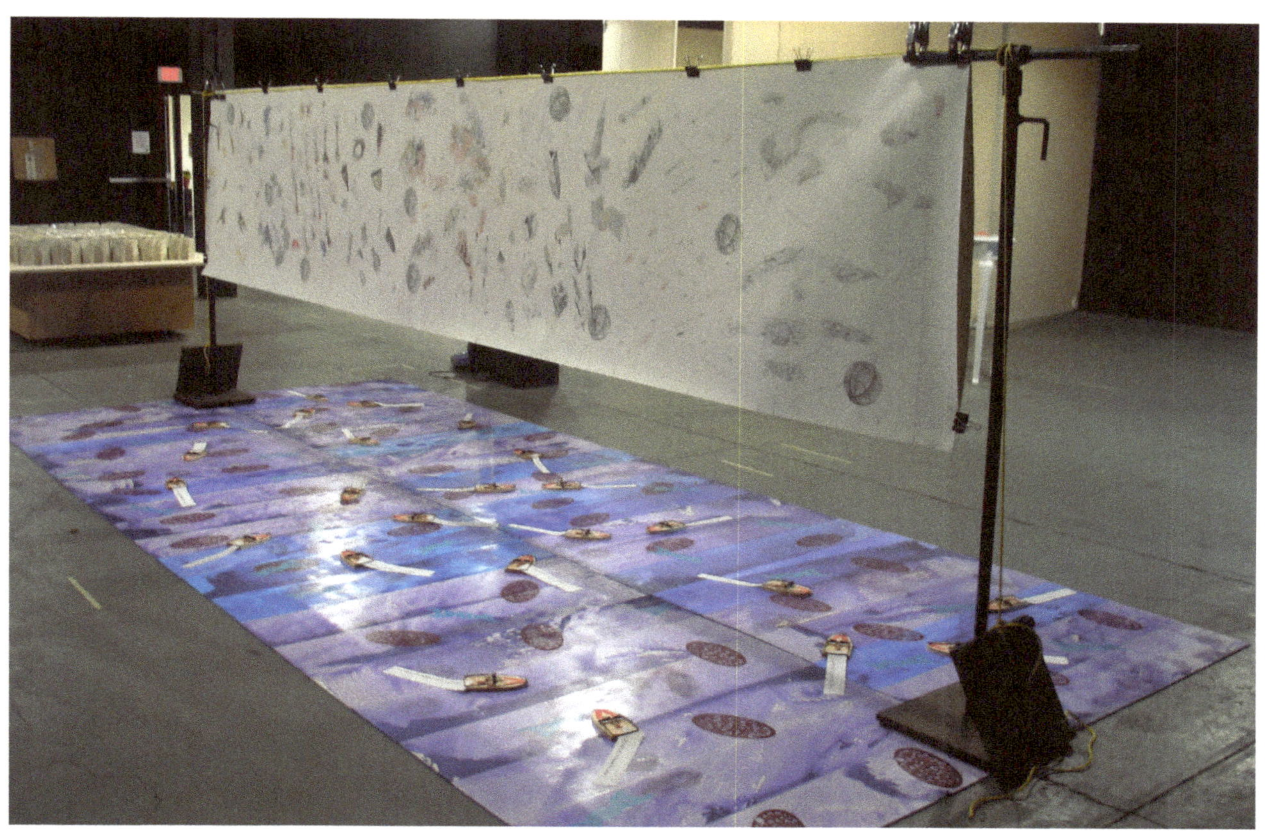

**Float World**, *2005, drawing/installation, Mid-American Print Alliance, University of Nebraska, Lincoln.*

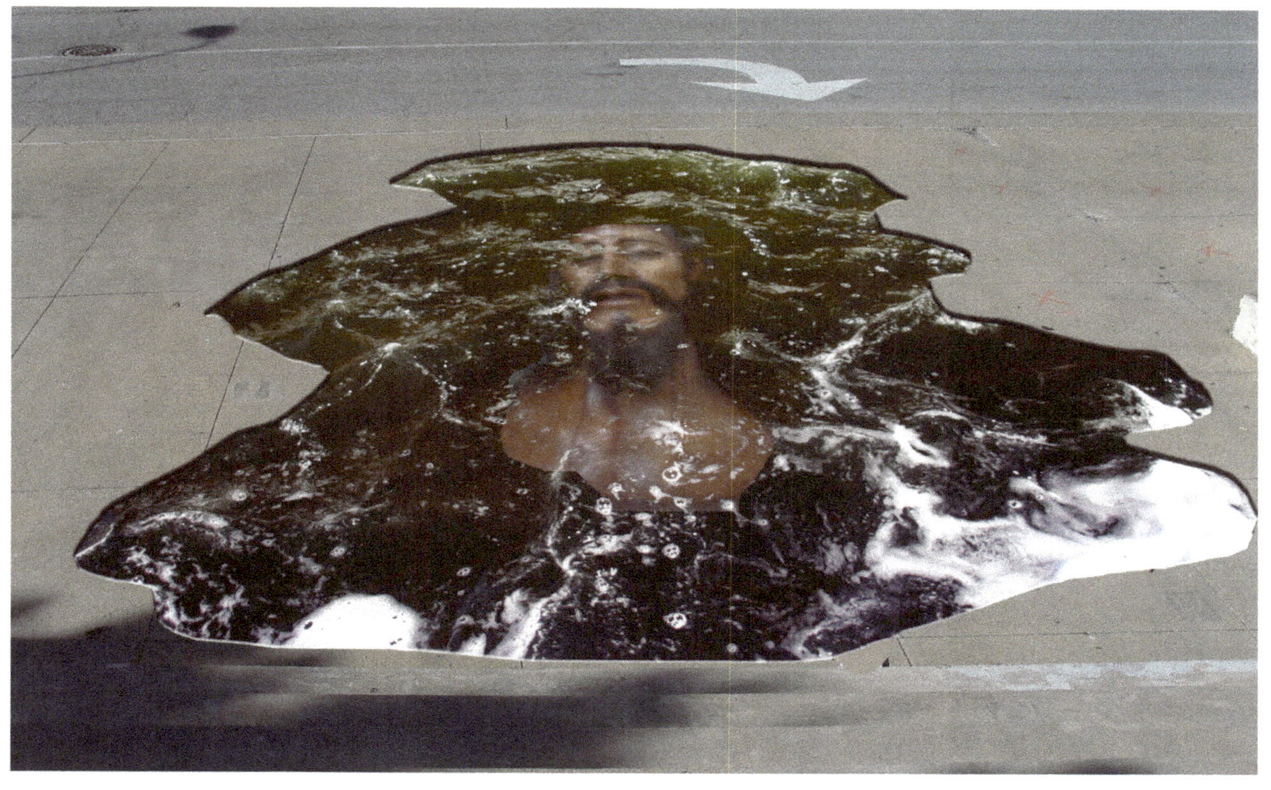

**Warrior**, *1990, proposed street graphic, 12'x12', Avenue of the Arts, Kansas City, Missouri.*

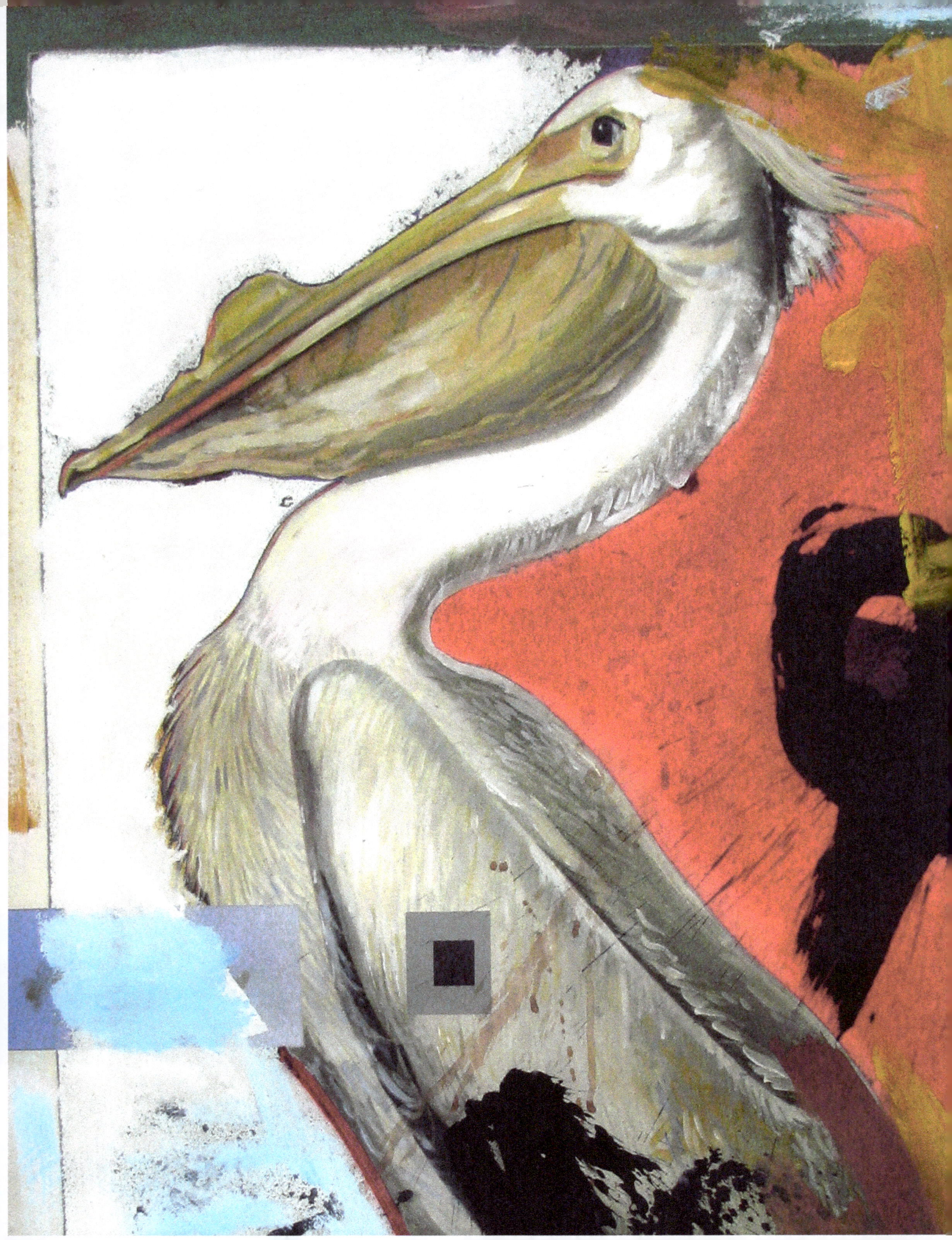

# Birds of America
## A re-interpretation of 8 prints by John James Audubon

Nothing conjures more images of birds in peril than the words *oil spill.* When Hugh Merrill first caught news of the 2010 BP Deep Horizon oil disaster his heart immediately turned to the plight of our wildlife who cannot speak for themselves. In his natural element of studying historical artists, this created the perfect storm of revisiting the great American naturalist and painter John James Audubon from the perspecitve of modern ecological distasters.

In this digital world, fewer and fewer folks have direct access to engaging with animals in the wild. Merrill, though, is one to walk and know the river, the pond, he is unafraid of the crow, eagle or egret. He understands the peace found in connection with nature, and as an arts educator is in a unique space to experience directly the disconnection the youth have with the wild world.

So while this re-imagining of Audubon's signature birds may at first breath seem pastoral, it is actually playing advocate for a re-connection with our natural past and is an important work in regards to understanding the value of wild-life in 21st Century Earth. The sequence also serves as an invitation to remember to look up from our phones and to see the migration, the life, and the stuggle of those beings which can actually fly.

The world watched dedicated volunteers delicately scrub thick, black scum off the feathers, from the fronds of our Gulf Coast shorelines. It is not just the birds unhoused by these disasters, it is the people. Merrill captures the panic-fraught loss of homes shown on every media outlet about a pelican or a tern, and we know it is a metaphor for the families displaced as well. So many living beings being sacrificed for the ongoing carbon-wars. So many displaced people unaccounted for and anonymous. Each of these birds is a child without school for the semester, a man who lost the house he raised a son in.

Merrill reminds us of why we should love these birds while reminding us that more than just birds are the victims of disasterous energy systems. They are the bonding agent which reminds us that when our resources are suffocated, we are suffocated.

*--Jeanette Powers*

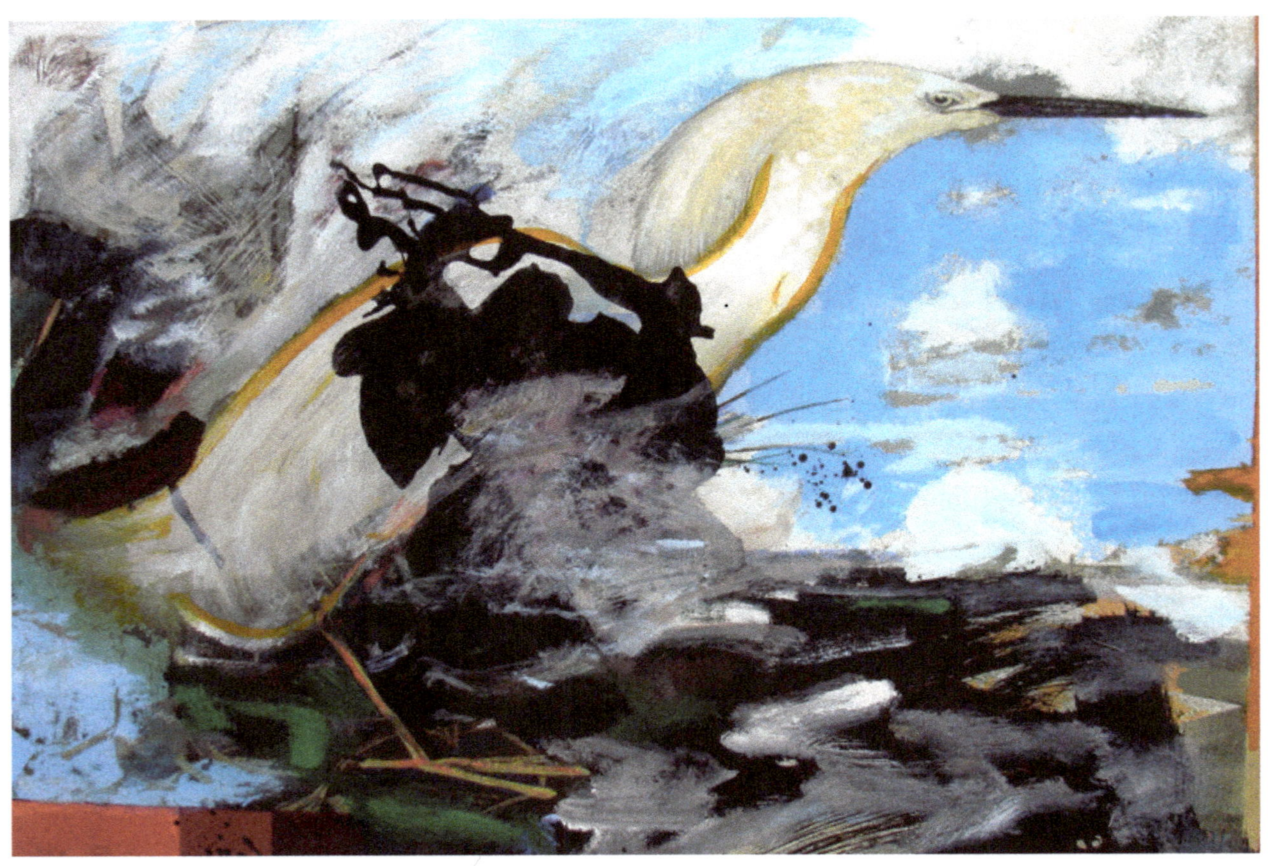

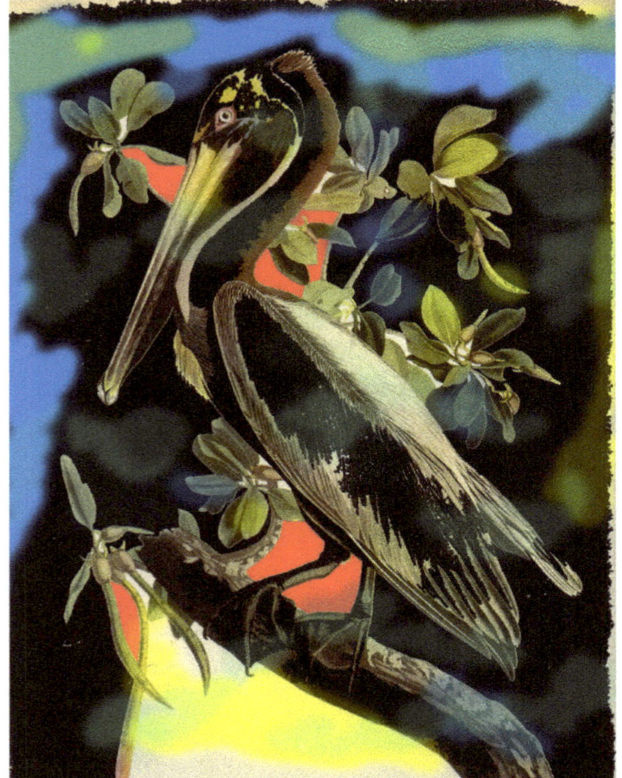

*Top:* **Snowy Egret**, *2010, painting and digital print, 32"x40", collection of the artist.*

*Left:* **Brown Pelican**, *2010, painting and digital print, 40"x30", collection of the artist.*

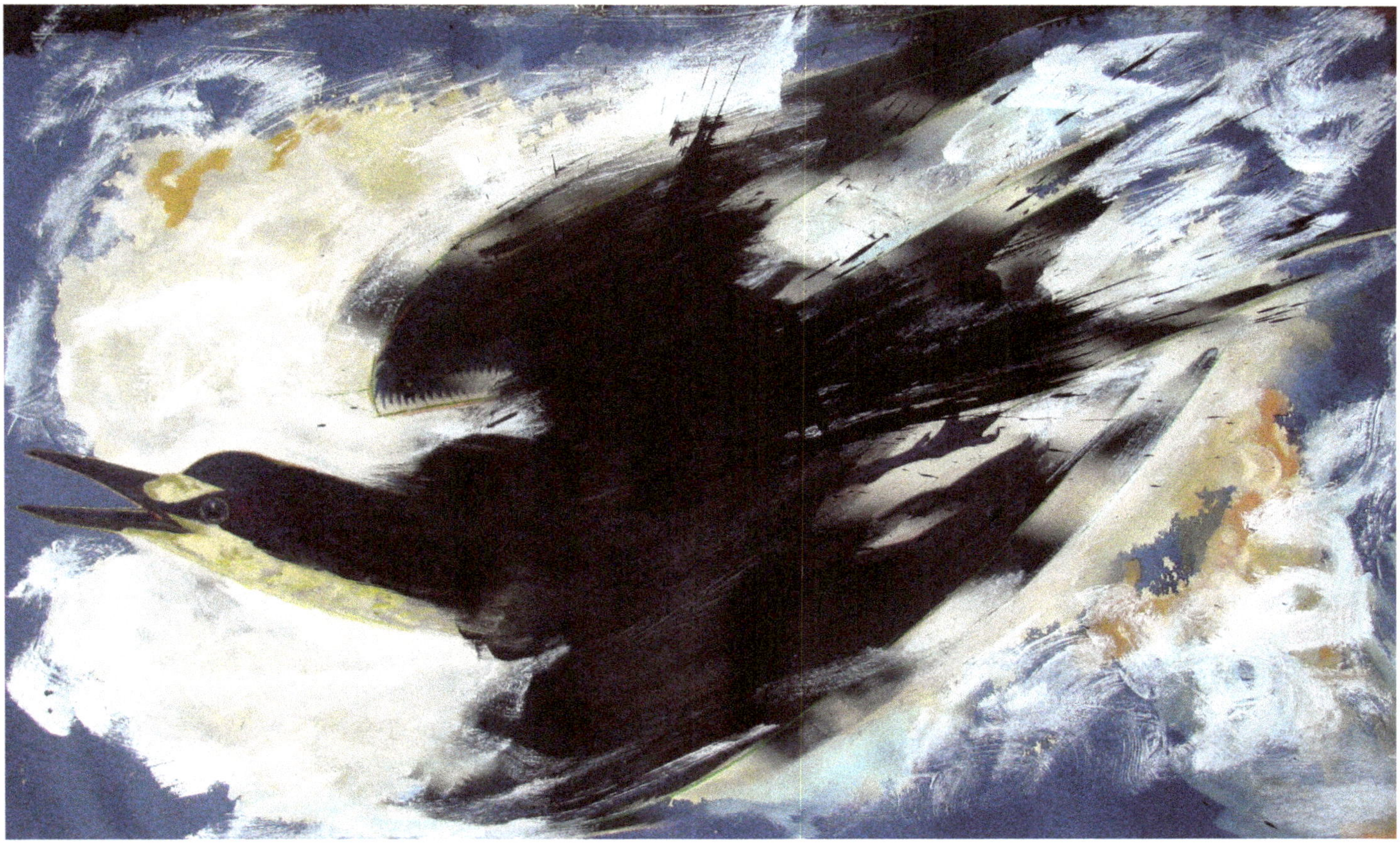

*Top:* **Tern**, *2010, painting and digital print, 38"x23", collection of the artist.*

*Right:* **Manowar**, *2010, painting and digital print, 40"x42", collection of*
*the artist.*

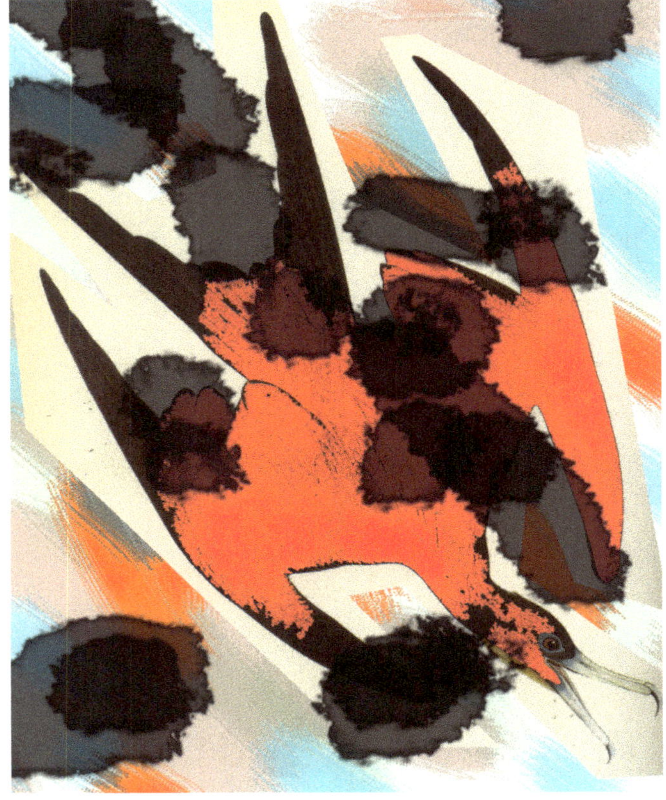

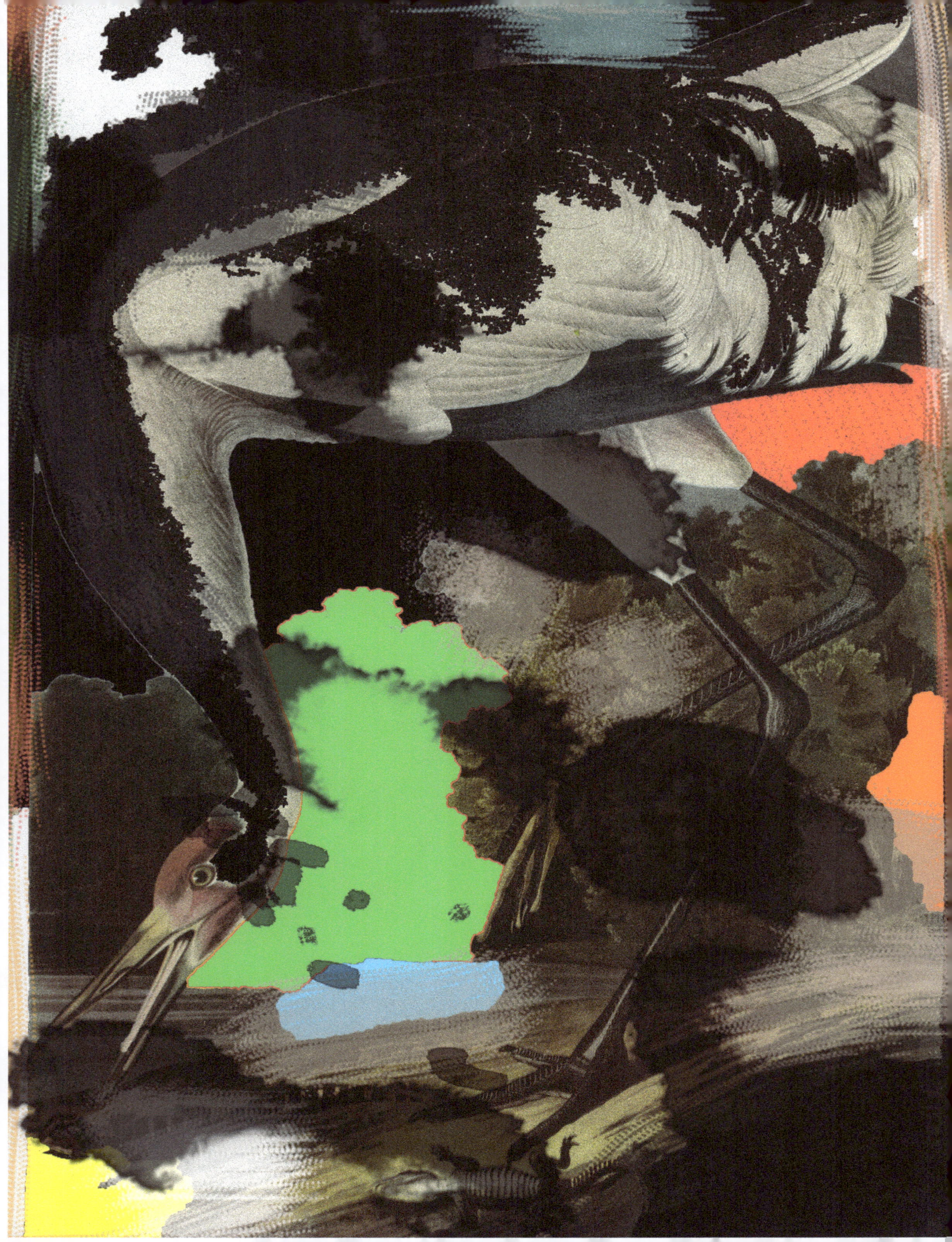

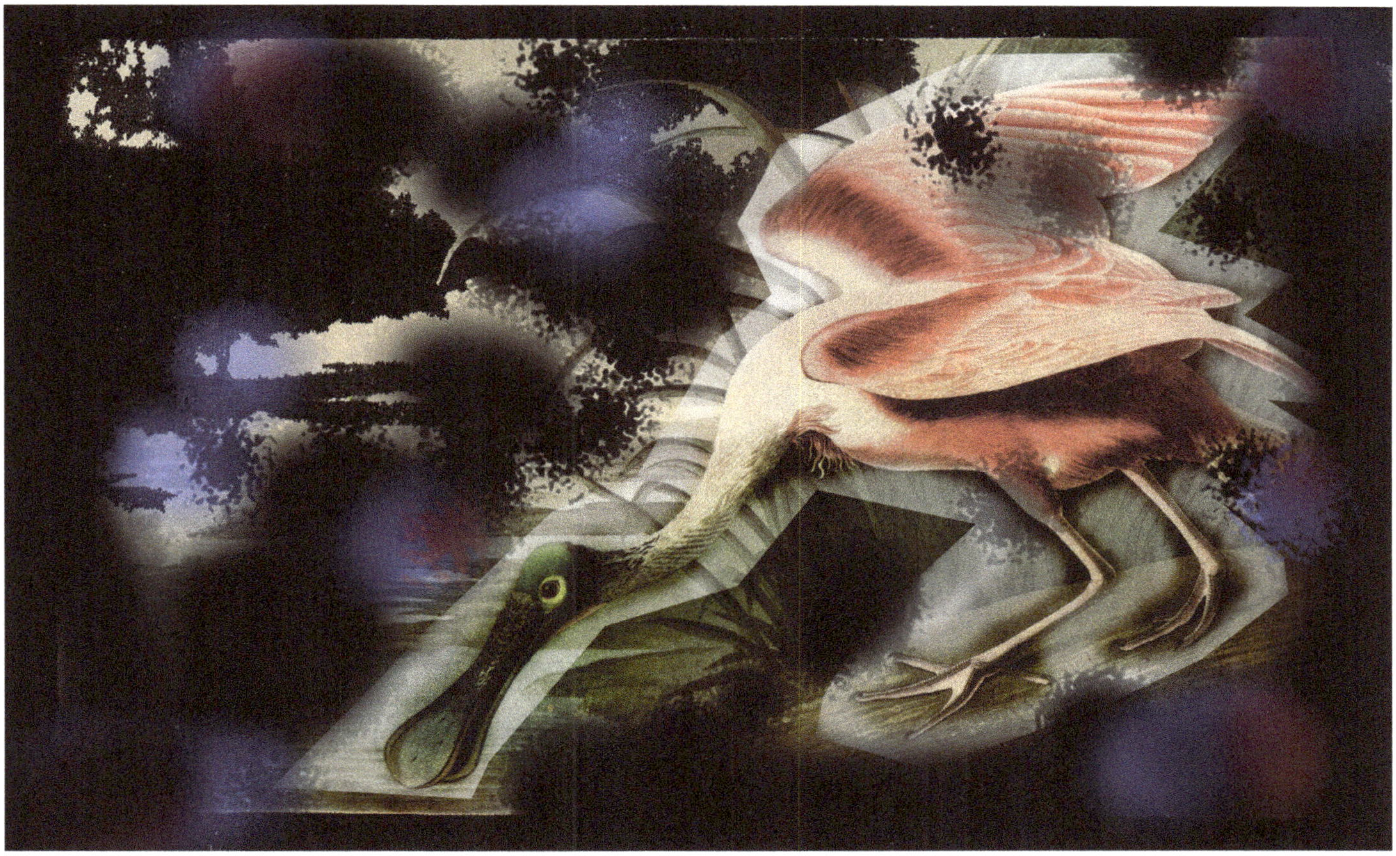

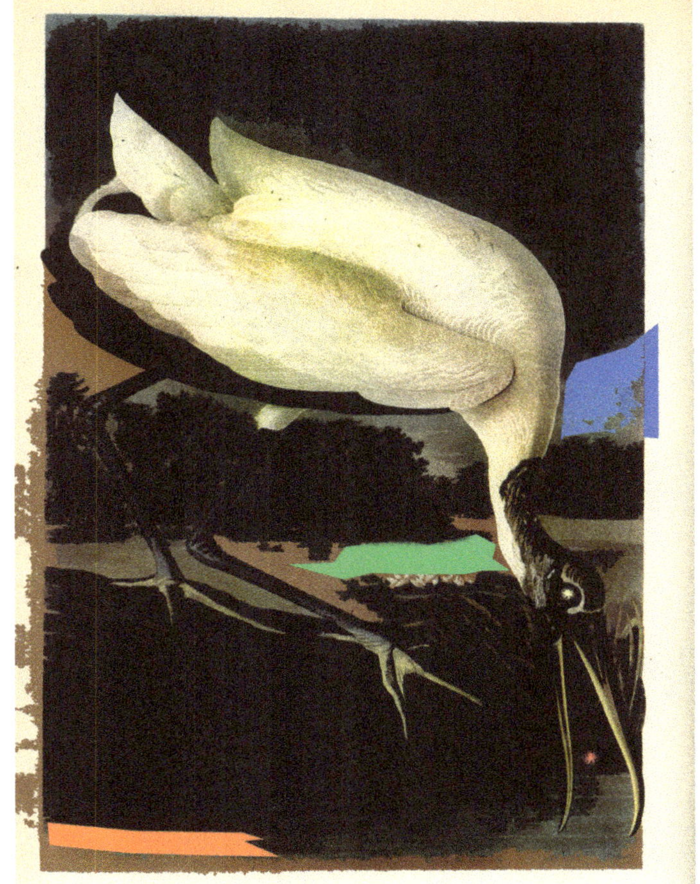

Top: **Spoonbill**, 2010, painting and digital print, 40"x25", collection of the artist.

Right: **Ibis**, 2010, painting and digital print, 29"x40", collection of the artist.

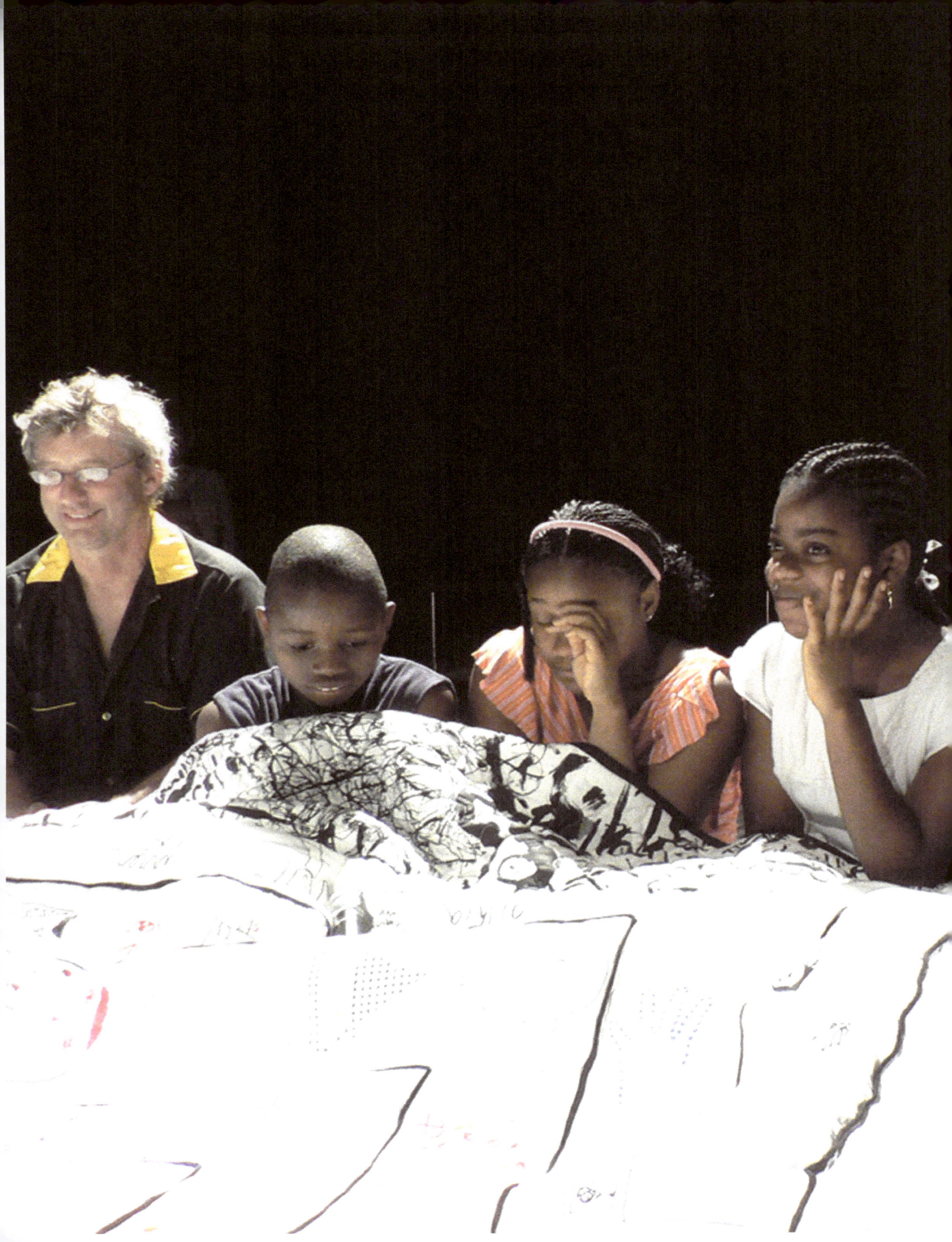

# Community Art
## Introduction

Hugh Merrill sensed something was amiss as a young man, and no matter how the adults in his life assured him all was right with the world, he couldn't unsee the injustice he saw every day. Merrill attended the inauguration of John F. Kennedy with his parents, and this moment is a seminal aspect to the ethics with which he has conducted his life. When the newly elected president spoke, Merrill took note:

*"We shall pay any price, bear any burden, meet any hardship, support any friend, oppose any foe to assure the survival and success of liberty."*

What Merrill found was less hardship and more enlightenment. By pursuing justice, by engaging marginalized communities, by acknowledging and utilizing his privilege to provoke social change, Merrill has fundamentally altered the artistic landscape of both modern printmaking and the modern intersection between arts and activism. He has passionately engaged with the civil rights movement, the anti-war movement, the Act Up AIDS awareness movement, the modern trans-rights movement, the immigration movement and continues to listen and engage with all marginalized peoples.

Merrill's viewpoint is inherently holistic, his view is that any disadvantaged peoples are a direct reflection of the advantaged whole. If some flourish extravagantly, all should flourish basically. Merrill percieves economic disadvantages as inconsequential to the value of a human being and insists on equality of beings. There is no option for humanity to disconnect from itself, and therefore Merrill advocates for the voiceless moreso than he advocates for himself.

Working with Chameleon and other arts organizations, Merrill has facilitated arts education for thousands of inner-city children over the thirty-year history of the non-profit. Exposure to art, theater, and dance programming transforms the lives of these children and helps them to understand that their personal narratives are singularly art artifacts by nature of the experience.

This teaching and nurturing ethic is also what makes Merrill such a transformative educator. He instills and advocates a deep sense of worth and responsibility in his undergraduate students. This sense of connection and value creates young artists to continue the mission of community building through the arts. Merrill says:

*"In community art you must go out before you go in to the studio. You need to connect, collect resources and stories. You must become part of the community through trust and the gift of those stories. It is this that establishes the collaboration from which the art will be made."*

*--Jeanette Powers*

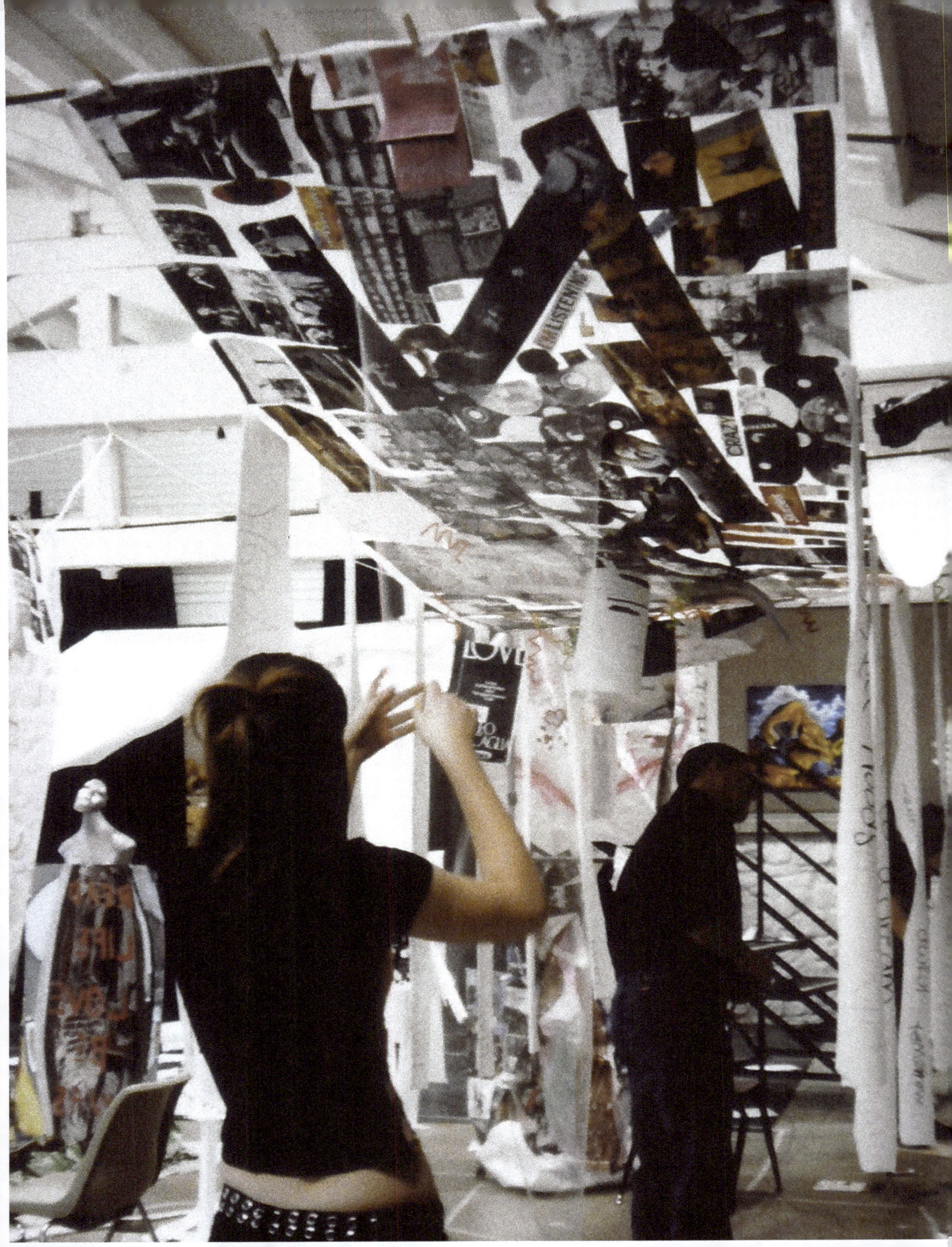

# Portrait of Self

*"Community art is a process that nurtures awareness and celebrations of others' aliveness . . . a process to move the community from the habit of consuming and watching culture to the ritual of producing and articulating culture."* remarks Merrill, explaining the underlying inspirations for the development of his acclaimed archiving process, *Portrait of Self* (*POS*). This series of explorations is universal in its ability to bring out the inner artist in anyone who participates. By paying close attention to nothing more than everyday life, participants suddenly find the ability to create personalized original images and participate in social dialogue.

*POS* is an arts and educational process designed to help people express the many factors that create a personal sense of who they are. An artistic self-portrait in the most traditional sense is the reproduction of one's own reflection in a mirror. *POS* is an archive of drawings, poetry, writing, photography, daily lists, and other documentation. Participants create chronicles as a representation of the complexity of everyday life. This project is an investigation of the sources that make us who we are.

Through a process designed to help challenge habitual ways of approaching issues of social and personal content, *POS* is a means to react to and investigate heritage, families, lifestyles, memories, and values using artistic practice. It allows communities to investigate issues within a neutral context; race, consumer culture, sexual orientation, gender, and religion are popular subjects. The process is not meant to solve social or personal problems, but to provide the participants with an ongoing means for reflection.

This project represents the evolution of a collaborative undertaking with French artist Christian Boltanski, aptly titled *Our City, Ourselves*. This innovative project was exhibited in 1998 at the Kemper Museum of Contemporary Art in Kansas City, Missouri. Merrill built on this idea and produced *POS* by archiving and documenting their activities. Visual artworks produced create unique exhibitions with a strong point of view and raw intensity. These complex and insightful works of community art become points of pride for participants and their families. Merrill originally worked with 30 high school students from Kansas City, Missouri inner city schools. The students produced vast personal archives documenting in detail 16 weeks of their lives. Subjects depicted in the work covered a broad range, from gun violence to wedding vows and family squabbles. These archives were then exhibited simultaneously at the Kemper Museum and Paseo Academy, a fine and performing arts high school in midtown Kansas City, Missouri.

*Opposite Page:*
**Portrait of Self**, *2000,*
*FutureSelf, Colorado*
*Springs, Colorado.*

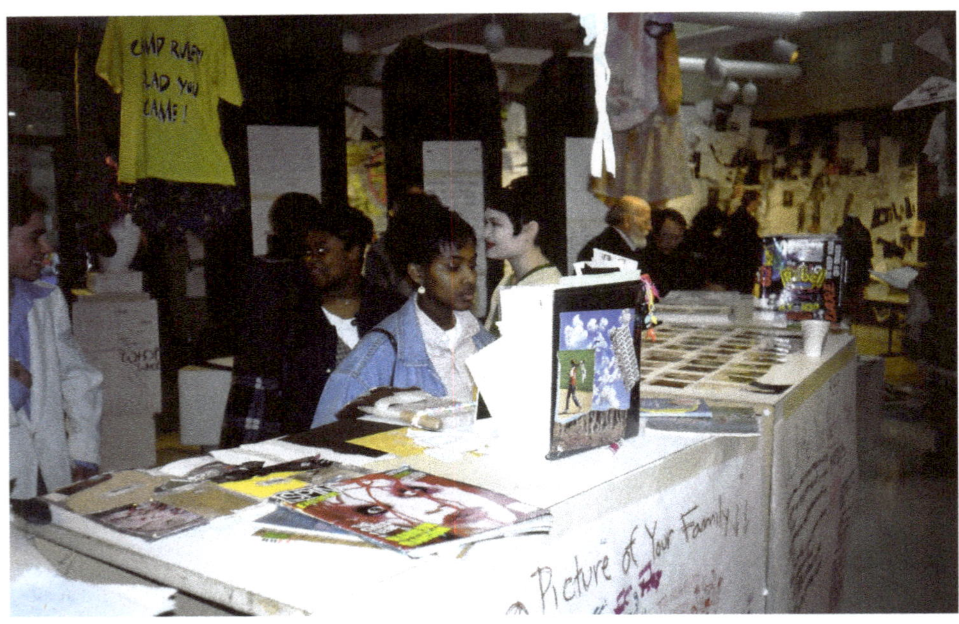

**Portrait of Self**, *1998, Kemper Museum of Contemporary Art and Paseo Academcy of Visual and Performing Arts, Kansas City, Missouri.*

*POS* has been the core process in over 30 community arts actions internationally and has received recognition from the National Endowment of the Arts. Through a grant from the Missouri Juvenile Justice System and the COMBAT program in Kansas City, Merrill organized programs for incarcerated youths and at the Kansas State School for the Blind. Kansas City Art Institute students provided arts therapy programs for Holocaust survivors at Village Shalom retirement home in Overland Park, Kansas. These images were printed on postcards and sold at the gift shop in the facility. Elders of an inner city nursing home also benefited from the students' teachings.

This project has inspired creative thinking and visual literacy curricula at many educational facilities including: the Missouri Academy of Fine Art in Springfield, Missouri; Manchester Craftsman's Guild in Pittsburgh, Pennsylvania; Eagle Rock School in Estes Park, Colorado; Western Sydney University in New South Wales, Australia; the Academy of Fine Arts Dublin, Ireland; the Goddard Gallery at the Daum Museum in Sedalia, Missouri; and the Kansas City Art Institute in Kansas City, Missouri.

The popular Percent for the Arts programs also brought the artist a commission for graphic murals at Dania Beach Elementary School. The title, *Millennium Voices*, reflects the striking imagery contained in the pieces. Sponsored by the Art and Culture Center of Hollywood, Florida, these large-scale photographic murals depict the history of the area as well as many of the participants and their families. Other Percent for Art projects included the Sanford-Kimpton Health Facility in Columbia, Missouri and a series of interpretive sculptures in conjunction with a sequence of literary plaques installed at the Roeland Park Skateboard Park, in Roeland Park, Kansas.

The full text and Portrait of Self workbook/curriculum can be downloaded online at www.hughmerrill.com.

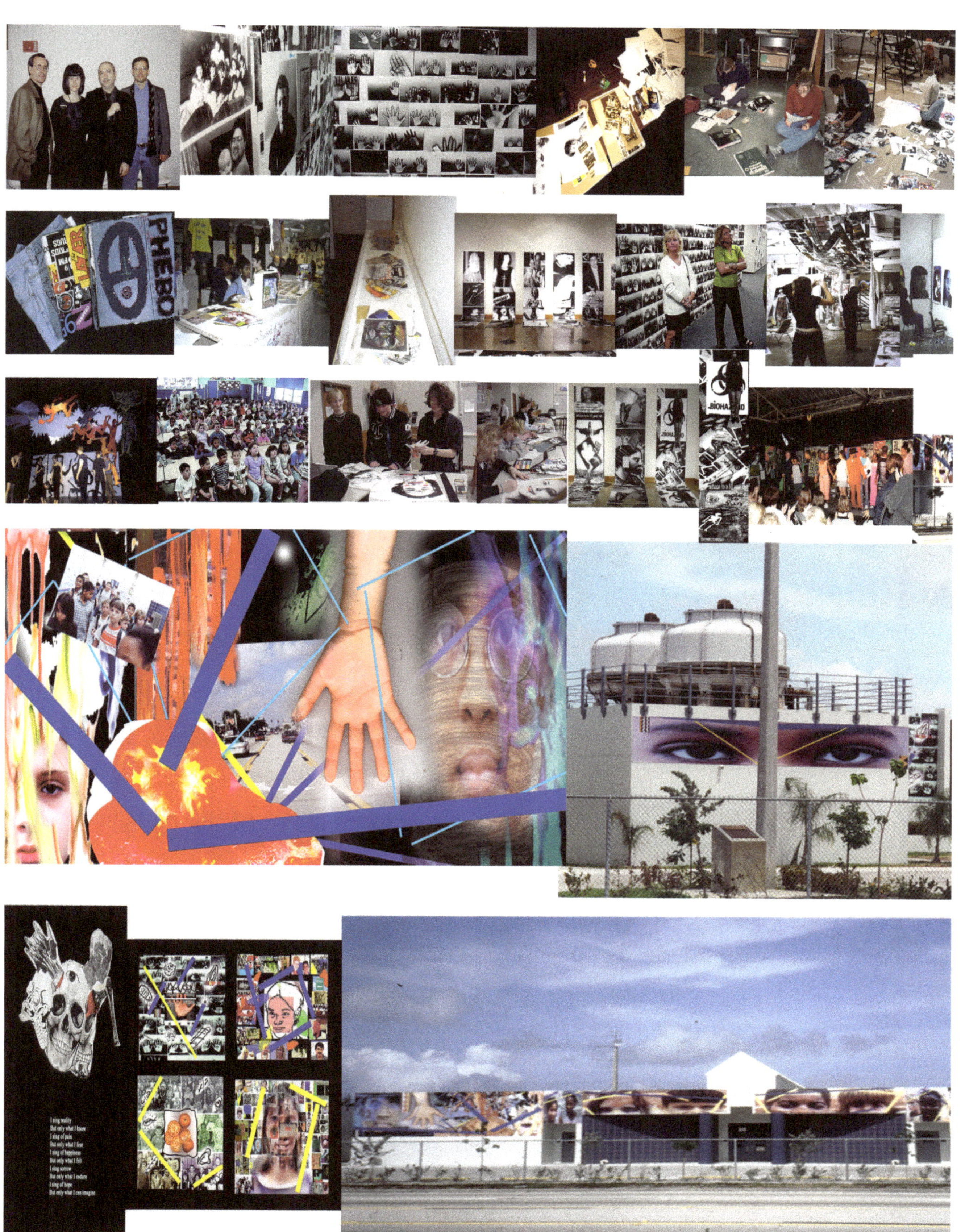

**Montage Portrait of Self installations**, *1998-2001*

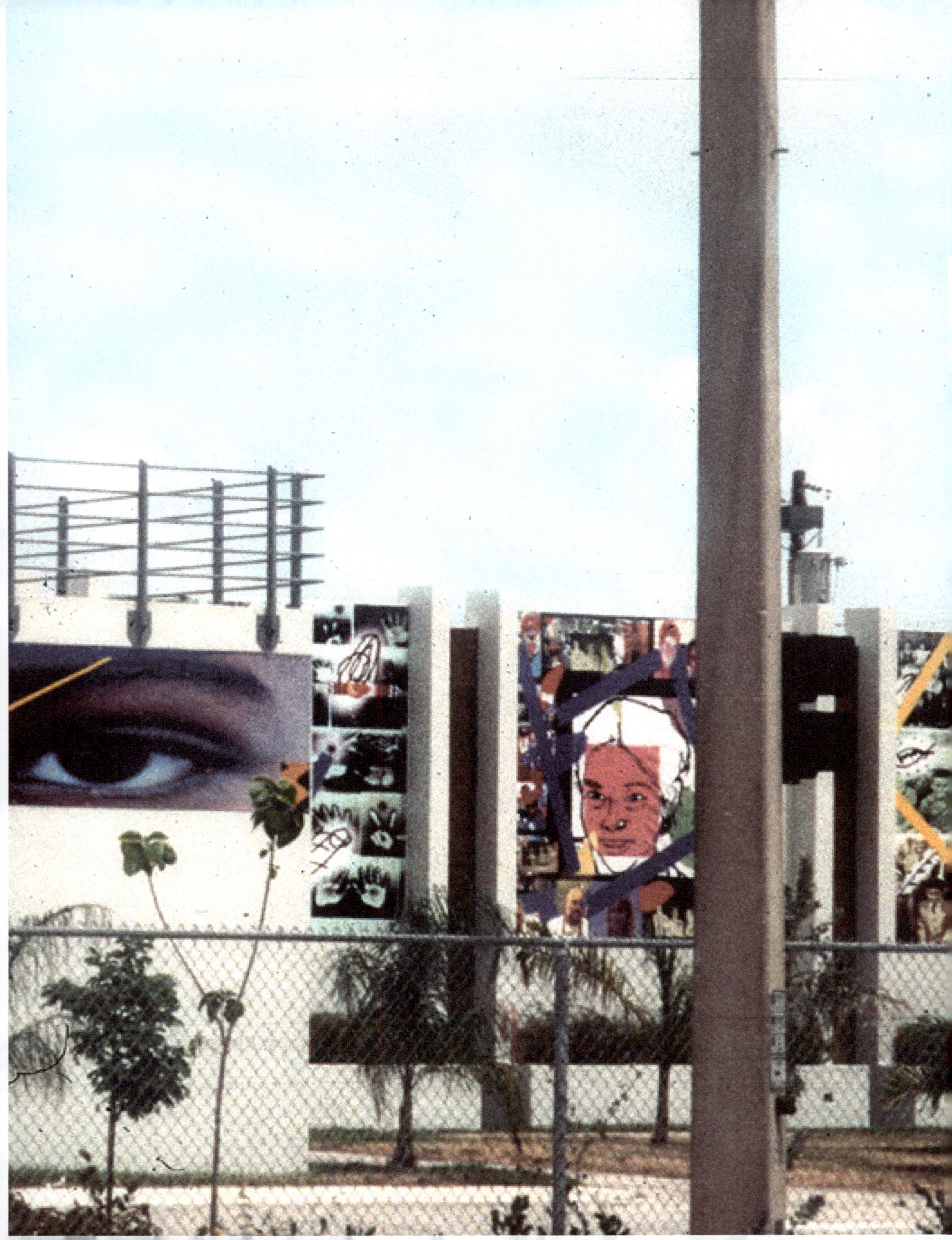

# Millennium Voices
## Recreating a Community Through Listener-Centered Art

Many artists are increasingly finding voices and roles within the public sphere. Dialogues based in creative thinking and collaboration guide successful community based art, posing new challenges for artists. The dissolution of Modernist canons espousing elitist distinctions between artists and members of society is a triumph of Post-Modernist praxis, encouraging reinterpretation of the contemporary artist's role as a member of society rather than a distant, disengaged observer. Coined "new genre public art," this art form is experiential and based on interaction with an audience and place. Collaborating and communication within a public sphere, artists working within this genre create participatory strategies for engagement and exchange between themselves and community.

Artist/Educator Hugh Merrill enacts such methodologies through community art projects encompassing participation, self-affirmation and youth education. Heightening a sense of community through investigation of self-identity and collaboration define the project, *Millennium Voices/Portrait of Self*, in Dania Beach Florida. This project involved the entire community of Dania Elementary School. Lasting nearly one year, from May 1999 to May 2000, Merrill made five trips to Dania to organize and facilitate this unique, creative interaction.



Three distinct components frame *Millennium Voices/Portrait of Self*. One aspect engaged the students in collecting personal archives, including copies of old family pictures, documents such as birth certificates, images of favorite objects and toys, personal notes, drawings, scraps of material, and the like.

Collected and compiled into notebooks over the course of several months, the process was an exercise in self-identity and memory resulting in what Merrill describes "as a lifetime living work of art having both function and a lifetime goal outside style and aesthetic content."

The creation of "a living communal archive" through collaboration between students teachers, parents and administrators, was then created inside the school. Collections of black and white photocopies included images of students' hands, toys and objects, family pictures, old class photos of teachers and candid photographs of students and teachers taken by Merrill. In a group effort, the students and teachers installed these archival images in a layered collage covering the various walls of the school. Merrill explains the premise for *Millennium Voices/Portrait of Self* as follows:

*"The issue is how we use art to change a community's relation to an institution–then change the way an institution sees itself so as to support the*

*identity of the community—giving itself up to acknowledge your life and your heritage. Letting all of the kids put up photocopies of their family archives on the walls of the school is the creation of such a relationship. With the images up, the kids own the wall space; it's about them individually and about creating individual ownership of a public institution."*

As a lasting component of the process, Merrill selected from the collage, creating a 150 foot graphic mural he describes as a "distillation" of the many images and experiences of the community interaction. The mural–a combination of painting, drawing, and traditional printmaking–is a digitally manipulated montage. Ultimately printed onto vinyl with special ink, the mural is a permanent installation spanning three buildings of the school and fastened directly to the concrete walls. It faces a busy highway (Dixie Highway) dividing the school from a failed vacant strip-mall. Abundant billboard advertising along the highway reinforces the commercial environs of the school and surrounding neighborhoods. Merrill refer-ences these factors in the mural augmented by a temporary installation of complementary graphic adhered to the school's surrounding sidewalks, a spontaneous encounter and visual cue for pedestrians to contemplate the nearby mural.

Looming eyes of children stare out from the mural, interspersed with fragmented portraits and vernacular images articulating a sense of history and place. Colorful strands of Seminole Indians, indigenous to the area but displaced in the event of colonization, also appear. Slices of red tomato reference Dania as a farming community that once produced huge crops of tomatoes eventually supplanted by housing and development. Collages of individual teachers past and present, group school pictures, images of children's palms, and the dangerous highway commingle. Bright yellow and blue skids transverse across and amidst the images, suggestive of speed and direction.

Through this visual mélange, Merrill creates a subtle subversion–a critique of commercialism, mass media influences, and the commodification of children–by creating an artwork that duplicates a commercial construct, but defies commercial aims. The piece is a hybrid of vernacular murals and billboard advertising. The eyes of the children–unblinking, questioning, and disquieting–are not trying to sell a product, although the nature of the work begs this question, provoking a complex array of interpretations.

An interest in populism and consideration of audience has guided Merrill since graduating with an MFA from Yale in 1975. At that time, many artists heralded a more democratic inclusive way of making art; environmental concerns, issues of equality for women and minorities, and a desire to affect commu-nities in a positive way informed their conceptions. For example, Judith Baca, a native of Los Angeles, enacted community art projects through largescale murals such as the *Great Wall of Los Angeles*. Be-gun in 1976, it was intended as an exercise in free speech, expression, and cooperation among a wide range of participants. Spanning 2,400 feet along a flood control channel wall of the Los Angeles River, a vast mural depicts the cultural history of Los Angeles, replete with minorities, immigrants, and women. Baca directed the project, employing hundreds of inner city teenagers, including gang members, who painted the mural over the course of several summers. Cooperation from various organizations and community members exemplified an artistic endeavor where many voices and views were expressed and heard.

Hearing and imparting community voices through engagement and collaboration are inherent in *Millennium Voices/Portrait of Self*. Confronting a broader audience via subversion of public, commercial advertising is also a key component. Merrill incorporates both interaction and process into a public message intended as a layered, pointed dialogue.

Utilizing euphemistic visual and text based language, artists have used billboards to impart often hard-hitting acutely politicized messages to the masses over the past several decades. Barbara Krueger, David Hammons, Flex Gonzalez-Torres, and the New York artist collective Group Material are just a few examples of artists who have sought voices outside the museum confines to confront broad audiences with highly charged social and political issues.

Since the late 1960's, many artists have incorporated visual education and creative expression to augment literacy outside of an institutional framework, such as Allen Kaprow, with his endeavor *Project Other Ways* involving elementary students in Berkeley, California. Since the early 1980's, New York artist Tim Rollins has led young people in the South Bronx to aesthetic expression under the collaborative name *Tim Rollins and K.O.S. (Kids of Survival)*. Merrill also conflates the educational process, community involvement, and sociological critique in all of his community art projects.

Merrill began teaching at the Kansas City Art Institute in 1976 where he soon became a professor of painting and printmaking. Utilizing both traditional printmaking techniques and cutting edge digital technologies, Merrill enacts a crossover praxis within his teaching, studio practice and community-based art. From 1985 to 1998, he organized a collaborative print exchange program with two high schools—one in Kansas City and one in Spring, Texas. Merrill's curricula also includes courses in which art students collaborate with veterans, senior citizens, and homeless children.

He considers his studio work as visionary and personal, informed by his inner voice. As a teacher and artist he encourages others to use their own inner voices, which within a public milieu became collaborative and communal. For Merrill, these processes are mutually supportive, intermingled, and organic. Like-minded approaches and philosophies indicate a growing interest among educators in fostering creativity through exchanges between artists, community members and institutions, expanding a pedagogical idiom within educational systems that proactively engages the arts.

*Millennium Voices/Portrait of Self* is the most recent chapter in a continuing project, *Portrait of Self*, begun by Merrill in 1998 in Kansas City. As a visiting artist at the Kemper Museum of Contemporary Art, Merrill conceived his first archiving collaboration with a group of inner city at-risk youths from an area high school, the Paseo Academy. For one year, the students created visual archives in notebooks, like the process enacted by the Dania elementary students but more highly charged with references to sex and drugs, as one might expect from inner city teens.

Ultimately, the archives were shown at the Kemper Museum in tangent with an exhibition of assemblages by Christian Boltanski, who collaborated with Merrill on a large community art project at the Kemper Museum of Contemporary Art, *Our City, Ourselves*. Area residents were invited to bring photocopies of their first relative known to come to Kansas City to the museum. These photocopies were hung in a wall montage in one of the galleries. Through this collaboration with Boltanski, whose assemblages depicted haunting portraits of child victims of the Holocaust, Merrill honed his strategies towards educational, interactive projects within communities. A recently implemented community project in Kansas City's Studio 150 further illustrates this intention. Involving 60 area teens in a two month long project aimed at job training through the arts, Merrill participated by heading a program called *Portrait of Self: Studio 150*. Integrating philosophies of visual literacy and creative thinking with digital photography, drawing, and other media, Merrill constructed an atmosphere of collaborative thinking and experimentation with teens of varying backgrounds. Within the context of a public park, the teens were removed from constrained institutional constructs, thus fostering an integrative acceptance among the participants. Merrill says, *"You have to get beyond the confrontation . . . the art making takes them out of socially restrictive confines and builds relationships where there was once suspicion, even hate."*

Traversing territories of education, community, and art, Merrill is an example of an artist working within a new genre sensibility of art focused on educational and healing values within communities. Of utmost concern for Merrill and others in the 21st century is the enforcement of community restoration through the arts as a part of daily life. The philosopher John Dewey, in 1934, expressed great concern over the separation of art from everyday experience. "When artistic objects are separated from both conditions of origin and operation in experience, a wall is built around them that renders almost opaque their general significance." He found that the solution to this dilemma would be to restore continuity between the refined and intensified forms of experience that are works of art and the everyday events, doings, and suffering that are universally recognized to constitute experience."

Art and cultural critic, Suzi Gablik, expands upon this notion, suggesting a "paradigm shift" for an art based in community, empathy, and listening, rather than isolated vision-based creations that exclude an audience:

*"Because this art is listener-centered rather than vision-oriented, it cannot be fully realized through modes of self expression: it can only come into its own through dialogue, as open conversation, in which one listens to and includes other voices. For many artists now this means letting previously excluded groups speak directly of their own experience. The audience becomes an active component of the work and is part of the process."*

*Millennium Voices/Portrait of Self* exemplifies a strategy of engagement between artist and community, self-expression through the visual arts and education through creativity. The result of Merrill's strategy, an aesthetic distillation of an internal community process, becomes a revelatory window for an external public.

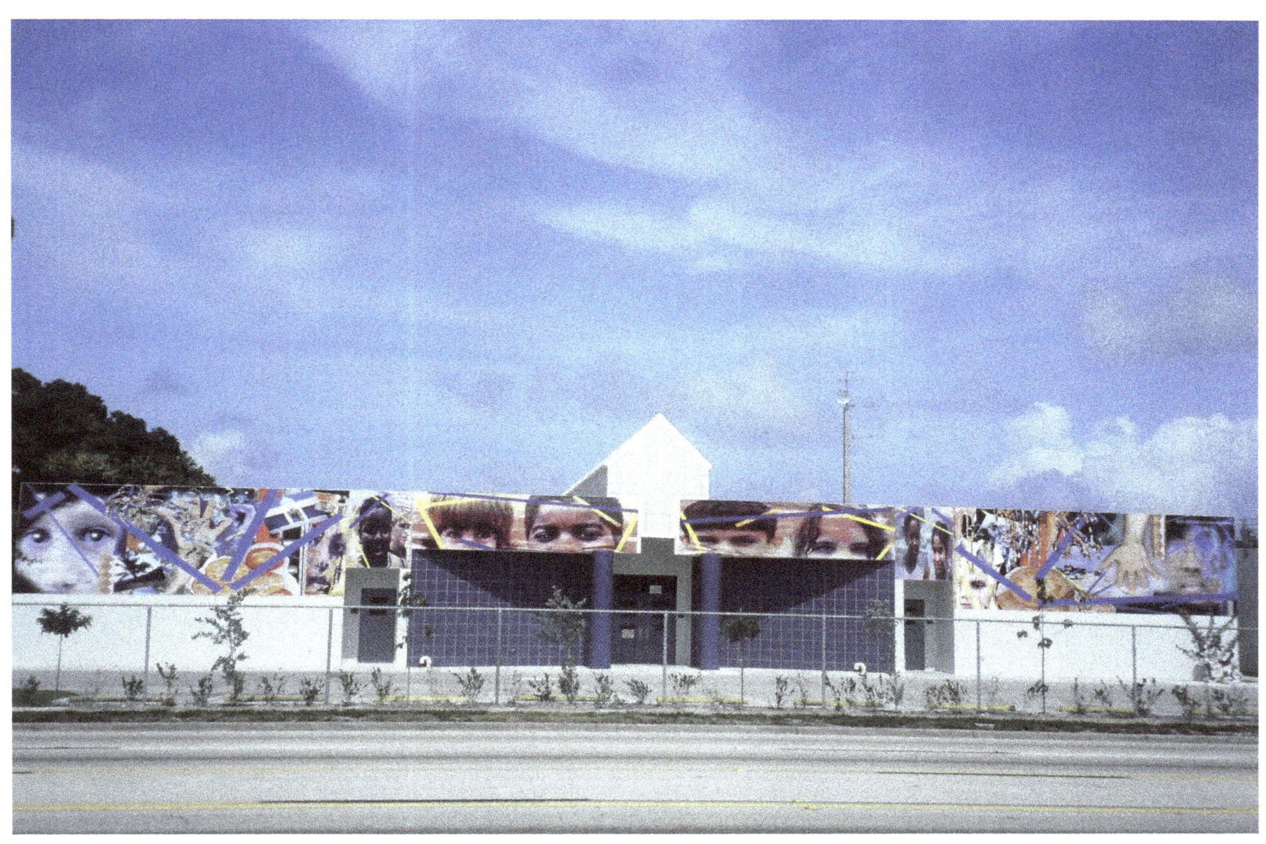

**Millenium Voices**, *2000, digital mural, Dania Beach, Florida.*

It entices a viewer through lively colors and graphic manipulations within its composition. But more importantly, it poses questions, challenges and inferences, all of which will strike a random observer differently. At its heart, the mural implores a viewer through the eyes of children who look toward us for guidance. In a world that too often manipulates young people, viewing them once as commodities and marketing tools, we must ask ourselves if the guidance we offer is enough.

*--Heather Lustfeldt*

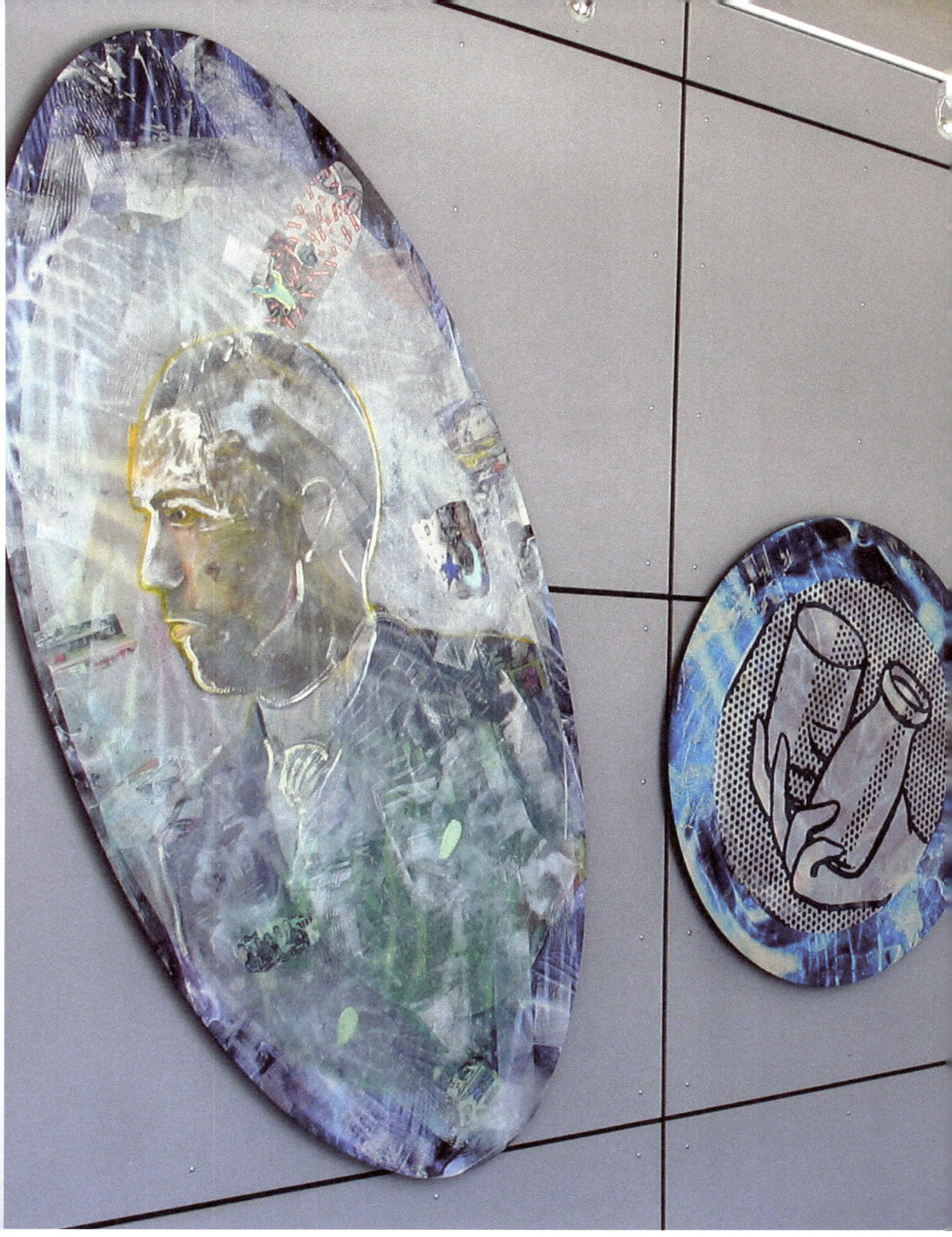

# The Art of Memory
## Sanford-Kimpton Health Facility, Columbia, Missouri

*It is a rare opportunity when artist and architects collaborate in a major way to bring an art form into the public eye. While artists tend to remain public as singular creative entities, collaboration has the potential to engage the public on multiple levels and broaden each field in a way that is both deliberate and participatory. Art of Memory brought together the Health Department of Columbia Missouri, artist/ educator Hugh Merrill and architect Kaylyn Munro of Raphael Architects in Kansas City, to complete the Sanford-Kimpton Health Facility.*

*—Eleanor Erskine*

**Interview between artist/educator Hugh Merrill and Associate Professor Eleanor Erskine of Portland State University, Portland, Oregon**

*Eleanor Erskine: Hugh, what was your approach to the **Percent for the Arts** Health Facility Project for Columbia, Missouri and how was it different from other public art projects you have created?*

Hugh Merrill: My approach to public and community work is consistent in process and varied in outcome. I start with getting to know individuals in the community. I do that through an archiving process called *Portrait of Self*. It is a process in which I interview and get people to provide me with their life stories, their family histories, documentation and photos. The archive of collected information becomes the resource for the images to be created.

*EE: How did you apply that process to the health facility in Columbia, Missouri?*

HM: First, I had to understand what the health facility does—who it touches. The Health Department and Family Health Clinic are comprised of a series of scientific and medical services. These include animal control, public health, a family clinic, and environmental science, among others. The clinic serves a broad and diverse population and is staffed by a committed group of professionals. I felt that the artwork for the building should respond to the function of the department, essentially reflecting the lives of the clinic's clientele. I wanted to create a visual environment that flowed through the architecture, unifying the various services and public spaces.

*EE: Part of the investigation is focused on the community, getting photos from people, hearing their stories and part is on a formal response to the architecture. Is that right?*

HM: Yes, absolutely. It's partly a collection of imagery and stories from the community and partly a search for what will best function as an interactive

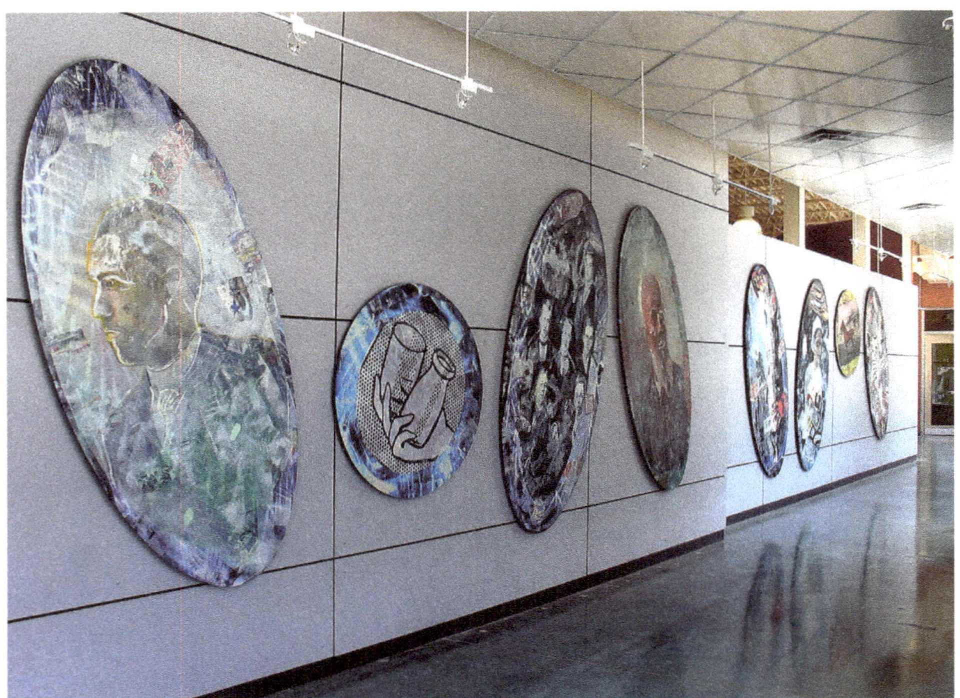

**The Art of Memory**, *2002, installation/digital print, Sanford-Kimpton Health Facility, Columbia, Missouri.*

with the wonderful architectural plans of Kaylyn Monroe. I wanted to make artworks that would take advantage of the openness of the space and the beautiful natural light she designed into the building. I wanted the artwork to resonate with the richness and variety of construction materials used in the building: wood, concrete panels, translucent plastic, sheet metal, and stained concrete.

*EE: What made you place the work in the building at tilted angles and at unexpected viewing levels?*

HM:  The oval shapes and the decision to install the works throughout the building at raking angles and in unexpected wall positions reflected a counterpoint and complement to the beauty of the architectural grid. The building is a complex layer of grids, of visual starts and stops, of changing speeds and sounds. I wanted to create organic forms that fall at obtuse angles across and in opposition to the grids.

*EE: How did you begin? What is the first thing you do when you start a public or community art project?*

HM:  Rather than coming to the project with a pre-conceived idea of what the final work should look like, I employed the *Portrait of Self* community archiving process. I have used this process for nine years to collect content and visual information from communities internationally. Then I use the collected information to make images concerning the community. Each project is different, with differing environmental and architectural spaces. The outcome is designed to best suit the specifics of each community and institution.

*EE:  Can you take me through the process?*

HM:  Let me start with a short history. In 1996, I was invited to produce a collaborative installation with Christian Boltanski for the Kemper Museum of Contemporary Art in Kansas City.  Boltanski and I came up with

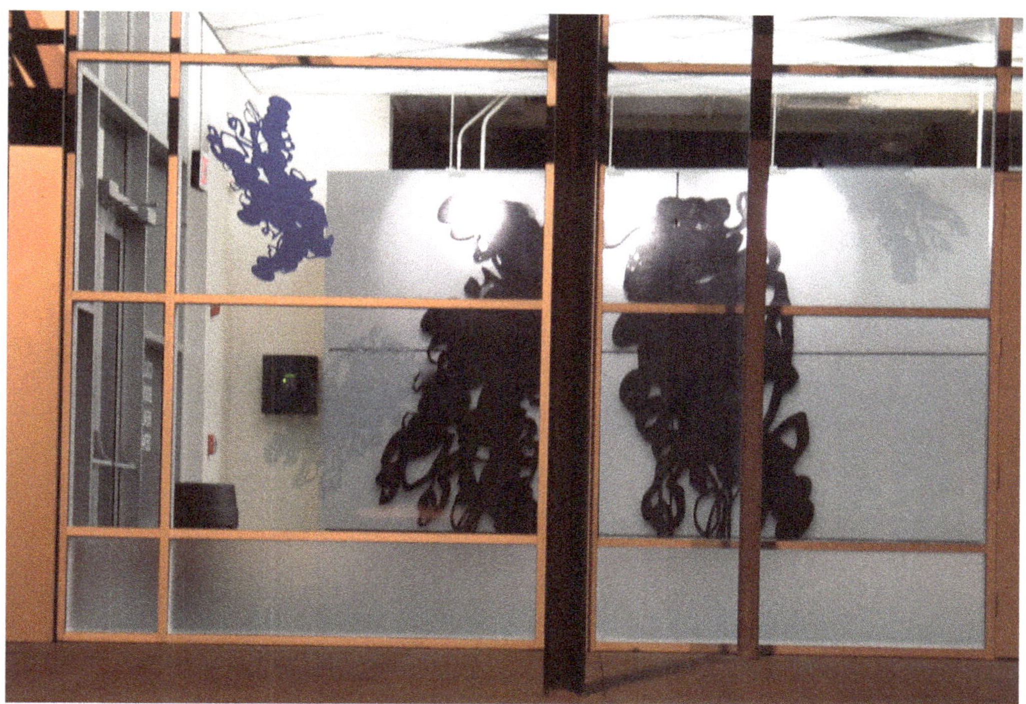

**The Art of Memory**, *2002, installation/digital print, Sanford-Kimpton Health Facility, Columbia, Missouri.*

a citywide installation project titled *Our City/Ourselves*, which invited the residents of the Kansas City metropolitan area to bring their family photographs to the museum, copy them, and install them on the walls of the museum. Several thousand people brought their family photographs to the museum, copied them and pinned them to the walls. Soon the gallery was covered with Xerox prints from floor to ceiling.

Building on *Our City/Ourselves*, I devised a workbook/process for *Portrait of Self*, to assist in the recall of lost memory and to help a community document its daily life. I used the process to work with inner city high school students. The archives the students created were exhibited at the Kemper Museum in conjunction with the Boltanski exhibition.

Since then, I have used the *Portrait of Self* process for collecting content to produce public community and percent-for-the-arts commissions and installations. *Portrait of Self* has been used to produce large graphic murals in Hollywood/Dania Beach, Florida. It also acted as the source of the installation for the Daum Museum in Sedalia, Missouri; an installation at the Manchester Craftsman's Guild in Pittsburgh, Pennsylvania; and *FutureSelf* in Colorado Springs, Colorado.

*EE: How did you begin to collect community information and stories in Columbia?*

HM: I began the process with an artist-in-residency grant given by the City of Columbia, Missouri Office of Cultural Affairs and the Missouri Arts Council to work with high school students at Hickman High School in Columbia. We created large digital collages from the items the students carried in their pockets and bags. These collages became the first layer of content for the images created for the health facility. The archiving with high school students at Hickman High School in Columbia. We created large digital collages from the items the students carried in their pockets and bags. These collages became the first layer of content for the images created for the health facility. The archiving process then shifted to the staff of the health facility, who provided family photographs. Other images were taken from health department past publications of the 1940s and 1950s. I was invited to look at archival photographs from the Boone County Historical Society and glass plate photographs from the 1890s that belonged to a staff member at the health department. From these I selected a number of images that became the base layer of the digital prints.

*EE: What was the final outcome of the project?*

HM: I designed six series of prints for the building: the large oval digital prints mentioned before, four polysilk banners, 27 silkscreened text plaques of quotes given by the health staff, vinyl decals based on DNA structures, and digitally printed canvases. The works are non-stylistic, yet I attempted to achieve a thematic and formal continuity. All the various works were then installed in the building.

*EE: You said it was important for the work to flow through the building. Did the installation achieve what you expected?*

HM: Yes. I was very pleased with the outcome of the installation, and the works flow well from room to room. I received the favorite quotes, lines of poetry and lyrics from the staff at the medical center, and these were printed on colored text plaques to activate large empty wall spaces. I think it all came together very well.

The people at the heart of the project were the wonderful staff at the health facility. Students at Hickman High School, project architects, and individuals involved in the political logistics of the project contributed an immense amount of work and inspiration. Marie Hunter's gifted work brought the project to fruition, as well as the artists that assisted on the project. These include: Adelia Ganson, Caleb Hauck, Patrick Moonasar, Miranda Young, Eleanor Erskine, Staci Pratt, and Greg Thompson.

*--Eleanor Erskine*

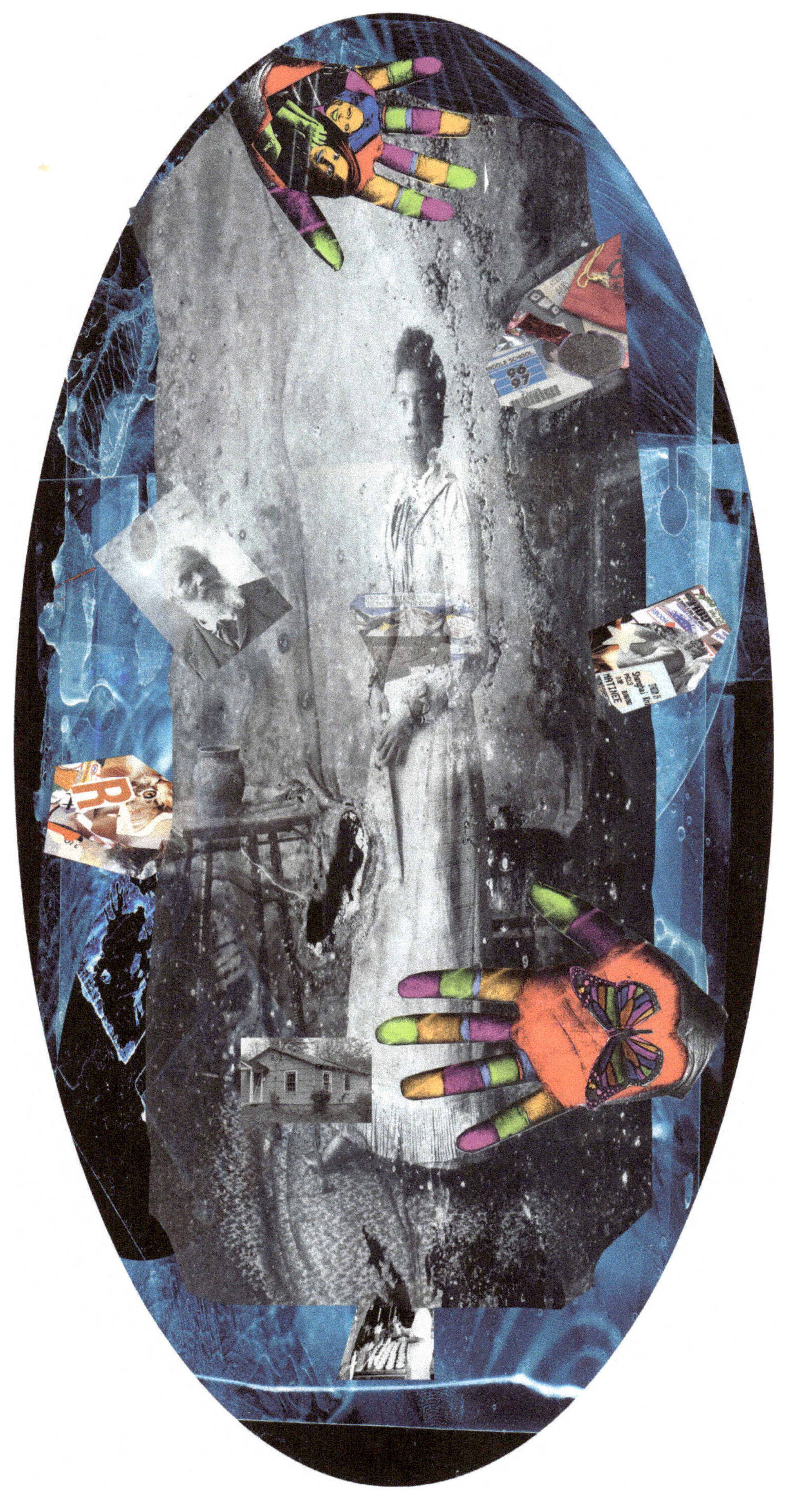

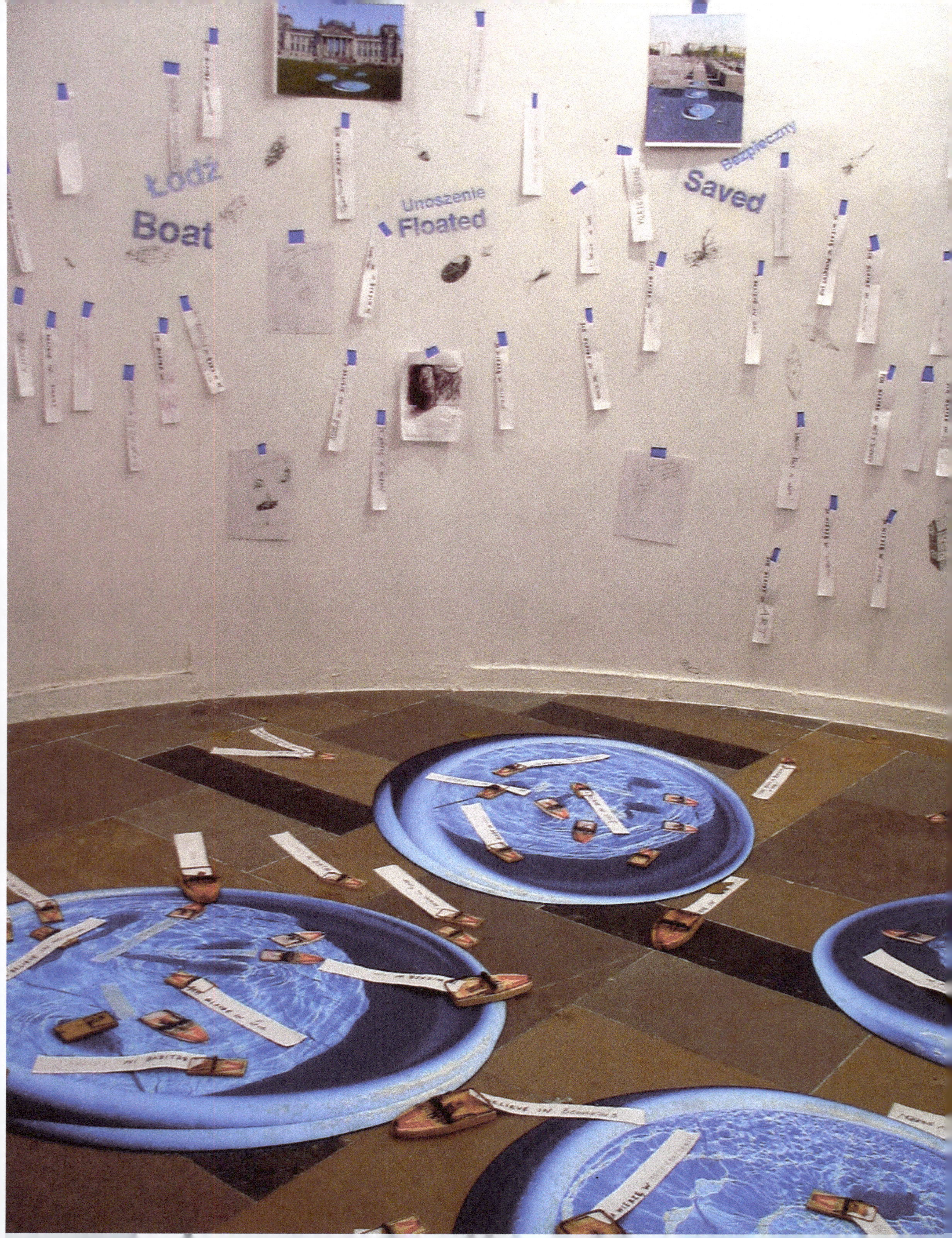

Łodź
Boat
Unoszenie
Floated
Saved
Bezpieczny

# Pools of Belief



*Max Skorwider is a graduate of the Academy of Fine Arts in Poznan, Poland. Max lives in Poznan and is a noted poster designer, artist, and contributor to the art magazine,* **Areton**. *He and Maja Wolna interviewed Hugh over a Piwo (beer) in The Proletarist Bar in Poznan, Poland, September 2005.*

*Max Skorwider: Can you tell us about* **Pools of Belief**?

Hugh Merrill: *Pools of Belief* is a community art piece, performance, installation, and exhibition. I created four graphic images of a children's swimming pool filled with water. Each was about 4x4 feet in diameter. Floating in the pools are images of mousetraps shaped like boats. Trailing from the traps are narrow sheets of paper with the text "I believe in the New York Stock Exchange" and other such answers. The graphic pools are adhered to rubber mats that are easily moved from place to place. The pools were displayed in public places in Berlin and Poland where the people walking by are asked to participate by writing their own answer to the phrase "I believe in__________" on a narrow sheet of paper. They are then asked to place their "I believe in __________" paper strips in a mousetrap and place the trap on one of the graphic pools. All of their responses were kept for later exhibition. I was able to work with a group of Polish art students who helped with the performances and installations. The Pools were taken out to locations in Berlin. In Poznan they were installed at the National Museum of Poland and in front of the Zamek Cultural Center. The final installation/exhibition took place at the Academy of Fine Arts in Poznan.

*MS: Are the pools a metaphor, and if they are what do they stand for? Or, why pools? Why children's pools?*

HM: We are a light society, a society of consumer goods, material desires, a society consumed by what is fun, goofy and playful. We are desire and we are lifestyle driven. Our time is much different than the old oppressed societies of Eastern Europe under Nazi occupation, then under communist occupation. If Poland is occupied now it is by Nike, Reebok, and beer companies. So the first consideration was to create a visual metaphor for our consumer society and a shallow children's pool seemed perfect. They are beautiful, clear, not only shallow but lacking in depth. They are made for fun and play, and their borders are plastic and air. Old borders were steel and iron, barbed wire and guns; they called it the Iron Curtain. Now in the western world everyone lives in a continuous mall. The children's pools act as a metaphor for national boundaries.

*MS: What about the mousetraps? Where do they*

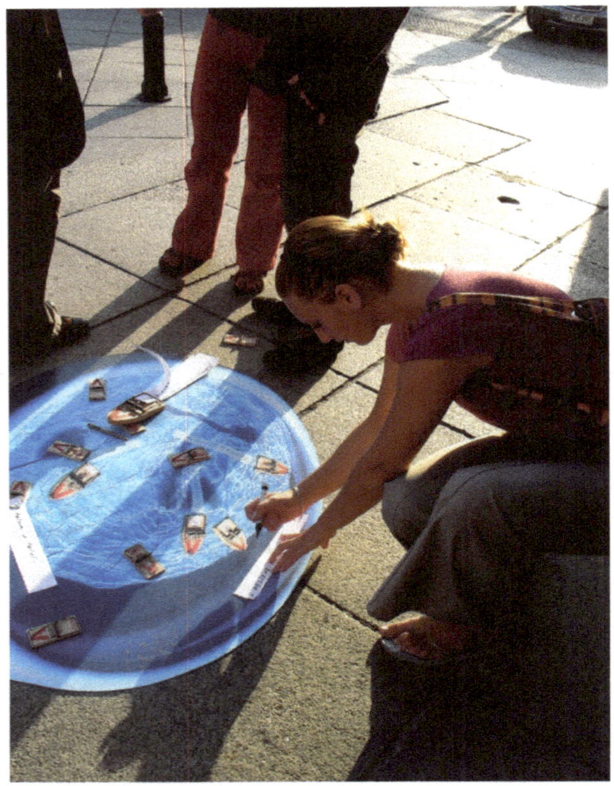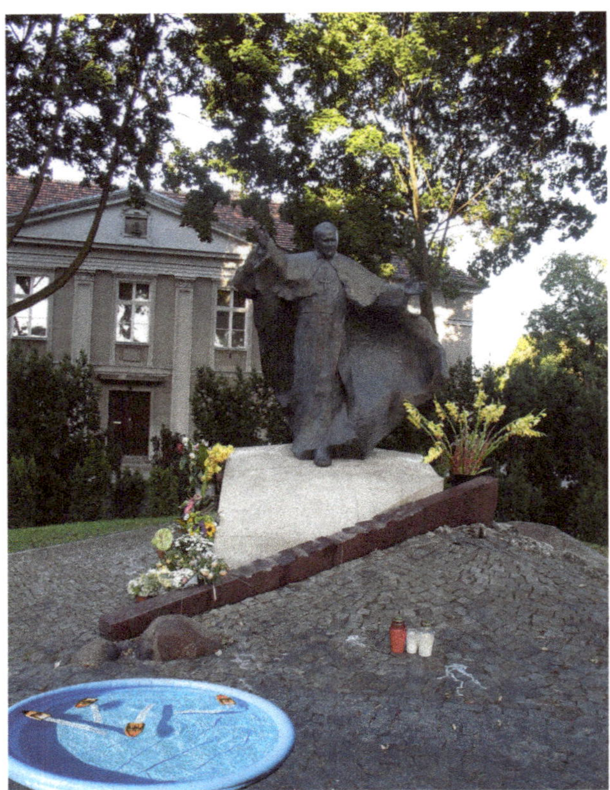

**Pools of Belief**, *2005, installation and performance, Poznan, Poland.*

*come in, and where does belief fit in?*

HM:  A belief system is double edged; the values that keep a person afloat in life are also a trap that blinds them from seeing the oppression they cause. A belief system centers us and provides moral and social guidance, political opinion and establishes our degree of tolerance. That same belief system is also the lens which prevents us from seeing others clearly. Belief is a trap that prevents us from seeing the harm and terror we do to others. So our belief system is both a trap and a boat and only when we see it as both can we step back and assess our actions. Absolute belief is like absolute power, it is corrupting and always leads to some one getting killed. The metaphor is simple: belief is neither good nor bad; it has both positive and negative qualities. Belief saves lives by giving people

context and meaning, but conversely narrows their abilities to perceive anything outside of their own self-imposed system.  That is what makes it possible for them to oppress others.

*MS: Have many people refused to put their beliefs in a trap?*

HM:  No! Its amazing. Hundreds of people have stopped to participate in the action, and no one, no matter how sacred their belief is, no one has not completed the act of putting their belief in a trap and placing it on the graphic pools. I am not sure what that means, but it is interesting.

*MS: You not only did public performances, but you did an installation of **Pools of Belief** in the rotunda at the Academia of Fine Arts in Poznan. How did the installation differ from the performance?*

HM: The installation of the pools at the Academia in Poznan is meant to have a deeper and darker weight than the public performance I described. The four pools and traps trailing people's beliefs are placed on the floor of the gallery. On the walls are stenciled the words *Belief Boat Float Saved Belief Trapped Confined Death Belief* in English, Polish, and German. There is a table in the gallery with pens and narrow sheets of paper and tape, so people can add their thoughts and beliefs to the installation. The gallery setting provides the audience time, space and quiet to consider their beliefs in a more thoughtful and in a less entertaining and active space than the public performance. I watched people read the work, read others' beliefs and contemplate the nature and meaning of the piece. They spent a good deal of time with the work.

*MS: What will happen to the **Pools of Belief**? Will you continue the project into the future?*

HM: Yes, I envision the pools as a two-year project ending with an exhibition in Kansas City in March of 2007 at the Southern Graphics Council conference. As the piece is performed/shown over two years, the weight and complexity of the piece increases with the documentation and records of beliefs accumulated. Where the pools are placed in the landscape determines or changes the reaction of the audience. Placing the pools in front of a histori historical site like the Jewish Cemetery in Berlin, Germany is much different than placing the pools in a mall in Colorado Springs. The final exhibit will document these changes.

*(Thanks to Max Skorwider, Miroslaw Pawlowski, Krztstof Molena, Beauvais Lyons, and Maja Wolna.)*

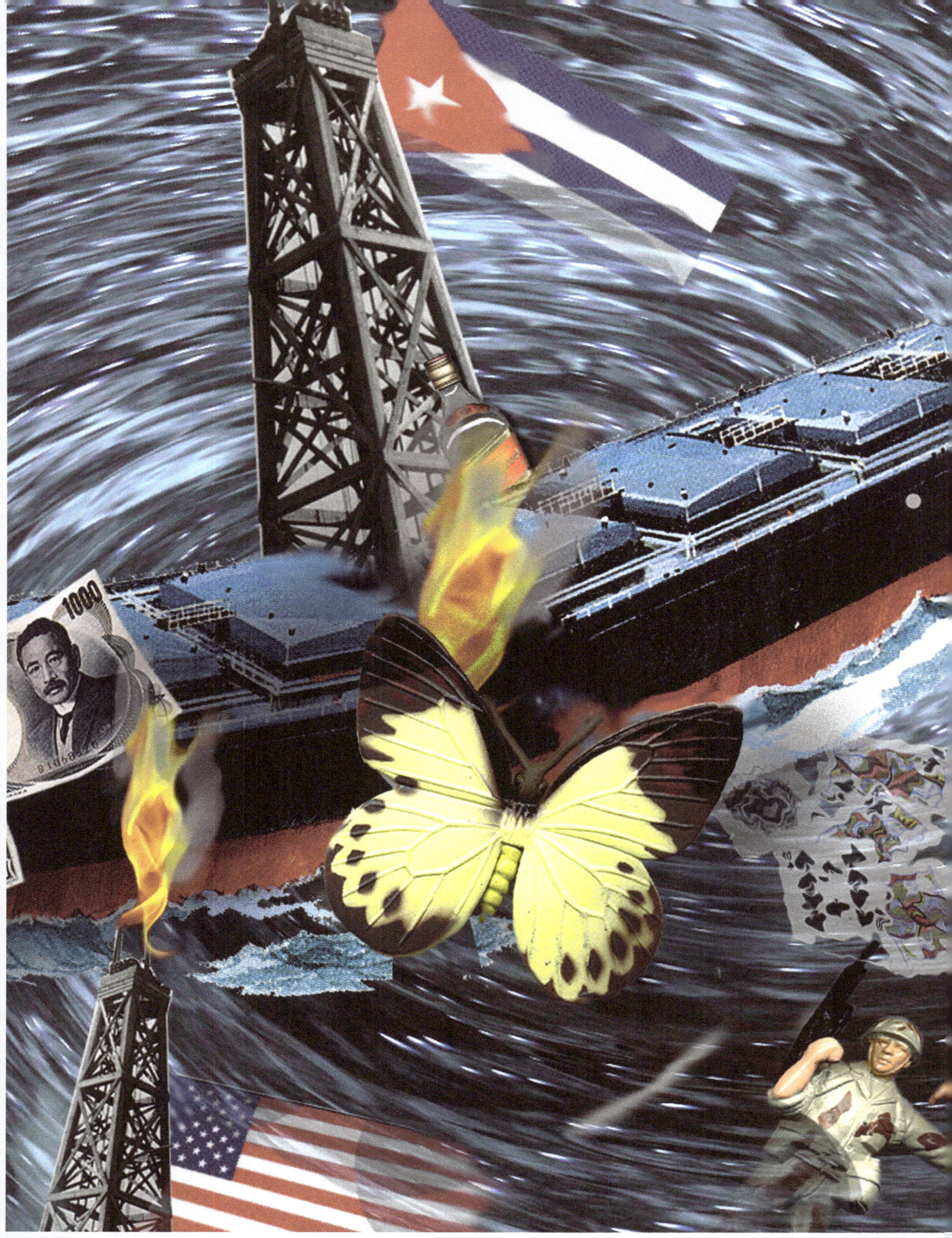

# Oceans of Desire

Merrill has explored his infatuation with Chaos Theory throughout all of his studio practice and it emerges in the *Oceans of Desire* installation series as well. This interactive artwork series was first commissioned by the Darlanas Museum in Falun, Sweden, for exhibition at their Print Triennial in 2007. In the following years, the concept has been re-visited and exhibited in many arts and public festivals with local communities.

*Oceans of Desire* is a natural extension of Merrill's *Pools of Belief* pieces, first exhibited at the Impact Conference in Berlin, Germany in 2005. After this initial display, Merrill conceived the concept of "Art Action Pieces." Merrill attended the Morgan Gallery opening one evening in summer 2005 and while none of the gallery staff was paying attention, he unrolled and displayed the floor-mat style artworks. The pieces display life-size photographs of children's wading pools full of both children's toys and full of oil rigs and fire and butterflies. Each of the repeating wading mats transforms from clear water to deeply oil soaked, black water.

These impromptu and spontaneous art installations were a perfect combination given the chaotic theme of the works which reference chaotician Edward Lorenz' famous butterfly effect.

Lorenz began his career with a pining interest in atmospheric effects. He studied climate and struggled with the immense complexity of global systems. Through methodical data gathering and a stroke of genius, Lorenz became a seminal thinker in what would be the most ground-breaking concept in physics since Newton's principia: Chaos Theory.

This new theory examines how large scales systems contain two essential elements: self-similarity across all scales and sensitive dependence on initial conditions. The world knows these concepts best as The Butterfly Effect, which is artistically described as the idea that a hurricane in the gulf coast might have been initiated by the burst of wind from a butterfly taking flight in Brazil. Merrill takes these mathematical concepts and merges them in unique and surprising ways into the realm of art and installation.

*Oceans of Desire* shows the syllogism of the ocean as to a child's pool and draws it further as the toys of men to the toys of children, combining the totality of both worlds to challenge the viewer to link the factual connection between the initial conditions of a child's life to the devastating effects of man's influence on our natural world. Inside the innocence of the pools are burning oil rigs next to rubber duckies, monetary currency next to plastic butterflies.

Installed as action pieces, these wading mats take curators and audience alike by surprise, just as a natural disaster does. Merrill's work explores how the unexpected is received, just as chaos theory explains how the unexpected emerges.

This series holds a level of intrigue as it comes well before the Deep Horizon Oil Disaster which inspired the Birds of America series. Merrill considers the artist acting as oracle, connecting to the deep anxiety of the earth in the face of industry, he is curious about the divining potential of the act of creation. He asks if the artist is speaking to the future, if the artist is not a theoretician, but a chaos practitioner.

Of course, *Oceans of Desire* is an incomplete installation without Merrill bringing community engagement in as a vital aspect.

Merrill joined forces with graphic designer Patrick Moonasar and the pair created display environments which included massive fabric butterflies transposed against projections. Mousetraps, that little metaphor for always seeking to build a better, were designed and shaped as boats. Gallery attendees were given small sheets of paper to pin to the traps and place on the wading mats. Each paper initiated a suggestion for a response to the statement "I believe in ___________."

This is a typical Merrill approach, to include ideas, concepts and input from the audience into his installation art. Responses ranged from trivial, "I believe in hot dogs," to sublime, "I believe in the American Dream."

The interaction of the audience with the art creates an active and engaging gallery experience, where the attendees share an experience and therefore begin to develop a micro-community thanks to the installation space.

*--Jeanette Powers*



*Opposite Page:*
**Oceans of Desire**, *2008, digital/video installation with puppet performance by StoneLion Puppet Theatre, YWCA, Kansas City, Kansas.*

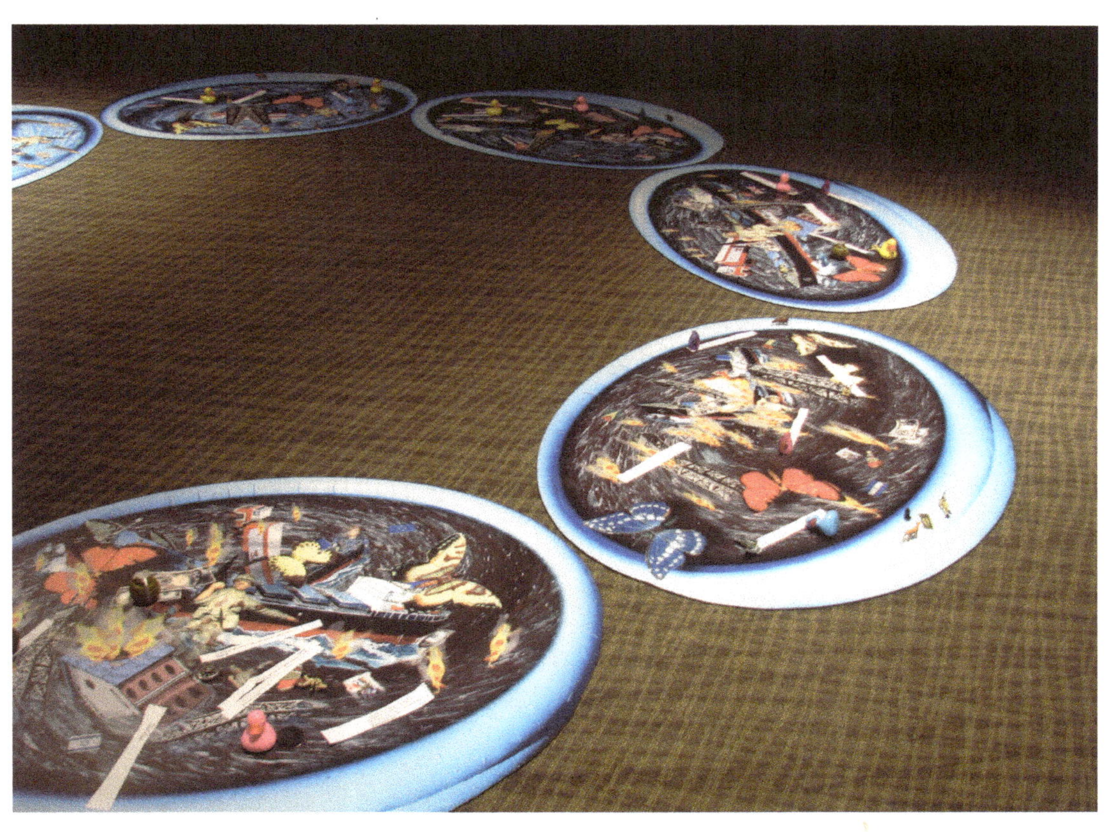

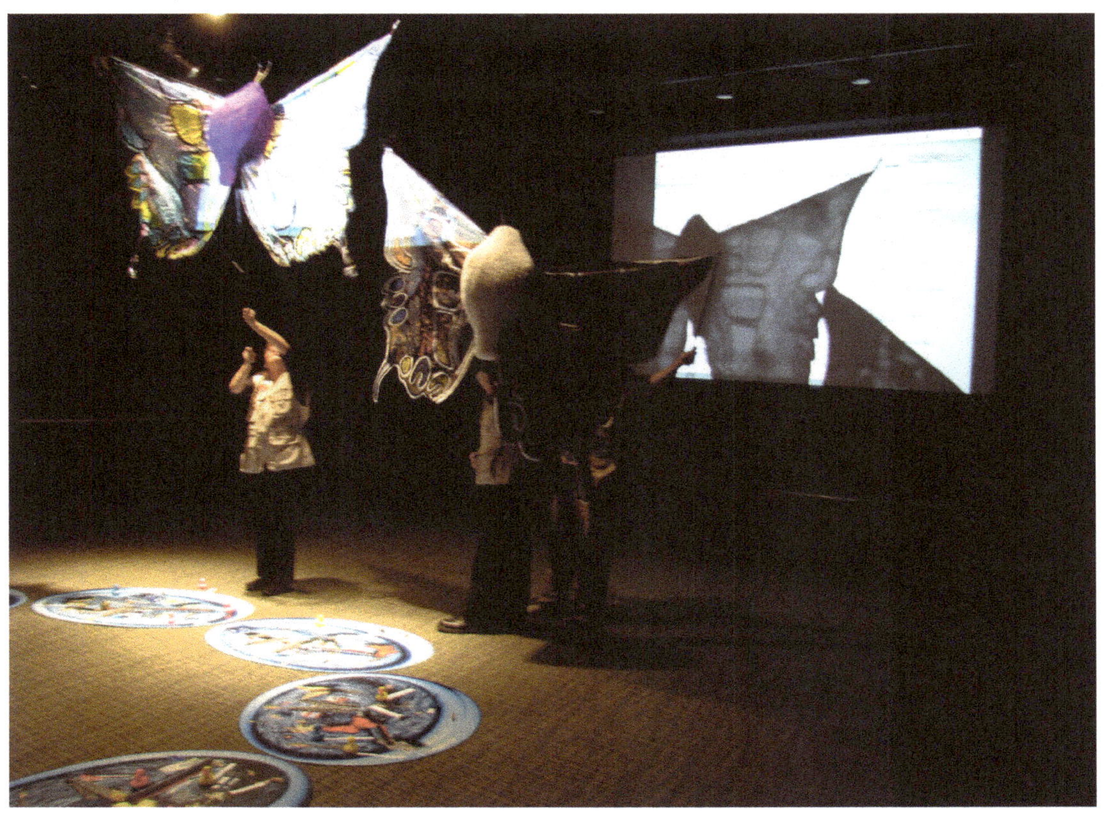

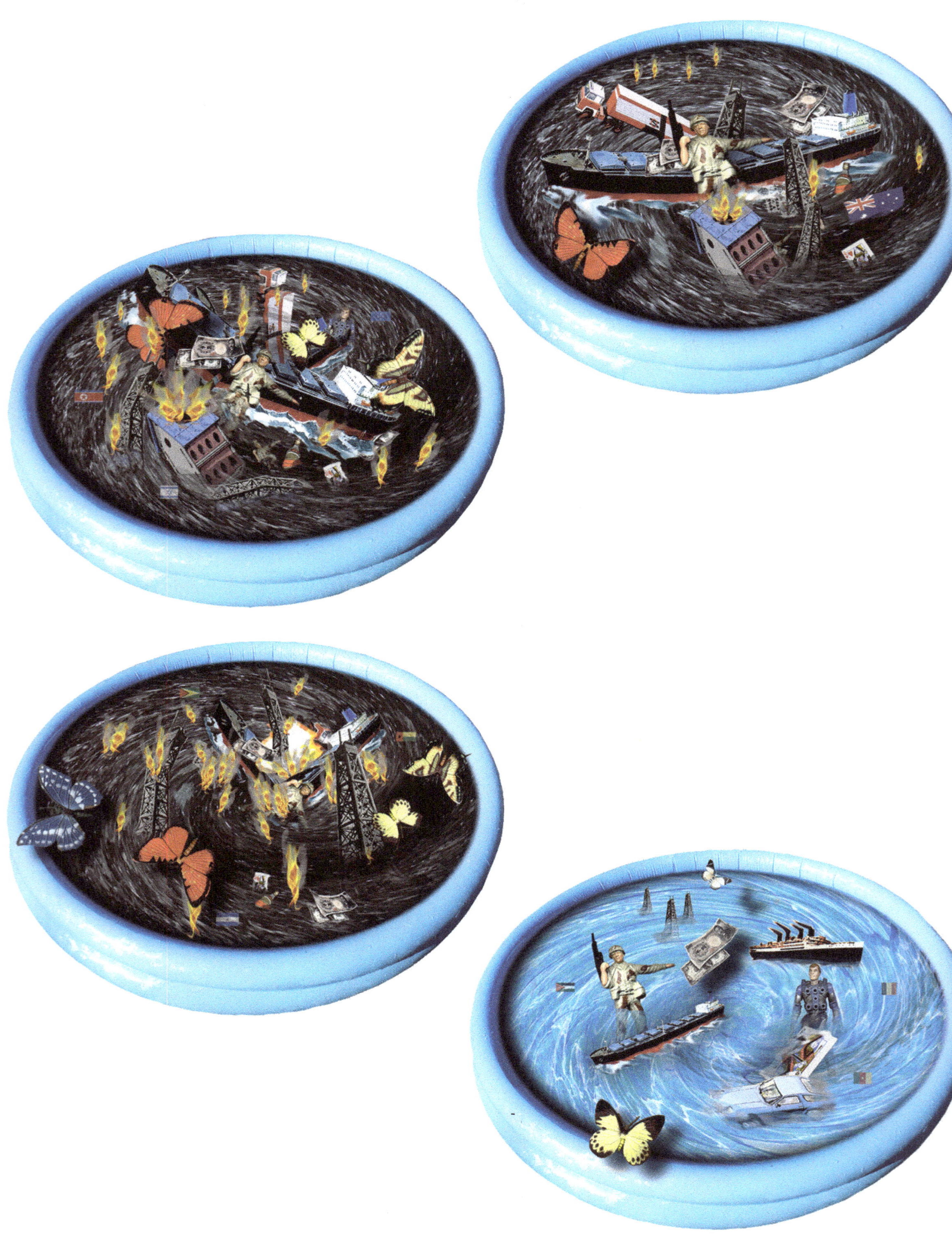

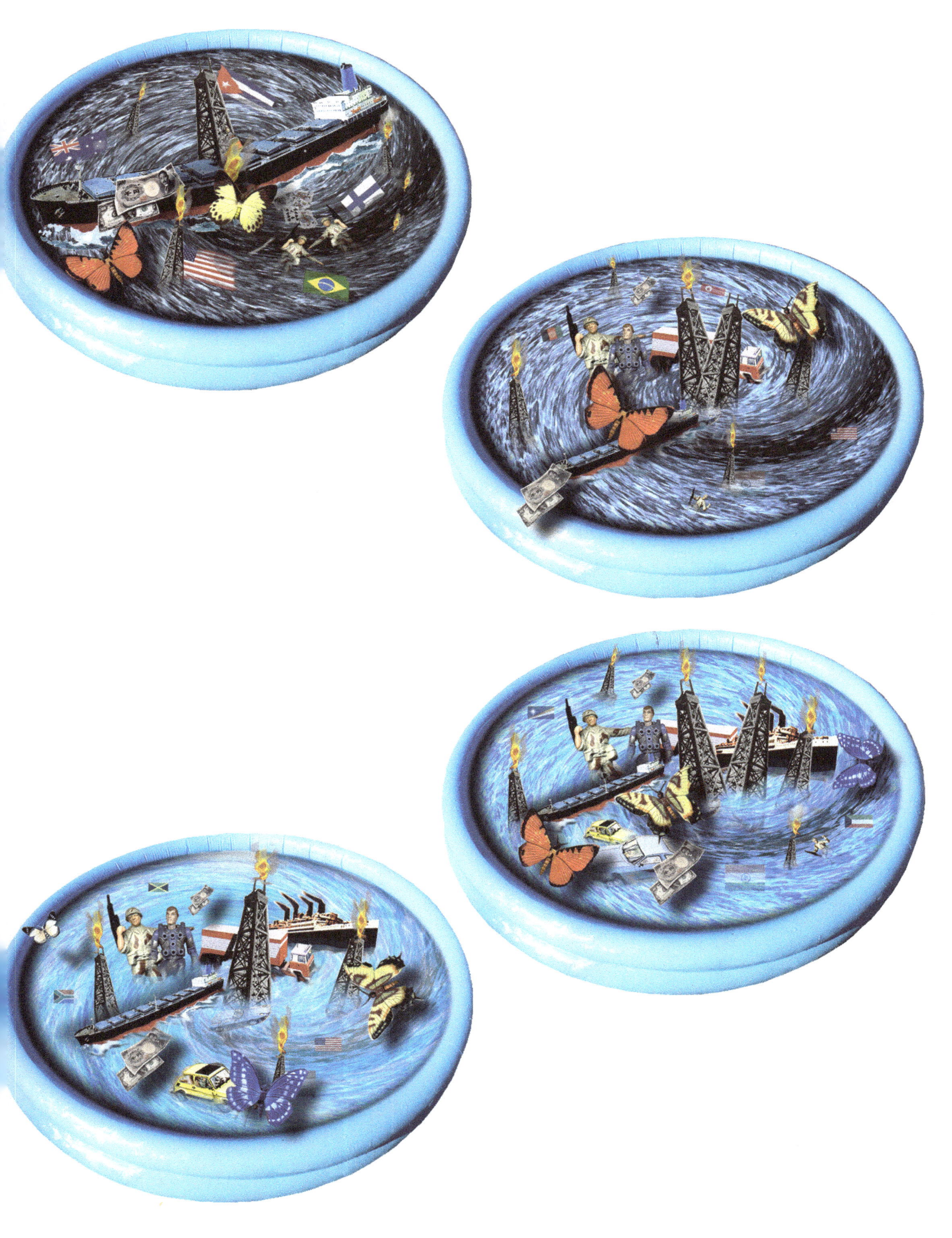

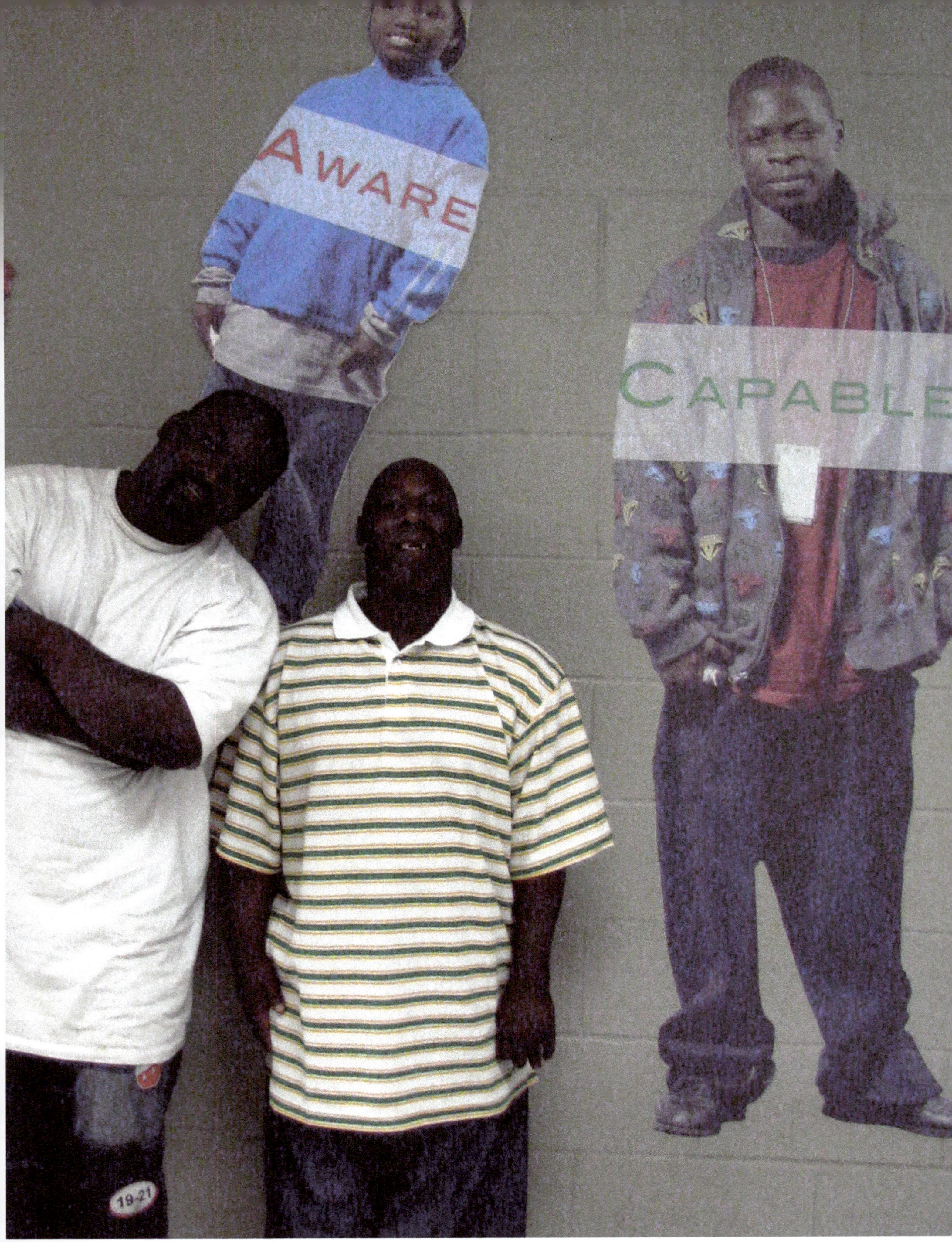

AWARE
CAPABLE
19-21

# Faces of the Homeless

When we think of the homeless, we often envision a tattered older man holding a sign by the off-ramp of a highway. The reality is far different. The average age of a homeless person in Kansas City, Kansas is seven years old. In order to bring this story to a broader public audience, artist Hugh Merrill and Chameleon Arts and Youth Development created the community arts project, *Faces of Homeless Youth*. The goal of this project was to increase the self-esteem of homeless teens, and enhance public understanding of the impact of homelessness on children.

Working in collaboration, Staci Pratt of the Kansas City, Kansas Public Schools Office of Homeless Liaison and Hugh Merrill guided a group of homeless teenagers living and going to school in Wyandotte County, Kansas. These students created personal journals, as well as fine art and performance projects. Their work led to the production of a series of posters and large-scale graphic images installed at the Willa Gill Resource Center in Kansas City, Kansas. The images helped others connect with the reality of homelessness and provided the children with the skills they needed to develop a coherent and insightful artistic voice. These skills served to support their academic ability, as well as build self-worth and community identity.

Homeless communities do not have many opportunities for positive reinforcement. In contrast, these residents had the opportunity to participate in the arts and have positive images they created exhibited at the soup kitchens and resource centers where they went for help. They remain passionate about the artwork installed in their facility.

Faces of Homeless Youth was first exhibited in Washington, DC during the Conference for the National Association of Educators for Homeless Children and Youth in late 2008.

Hugh Merrill produced the project with the assistance of Matt Hilger and Patrick Moonasar. Hilger, concept and project design manager, is a student at the Kansas City Art Institute. Patrick Moonasar is credited with photography and artistic consultation.

--*Staci Pratt*

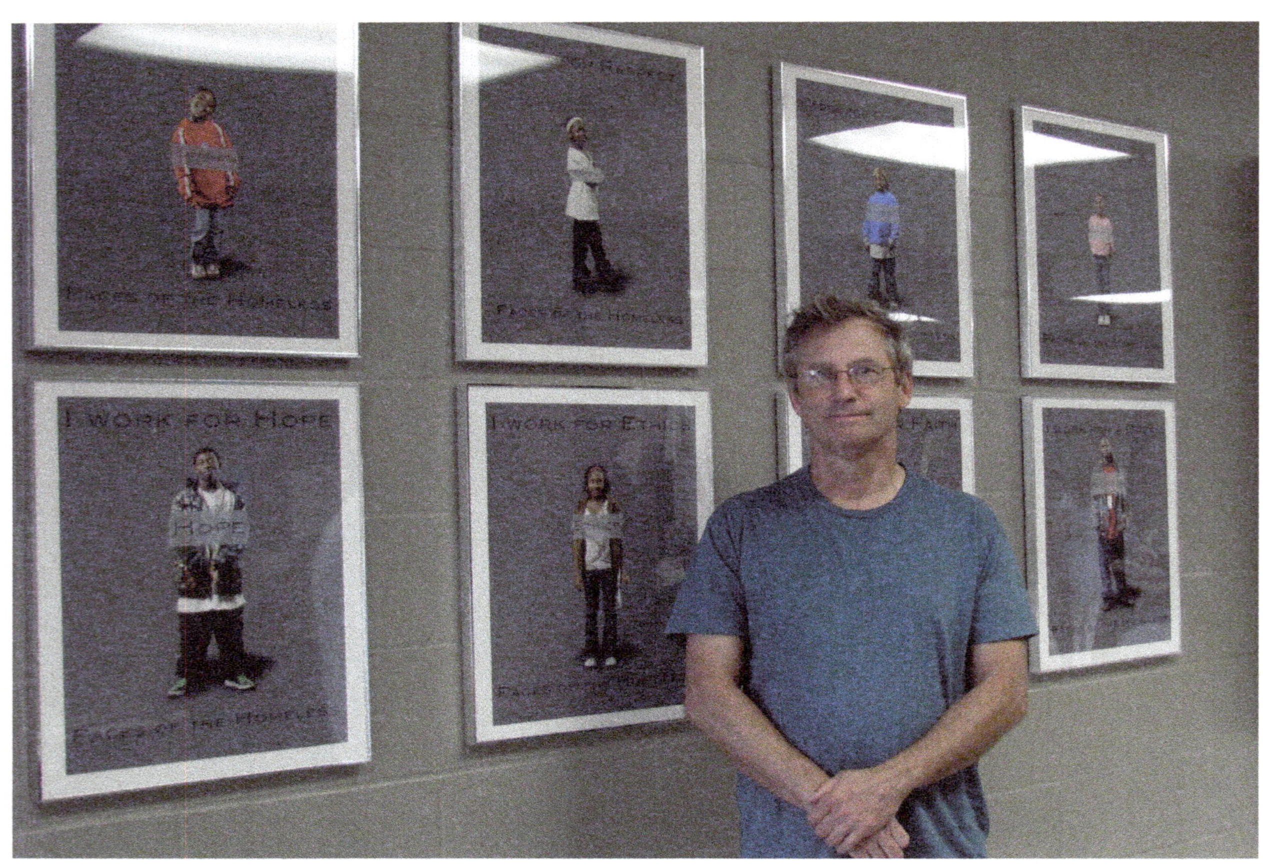

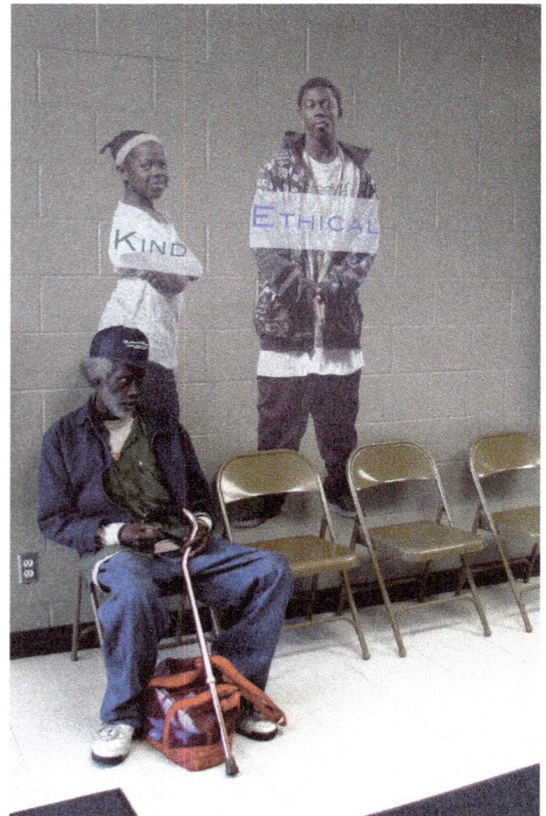



*Top: The artist pictured with the **Faces of Homeless Youth** posters, 2008, Willa Gill Resource Center, Kansas City, Kansas.*

*Left:  **Faces of Homeless Youth**, 2008, wall graphics installation, Willa Gill Homeless Resource Center Kansas City Kansas 2008.*

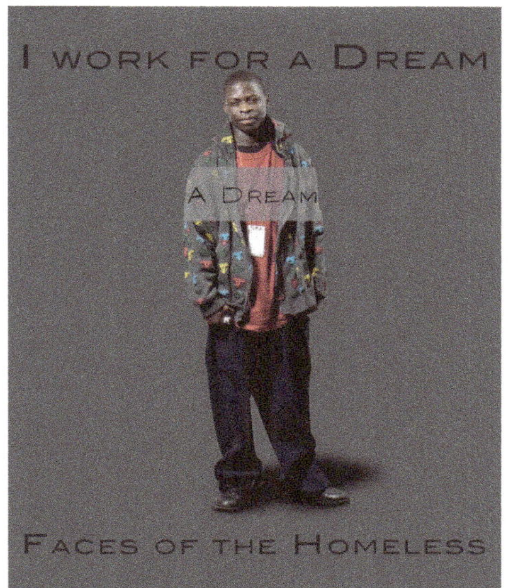

I WORK FOR A DREAM
A DREAM
FACES OF THE HOMELESS


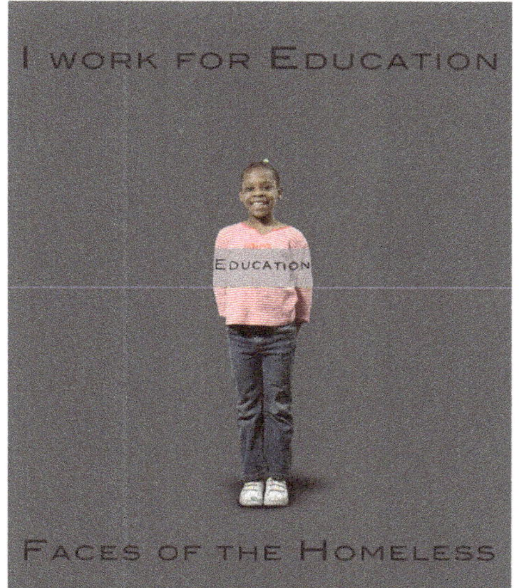

I WORK FOR EDUCATION
EDUCATION
FACES OF THE HOMELESS


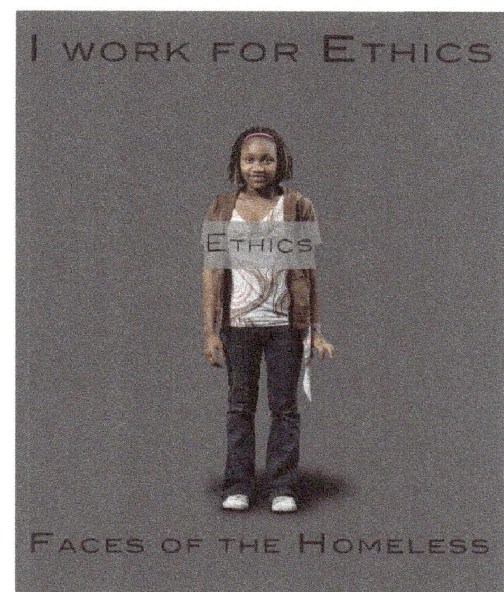

I WORK FOR ETHICS
ETHICS
FACES OF THE HOMELESS


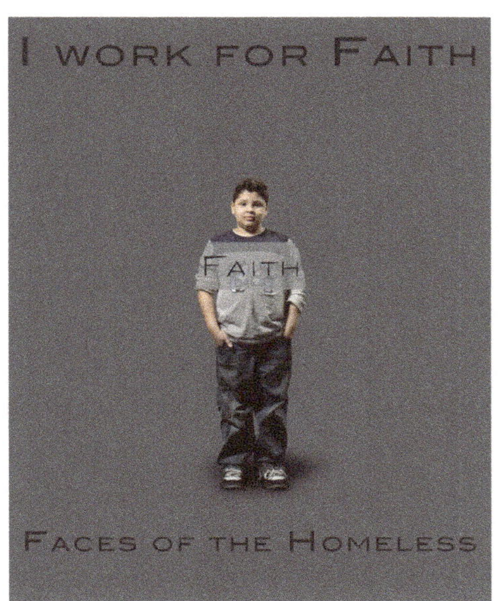

I WORK FOR FAITH
FAITH
FACES OF THE HOMELESS


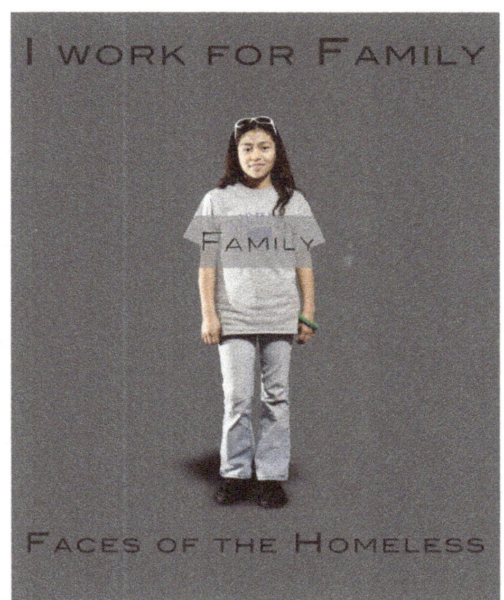

I WORK FOR FAMILY
FAMILY
FACES OF THE HOMELESS


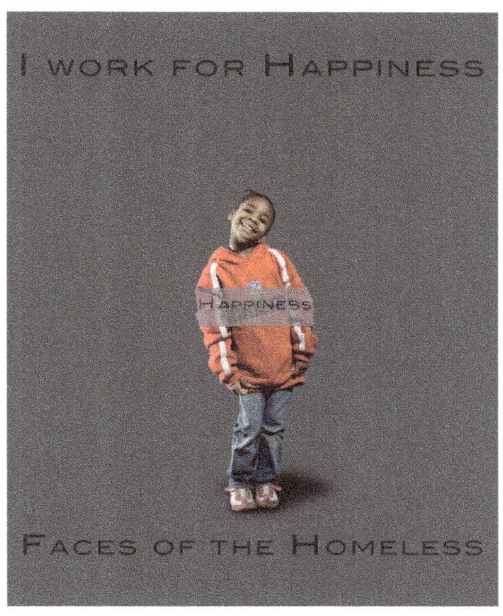

I WORK FOR HAPPINESS
HAPPINESS
FACES OF THE HOMELESS


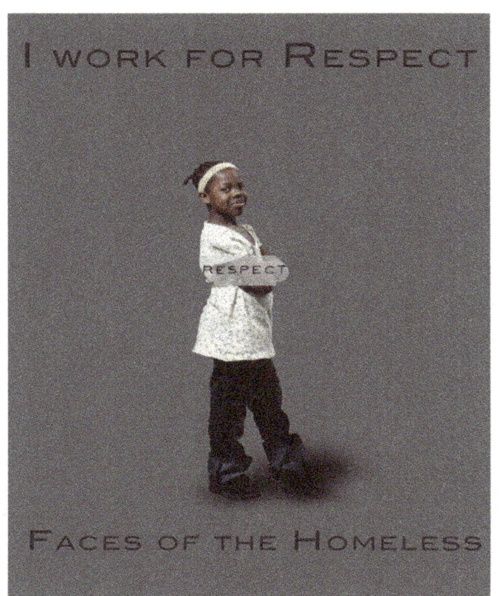

I WORK FOR RESPECT
RESPECT
FACES OF THE HOMELESS


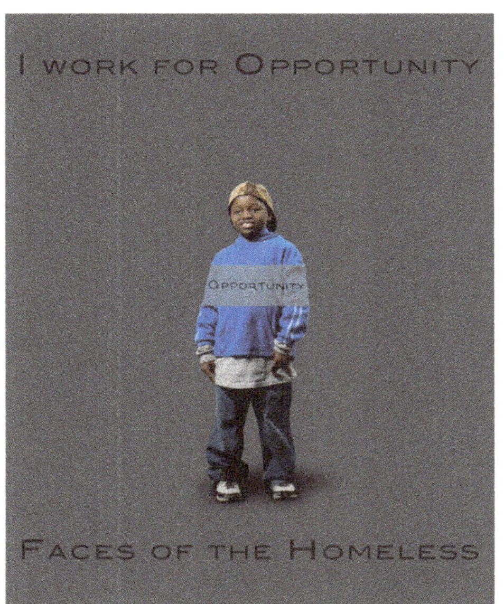

I WORK FOR OPPORTUNITY
OPPORTUNITY
FACES OF THE HOMELESS


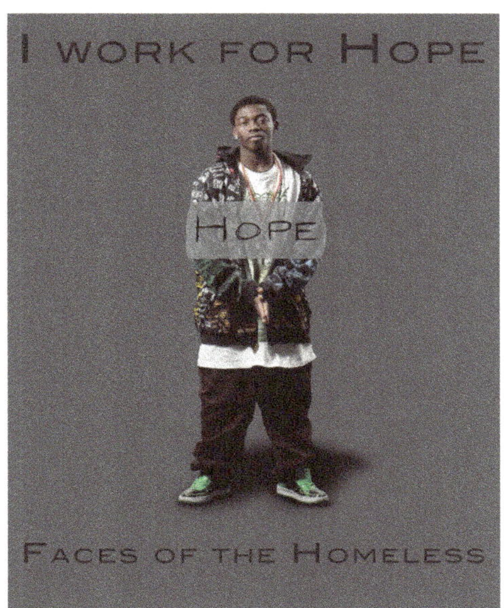

I WORK FOR HOPE
HOPE
FACES OF THE HOMELESS

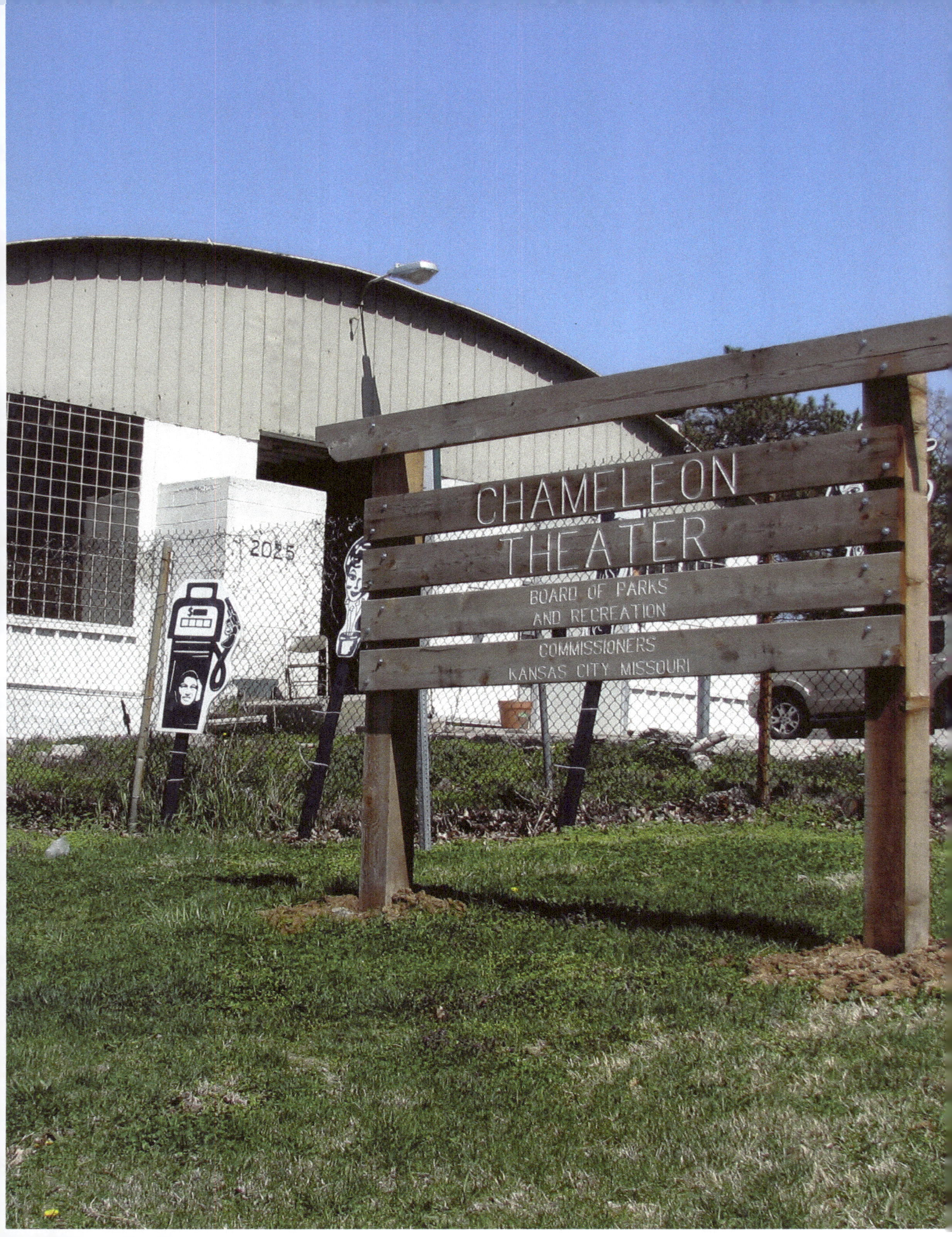
CHAMELEON
THEATER
BOARD OF PARKS
AND RECREATION
COMMISSIONERS
KANSAS CITY MISSOURI
2025

# Chameleon Arts & Youth Development

Hugh Merrill has worked with artists, educators, partners, and clients to transform Chameleon from a small theatre company into a highly successful interdisciplinary community arts agency. This decade-long endeavor has been a challenge. As an artist unraveling the mysteries of management practices and developing an effective board of directors, Merrill has created a well-run and transparent arts resource. With the help of Chameleon's new board, a consortium of small arts organizations, and excellent staff, they are able to bring arts projects and programming to marginalized populations, including homeless youth and families in domestic violence shelters.

With the generous support of many of Kansas City's largest philanthropic organizations, Chameleon expedited over one million dollars in community arts and youth development programs from 2006 to 2010. These generous supporters include: the Muriel McBrien Kauffman Foundation, the Francis Families Foundation, Bank of America, the R.A. Long Foundation, the Sosland Foundation, and the Oppenstein Foundation. The Missouri Arts Council and the Arts Council of Metropolitan Kansas City's ArtsKC Fund are also important contributors.

Even in a time of economic crisis, Chameleon has expanded programming and is presently serving these Kansas City, Missouri Parks and Recreation community centers: Office of Homeless Liaison of Kansas City, Kansas, Public Schools; Phoenix Families Housing; Rose Brooks Shelter; St. Marks Child and Family Development Center; and the Kansas City, Missouri School District. Through these alliances and interdisciplinary artistic practice, exceptional works of art that change and enrich the populations they serve are created.

Chameleon believes strongly that the success of its arts and youth programs is directly tied to its involvement with other small arts organizations. By providing access to creative studio space for six small arts groups, Chameleon is able to draw upon the skills, knowledge, and talent of passionate and committed artists to focus energy on youth development. By designing new arts curriculum and charting outcomes of programming, Chameleon maximizes its value to supporters. Management, evaluation, and financing of projects are part of the assistance the company offers. In turn, this guarantees educational and arts studies of the highest quality.

The Institute for Children, Poverty, and Homelessness in New York City focuses on action-oriented research designed not just to study family homelessness, but also to provide data and ideas that will inform and enhance public policy on serving homeless families.

Through collaboration with ICPH, Chameleon implements new arts and academic curriculum designed to meet the needs of homeless populations. Each of these programs meets national instructional standards. The Office of the Homeless Liaison works with certified school district teachers in a tutoring program to assist with the academic portion of these courses of study. The organization then trains artists and educators to provide studio response to the lessons and their themes.

This year's program interpreted Alvin Ailey's *Revelations*, a signature choreographic piece first performed in 1960 that continues to impact audiences today. *Revelations* has been performed worldwide and inspires an avid following in the United States and abroad. This compelling tale chronicles a culture grappling with the transition from slavery to freedom. The spectacular musical score is comprised of traditional spirituals and jazz compositions that express joy, sorrow, and transcendence simultaneously.

In early 2010, internationally regarded conceptual artist and sculptor Mel Chin personally invited Chameleon to participate in his *Fundred Dollar Bill Project*. The over-arching goal of this venture is to build creative capitol in the form of hand-drawn one hundred-dollar bills. Chin will then ask the U.S. Congress to convert these Fundreds into real money to clean up the toxic soil in New Orleans, Louisiana. Each participant is only allowed one Fundred, so over three million artworks are required to meet the goal of $300,000,000. This amount represents what it would take to clean up the lead-contaminated soil for the children of this Gulf Coast city. The ability for anyone to join in this conceptual sculpture provides participants with a means to explore their own ideas of social and political justice.

Merrill's commitment to art as a mechanism for pursuing social justice reflects a passionate and unwavering dedication to disempowered citizenry. "I have never met anyone whose soul, passion, and talents combine so powerfully to ensure we hear the voices of those who have been asked to be silent," observes Staci Pratt of the OHL. She expresses her continuing thanks:

*"Hugh is a force of nature, He will not let us forget the eyes of the children of Dania Beach, or the faces of homeless youth. For this, we cannot thank him enough. He is a witness to the story of our communities, their endeavors and attendant struggles, along with their triumphs and truths. His honesty calls us to action."*

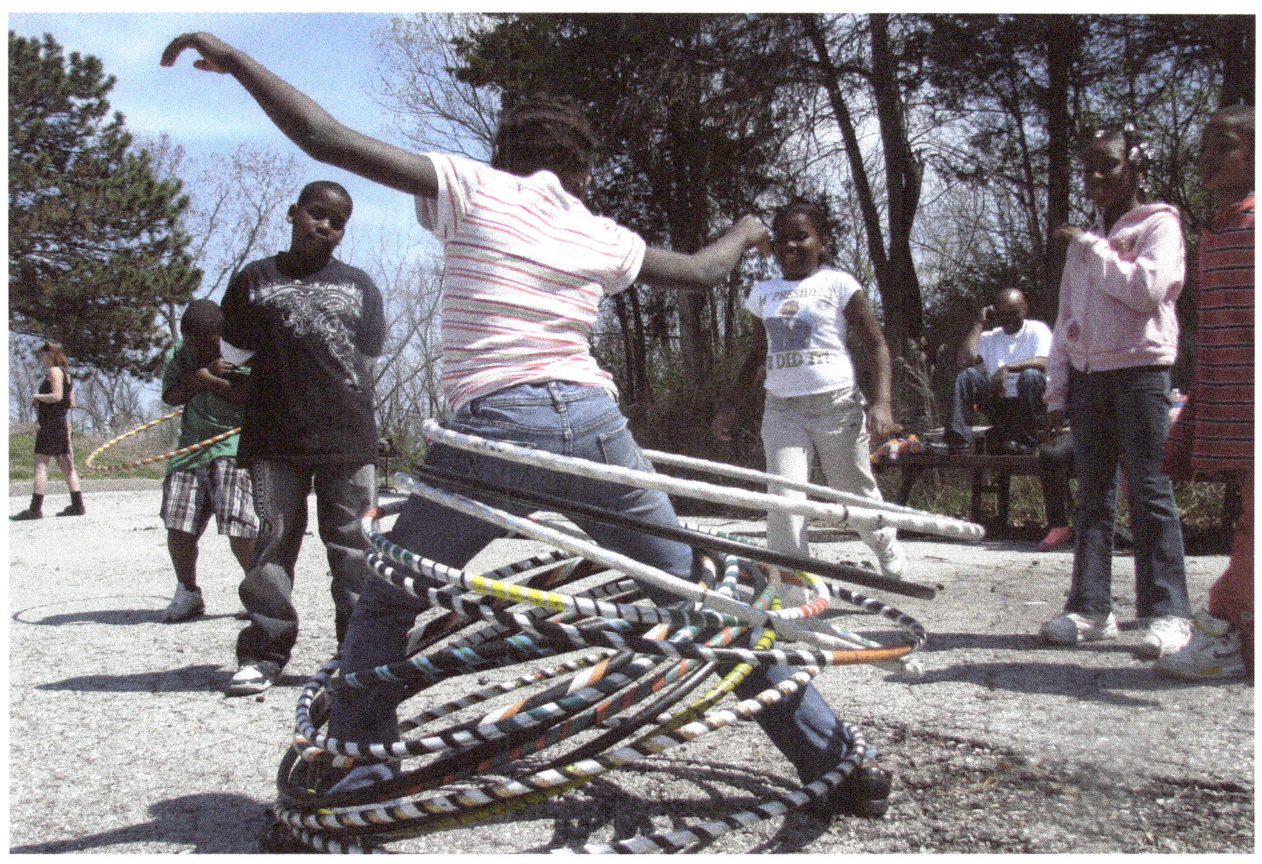

**EarthFest**, *2009, collaboration between Chameleon Arts and the Community Arts and Service Learning program at the Kansas City Art Institute.*

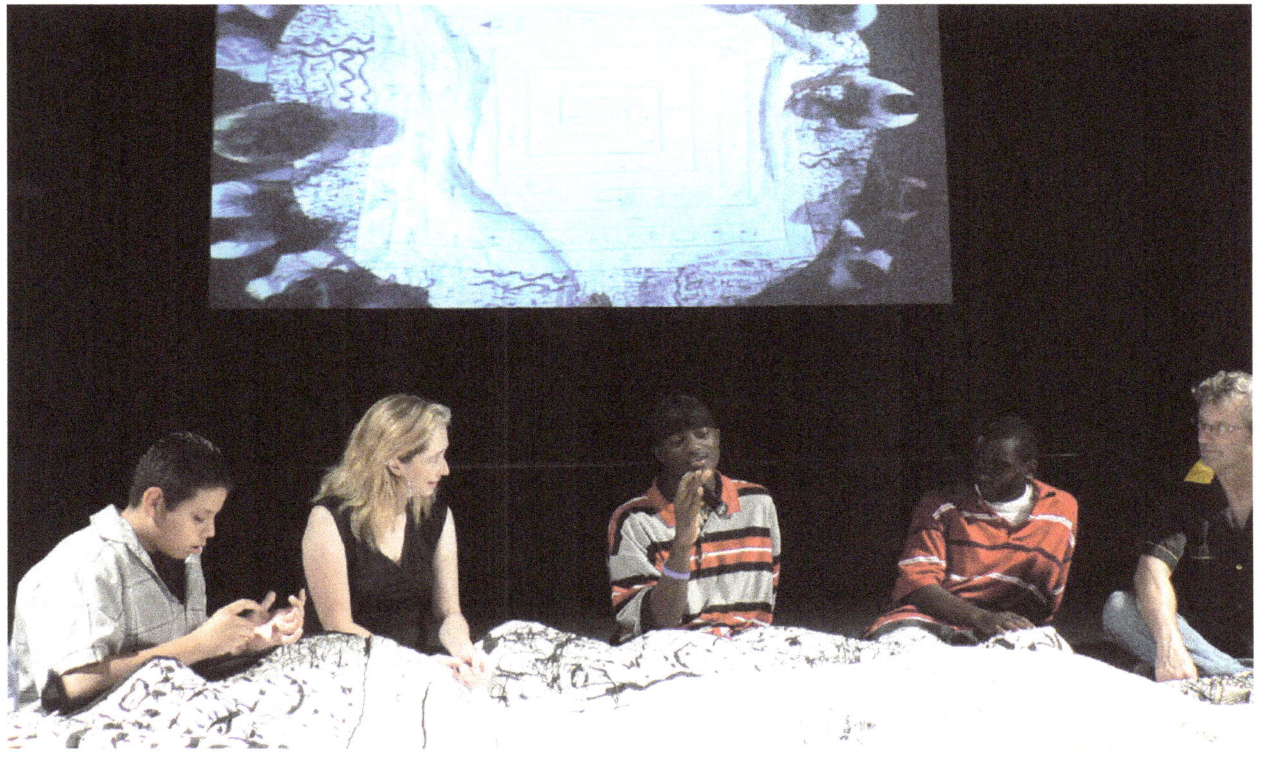

**Storytelling and Listening**, *2005, quilt project by So Yeon Park, YWCA, Kansas City, Kansas.*

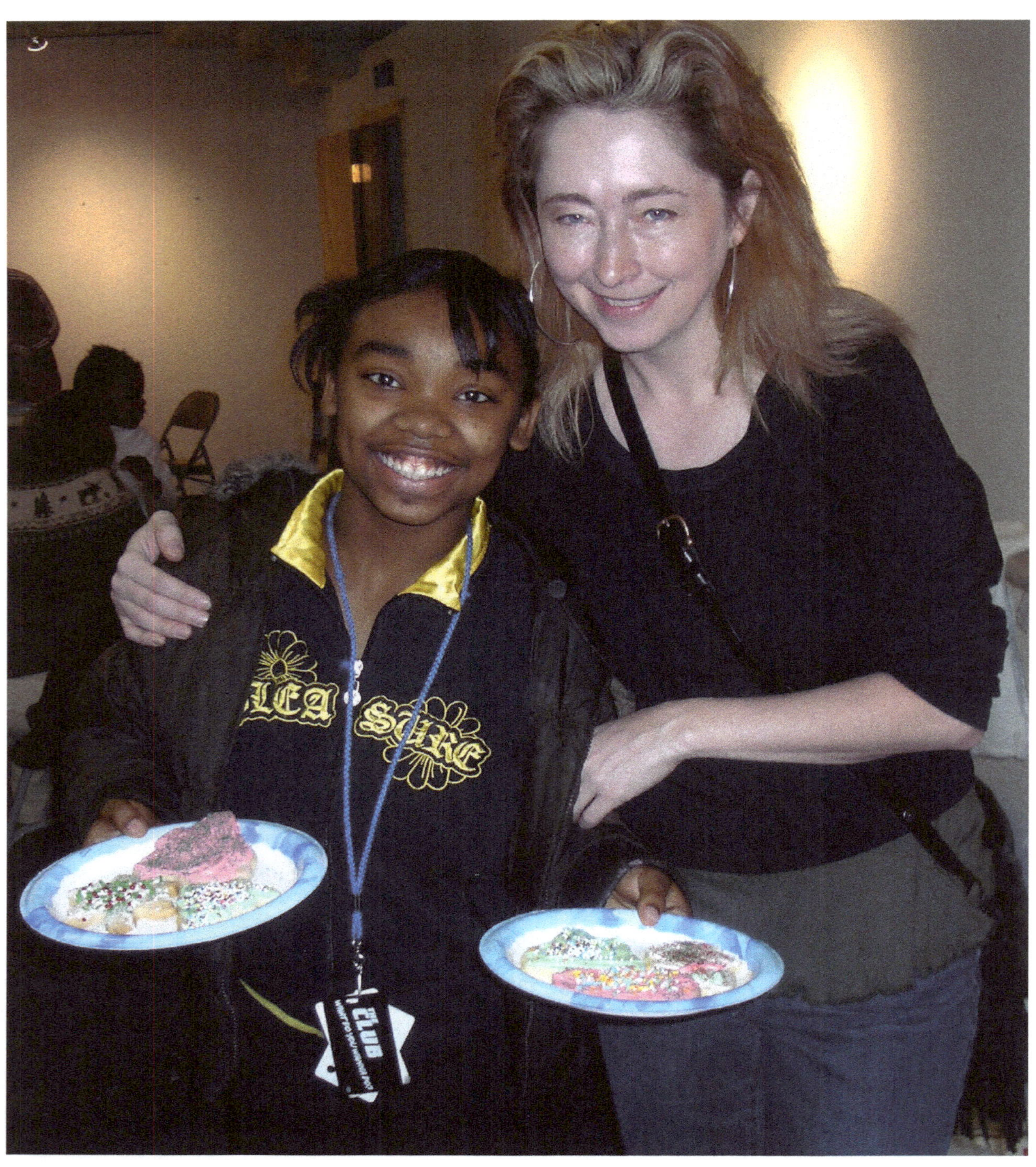

**Staci Pratt, Director of Office of Homeless Liaison Kansas City, Kansas, with Rita**, *2007, Chameleon Arts programming.*

"I credit Chameleon with significantly improving the lives and self-esteem of our homeless youth.  This consortium not only teaches art, dance, drumming, and creativity, they help participants to make art that validates their life experiences in society. Artworks by Mel Chin, So Yeon Park, Deanna Skedel, and Hugh Merrill celebrate the intrinsic beauty of our children. Through exhibitions and presentations at regional and national education and arts conferences, the works have both nationwide and international impact. They empower and propel audiences to question their understanding of who is homeless and require that viewers lose their detachment from this societal tragedy."

Staci Pratt, Director of the Office of Homeless Liaison of the Unified 500 School District Kansas City, Kansas.

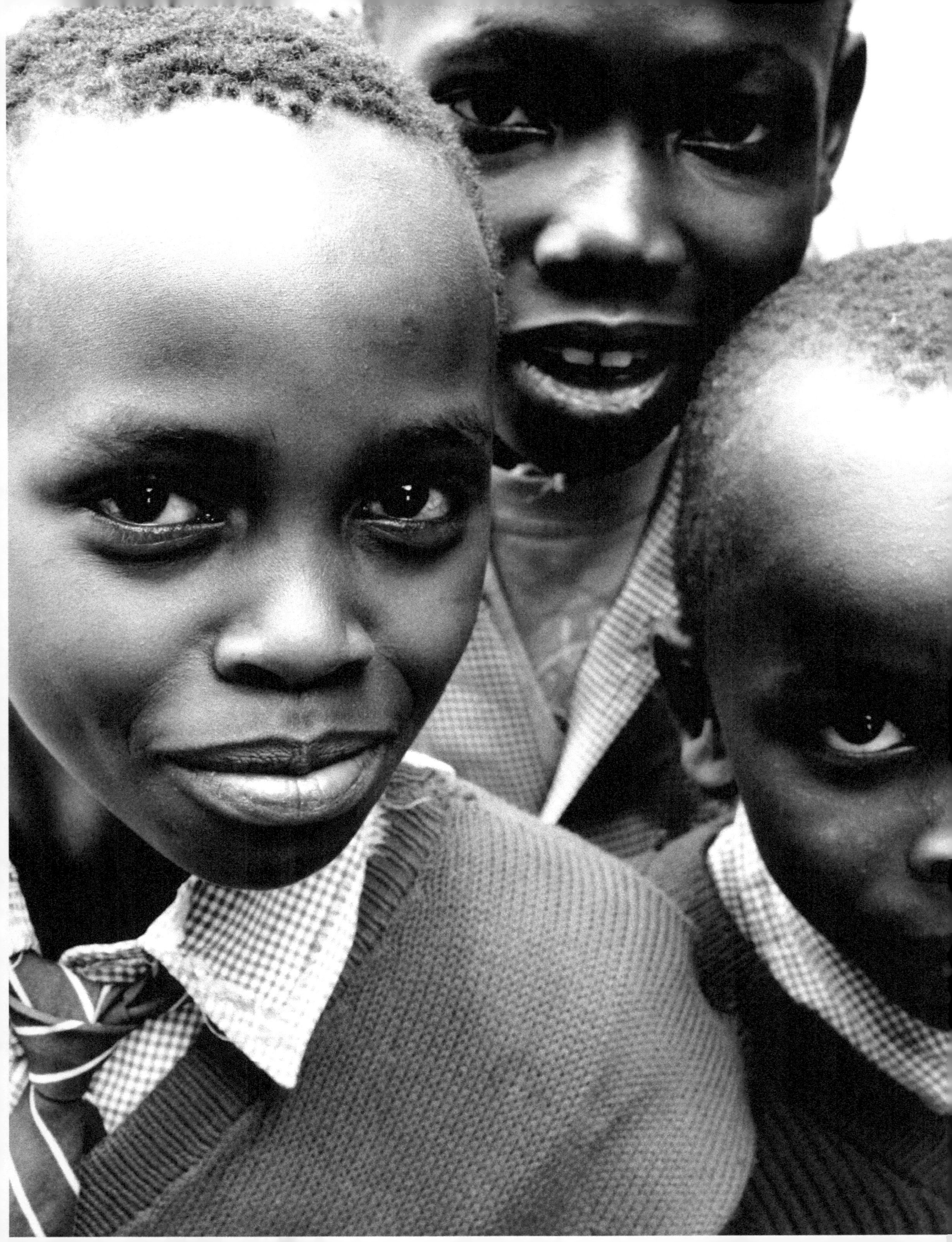

# International Travels

While Merrill is ceaseless in his coordination and advocacy for local communities, he has also traveled extensively internationally to create artworks, host seminars facilitating printmaking and to develop community art projects. Collaborations with Doctor Antonio and Luz Racela gave space for Merrill to work as community artist and photographer in the Philippines, Cuba, and Guatemala. These travels were part of the Medical Missions Foundation of Kansas City's outreach programs which are dedicated to generating community arts actions and mural making. In addition to the arts, this foundation provides medical services, including life-saving surgeries for communities lacking in many basic health services.

In 2001, Merrill traveled to Nairobi, Kenya with a number of artists and guided by Kansas Citian, Josie Mai. Here, these artists collaborated with Mother Theresa's Mission in Huruma to create a sculptural playground. Mai, Merrill and the other artists worked directly with local artists and crafts people. Merrill was fortunate to return to Nairobi with his son, Emmett, in 2009. The father-son artist duo traveled for five weeks working with village children in the art forms of photography, drawing and writing.

These international travels bring Merrill a deep respect for world citizens, as well as highlighting our American luxury and privilege. While he lodged with Mother Theresa's Sisters of Charity Orphanage, he wrote extensively on the dramatic life-style differences between his Kansas City home and students versus the orphaned children of Kenya, including this excerpt:

*A gate divides two worlds. They are inches apart, yet worlds apart. Masonry and steel serve as dual dividers, contrasting mirror images of each other. What do they tell us about the physics of heaven and hell? About the word and acts of gods, the words and acts of human kind? Is their meaning sacred, divine, or mundane and of this world?*

*Outside the gate is the nature of nature grossly abundant, uncaring, chaotic, and random. It is a jungle of cultural and economic survival. Here nature feeds on itself. Outside the gate is the abundant stench of life unrelenting. Humans forced to devour, to fight for every inch of space, every gram of nutrition. Fight for a bucket, fight to sell, to earn money, to simply fill the bucket with questionable tap water. They fight exhaustion and hatred while carrying the bucket, strapped to their heads, home to a black and blue hole of rusted tin and dank charcoal. They fight to sustain a battered body exposed to the elements, fight to clear the lungs filled with smoke, diesel fuel and the acrid perfume of garbage, rotting treasures of trash. Trash spread down streets seeping, picked over, resold and devoured. Garbage that has had the last bit of nutrition sucked from it. Everything is for sale, the sole of an old shoe, fruit, discarded corn oil plastic jugs. Old lead plumbing parts hanging like drying papers. Next to the fruit and tomatoes is a dying man, worn out, sitting, exhausted legs splayed akimbo. A girl with her baby, a pre-teen mother, shy and restrained by taboos and culture, fights for her son in a hopeless world of exquisite abject poverty. Glue sniffing teens dance like drunken Pans with poison pipes, weaving and bounding off imaginary walls.*

*A goat, a chicken, an African king in full regalia, swirl in a kaleidoscope of color in an atmosphere of choking dust. The man selling maize does not see the starving child but eyes the man in the business suit walking and talking on a cell phone. They all fight for sustenance, family, culture and self in a vast slum in contemporary Nairobi.*

*There is no solution for this vast sway. There will be no saving the desperately poor. No overnight solution or silver bullet. Gods will not descend tomorrow or maybe Tuesday to uplift and make the system equitable. Yet this reality of shaking color, smell, dust, sky and existence is sustained. The people and their meager products are illuminated by the same powers that value life on the distant other side of the gate.*

*Inside. Open the gate and step into the garden, to a safely ordered world. Chaos is vanquished behind the self-imposed prison walls. A touch of utopian architecture, a world pruned and painted white and blue. Swept, scrubbed, a world of balance, harmony and equality. Here the lowest is the most respected and compassion is the common cultural value. Compassion here is no big deal, it just is. Inside the walls nature's chaos is held at bay by duty, sacrifice, order, hierarchy and good management. The child from the dustbin, broken and malnourished is revived, body, mind, and spirit. The clock slows the focus of the community, narrow and sharp. A world made up of routines and values. Outside is the world of chaos, desire, need, competition, the natural order, the attrition of existence. Inside is a garden of nurturing kindness. But like the best Japanese garden, it is not natural; it is a transformed and artificial substitution for raw reality.*

*The common unbreakable thread that sustains a life in the chaotic/erotic outside world is the same force that sustains survival inside the gate. Joy, love, and beauty (JLB) exist in the dank malaria infested alleys of humanity. JLB guides communities, lost souls, families and children toward hope. JLB exists inside the gate, guiding a group of nuns to endlessly care for a microscopically small minority of children and women in need.*

*The big picture of emptying the ocean with a teaspoon only momentarily troubles the mind of the caregivers, on either side of the gate. The obligations of joy, love, and beauty are gravitational, the magical force that holds things together. The nun picks up the spoon and feeds the disfigured child while the teenage mother sitting in her dark charcoal dirt and tin hovel offers her breast to her giggling child.*

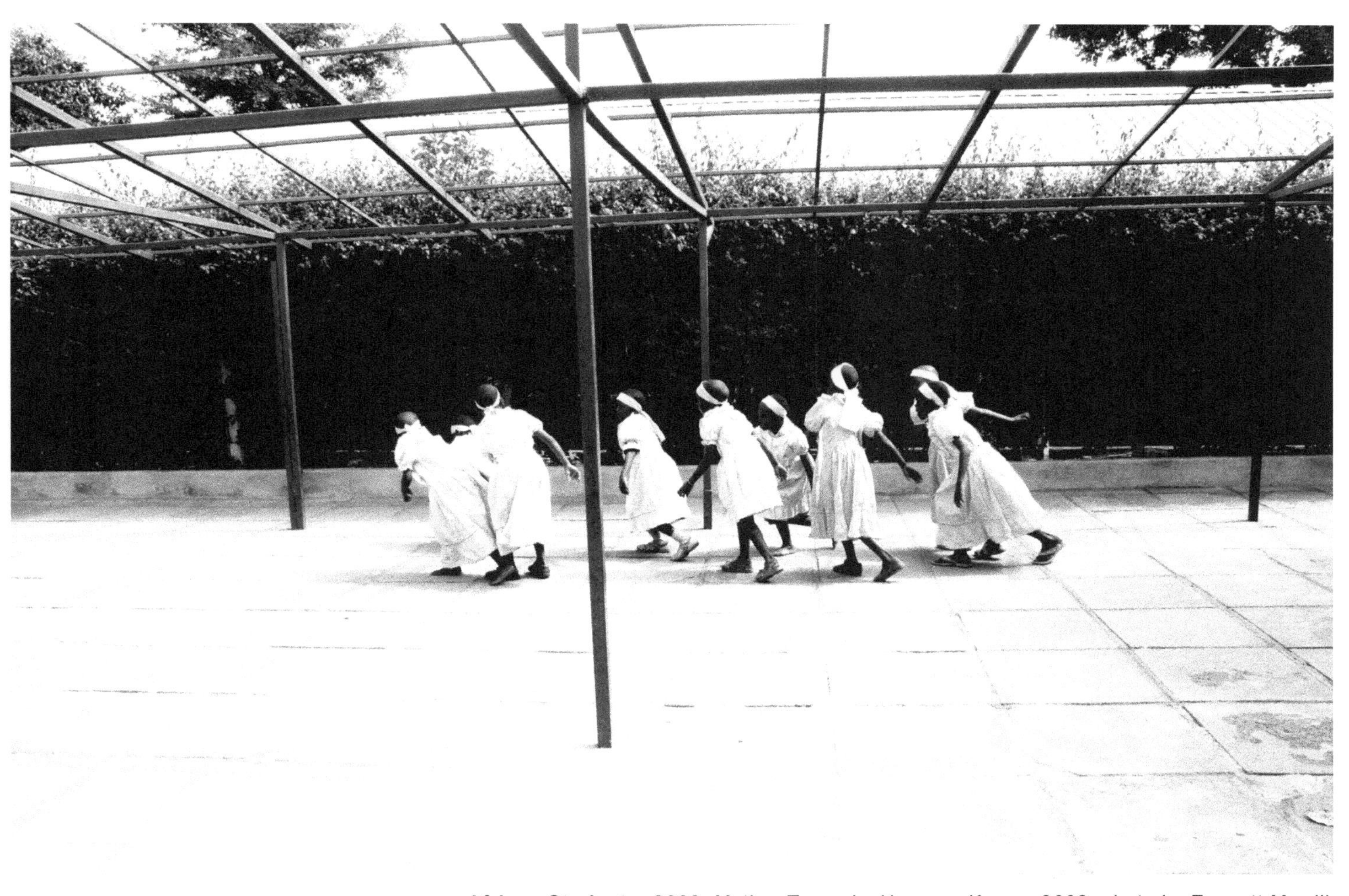

**African Students**, *2008, Mother Teresa's, Huruma, Kenya, 2008, photo by Emmett Merrill.*

# Chronology

**1949**        Born in Olney, Maryland.

**1973**        BFA, Maryland Institute College of Art, Baltimore, Maryland.

**1974**        Fellowship, Virginia Museumof Fine Arts, Richmond, Virginia.

**1975**        MFA, Yale University School of Art and Architecture, New Haven, Connecticut.

**1976**        Professor, Kansas City Art Institute, Kansas City, Missouri.

**1977**        Founder, Squadron Press, Kansas City, Missouri.

**1985**        *Lucky Dragon Suite*, Nelson-Atkins Museum of Art, Kansas City, Missouri.

**1986**        *Hugh Merrill Prints*, Springfield Art Museum, Springfield, Missouri.

**1987**        *Hugh Merrill Drawings and Prints*, Smith College, North Hampton, Massachusetts.

**1988**        *Art Across America: Artists and Their Students* (traveling exhibition).
            *Prints and Hidden Drawings*, Printworks Gallery, Chicago, Illinois.
            *Tenth Anniversary Exhibition*, Nelson-Atkins Museum of Art, Kansas City, Missouri.

**1989**        *Art from Academé*, Central Exchange, Kansas City, Missouri.
            *Dead Serious*, Davenport Museum of Art, Davenport, Iowa.

**1990**        *Los Angeles Print Society 1990*, Los Angeles, California.
            *Wallenberg Suite*, Tyler School of Art, Philadelphia, Pennsylvania.

**1991**        *Art Expo 1991*, Lakeside Gallery, Chicago, Illinois.
            *Cranbrook Collects: New Acquisitions*, Cranbrook Museum of Art, Bloomfield Hills, Michigan.
            *Fellowship: Hugh Merrill and Steve Murakishi*, Leedy-Voulkos Art Center, Kansas City, Missouri.
            *Wallenberg Suite*, Printworks Gallery, Chicago, Illinois.

**1992**        *Rosa Luxemburg Suite*, Art Expo 1992, Lakeside Gallery, Chicago, Illinois.
            *Dada Invitational*, Alpha Gallery, Denver, Colorado.
            *60 Square Inches*, Purdue University, West Purdue, Indiana.
            *Twelfth National University of Dallas Print Invitational*, Dallas, Texas.

**1993**    *Big Print*, University of Dallas, Irvine, Texas.

*Critical Impressions: Contemporary Print Arts and the Engagements of the Socio/Political*, Florida State University, Tallahassee, Florida.

*Facts of Fictions*, University of Puget Sound, Tacoma, Washington.

*Ink Visions*, Evanston Art Center, Evanston, Illinois.

*LA Print Society National Competition*, Los Angeles, California.

*Print Mural*, Edmonton Arts Festival, University of Alberta, Canada.

*Pulling Together*, Southern Graphics Council Conference, Baltimore, Maryland.

*Rosa Luxemberg Suite*, Navy Pier Exhibition, Printworks Gallery, Chicago, Illinois.

**1994**    *Life Cycles*, Indianapolis Art League, Indianapolis, Indiana.

*Life Cycles*, Santa Barbara Contemporary Arts Forum, Santa Barbara, California.

*Life Cycles*, Stephen F. Austin University, Nacogdoches, Texas.

**1995**    *25th Invitational Print and Drawing*, Bradley University, Peoria, Illinois.

*Art from Académé*, Central Exchange, Kansas City, Missouri.

*25 American Print Artists: La Jeune Gravure Contemporaine, Mairie du Sixieme*, Arrondissement Salle des Fetes, Paris, France.

*National Print Exhibition*, University of Hawaii, Hilo, Hawaii.

*Nova Huta Rising*, Edmonton, Alberta City Hall, Edmonton, Canada.

*Printmaking 1995*, Northern Arizona University, Flagstaff, Arizona.

*Print Masters*, University of Tennessee, Knoxville, Tennessee.

*Transparent Motives*, New Orleans Museum of Art, New Orleans, Louisiana.

**1996**    *Facts of Fictions*, Printworks Gallery, Chicago, Illinois.

**1997**    *Facts of Fictions*, Western Sydney University, Sydney, Australia.

*Shadow Plays*, Missouri Fine Arts Academy, Springfield, Missouri.

*Vitreographs from Harvey Littleton Studio*, Portland Art Museum, Portland, Oregon.

**1998**    *Martin Buber's Cat*, Leedy-Voulkos Gallery, Kansas City, Missouri.

*Our City/Ourselves, Portrait of a Community*, Kemper Museum of Contemporary Art, Kansas City, Missouri.

*Prints III, An Invitational of American Artists*, Ball State University, Muncie, Indiana.

**1999**      *Blue Print Portraits*, Buena Vista University, Storm Lake, Iowa.

Executive Director, Chameleon Arts and Youth Development, Kansas City, Missouri.

*Fast and Fugitive*, University of Sydney, Sydney, Australia.

**2000**      *Boston Printmakers 2000*, Boston University Art Gallery, Boston, Massachusetts.

*Bradley International 2000*, Bradley University, Peoria Illinois.

*Facts of Fictions: Prints by Hugh Merrill*, Art and Culture Center, Hollywood, Florida.

*Fast and Fugitive*, Daum Museum of Contemporary Art, Sedalia, Missouri.

*Is*, Leedy-Voulkos Art Center, Kansas City, Missouri.

*Midlands Invitational 2000*, Joslyn Art Museum, Omaha, Nebraska.

*Printology 1990-2000: Prints by Wycross Press*, Wiregrass Museum, Dothan, Alabama.

**2001**      *3-Ring Circus*, Leedy-Voulkos Art Center, Kansas City, Missouri.

*On/Off/Over the Edge*, American Print Alliance, (traveling exhibition).

*Persistent Prints*, Butters Gallery, Portland, Oregon.

*Reconciliation Project*, Dublin Ireland Academy of Art, Dublin, Ireland.

**2002**      *Small Paintings*, Weber State University, Ogden, Utah.

**2002-2004**      *Art of Memory*, Public arts commission at the Sanford-Kimpton Health Facility in Columbia, Missouri.

**2003**      *25th Anniversary Show*, Purdue University, West Lafayette, Indiana.

**2004**      *75th Honolulu Print Exhibit*, Honolulu, Hawaii.

*Drawings and Community Art*, Manchester Craftsman's Guild, Pittsburgh, Pennsylvania.

For Sydney, Printworks Gallery, Chicago, Illinois.

*Group Exhibition*, Morgan Gallery, Kansas City, Missouri.

*Group Exhibition*, Foresight Gallery, Kansas City, Missouri.

*KCAI Faculty Exhibition*, Block Art Space, Kansas City, Missouri.

*Magic Mats at SLOP Art*, Center of Creative Arts, St. Louis, Missouri.

*Multiple Perspectives*, Southern Graphics Council Conference Exhibition, Boston, Massachusetts.

*Pandora's Box*, Epic Center, Columbia College, Chicago, Illinois.

*Skate: A Metaphysical Park*, Public art commission, Roeland Park, Kansas.

*Truth*, Mid America Print Council, Lincoln, Nebraska.

**2005**      *Chameleon 10th Anniversary Exhibition*, Chameleon Arts and Youth Development, Kansas City, Missouri.

*Hugh Merrill: Drawings and Community Art*, Drury University, Springfield, Missouri.

*Pools of Belief*, Polish National Museum, Poznan, Poland.

*Thieves, Thugs and Liars*, Southern Graphics Council Conference, Washington, D.C.

*Touch and Language*, Morgan Gallery, Kansas City, Missouri.

**2006**      *31 @ Unit 5*, Unit 5 Gallery, Kansas City, Missouri.

*I'd Rather Be Drawing*, Morgan Gallery, Kansas City, Missouri.

*Lucky Dragon Suite*, Daum Museum of Contemporary Art, Sedalia, Missouri.

*Print at the Edge*, Cardiff Gallery, Cardiff Wales, United Kingdom.

**2007**     *Falun Print Triennial*, Darlanas Museum, Falun, Sweden.

*Further: Artists from Printmaking at the Edge*, Museum of Photography, Seoul Korea.

**2008**     *Ecoscape*, Leedy-Voulkos Art Center, Kansas City, Missouri.

*Print Lovers at 30: Celebrating Three Decades of Giving*, Nelson-Atkins Museum of Art, Kansas City, Missouri.

*Second International Print Biennial*, Beijing, China and Seoul, Korea.

**2009**     *Divergent Consistencies: 40 years of the Studio and Community Art of Hugh Merrill*, Leedy-Voulkos Art Center, Kansas City, Missouri.

**2010**     *5th Bienal Internacional Gravura Douro*, Teixeira De Sousa, Portugal.

*Community and Loneliness*, Paragraph Gallery, Kansas City, Missouri.

*Further: Artists from Printmaking at the Edge*, (ongoing international traveling exhibition).

*Mano/Mundo/Corazón: Artists Interpret La Lotería*, The Center for Book & Paper Arts at Columbia College Chicago, Chicago, Illinois.

*Spacium Tempus: International Exhibition of Contemporary Printmaking 2011*, Guanlan Printmaking Base, Shenzhen, China (international traveling exhibition).

**2011**     *Divergent Consistencies 2*, Downtown Public Library, Kansas City, Missouri.

*Guanlan International Biennial*, Guanlan Original Printmaking Base, Shenzhen, China.

*Plunder the Influence: An Examination of Visual Manifestations (and Sources) of Influence*, www.adrianeherman.typepad.com/plunder_the_influence/

# Collections

Albrecht-Kemper Museum of Art, St. Joseph, Missouri

Auburn University, Auburn, Alabama

Columbus College of Art, Chicago Illinois

Cranbrook Academy of Art, Bloomfield Hills, Michigan

Daum Museum, Sedalia, Missouri

Davenport Museum of Art, Davenport, Iowa

Franklin Furnace, New York, New York

Gravura Do Douro Museo, Sousa, Portugal

Guanlan Original Printmaking Base, Shenzhen, China

Hallmark, Inc., Kansas City, Missouri

Harvard Law School, Boston, Massachusetts

Harvard Museums, Boston, Massachusetts

Kemper Museum of Contemporary Art, Kansas City, Missouri

Minneapolis Museum of Art, Minneapolis, Minnesota

Museum of Modern Art, New York, New York

National Contemporary Art Museum, Poznan, Poland

Nelson-Atkins Museum of Art, Kansas City, Missouri

Nerman Contemporary Art Museum, Overland Park, Kansas

Purdue University Art Museum, West Lafayette, Indiana

San Antonio Art Institute, San Antonio, Texas

Sheldon Museum of Art, Lincoln, Nebraska

Silvermine Artist's Guild, Silvermine, Connecticut

Springfield Museum of Fine Art, Springfield, Missouri

Spencer Museum, Lawrence, Kansas

University of Dallas, Dallas, Texas

University of Mississippi, Oxford, Mississippi

Virginia Museum, Richmond, Virginia

Wright State University, Dayton, Ohio

Yale Museum of Fine Arts, New Haven, Connecticut

# Selected Bibliography


Agnew, Sara. "Drawing Outside the Box." *Columbia Daily Tribune*, February 23, 2003.

Akers, Jama. "Hugh Merrill: Prints, Politics and Perception." *Kansas City Home Design*, March, 1998.

Allen, Lynne and Phyliss McGibbon. *The Best of Printmaking: An International Collection*. Rockport: Rockport Publishers, 1997.

Asher, Dean. "Sol House Hosts events to raise Awareness for Homeless Youth." *Columbia Missourian*, November 4, 2009.

Baca, Judith F. "Whose Monument Where? Public Art in a Many-Cultured Society." in *Mapping the Terrain, New Genre Public Art*, edited by Suzanne Lacy, Seattle: Bay Press, 1995. 131-38, 202.

Berman, Laura. "Teaching Excellence: Hugh Merrill." *Graphic Impressions: Journal of the Southern Graphics Council* (winter/spring 2007).

Berry, Ian, Julie Ault, Susan Cahan, David Deitcher, et al. *Tim Rollins and the K.O.S.: A History*. Cambridge: MIT Press, 2009.

Calloway, Rebekah. "Divergent Consistencies."  Unpublished manuscript, exhibition documents, (2009).

Canelas, Nuno. "5th Bienal Internacional de Gravura Exhibition Catalogue." *Contemporary Museum of Art*. Douro: Portugal (2010).

Caruso, Laura. "Printmaker Pursues Metamorphosis of Ideas." *Kansas City Star*, March 31, 1991.

Casey, Betty. "Chameleon Community Arts Project: Art as Community." *Tulsa Kids Magazine*, May, 2004.

"Chameleon Celebrates 10th Anniversary." *Review* 7, no. 5 (April, 2005): 29-30.

Childers, Kara. "Skate Park Artist Making Kids His Partners." *Kansas City Star Neighborhood News*, December 10, 2003.

Conrad, David. "Community Murals as Democratic Art and Education." *Journal of Aesthetic Education* (Spring, 1995): 98-102.

Cook, Linda. "Printmaking Artist Teaches in Q-C." *Quad-City Times*, July 24, 1989.

Dewey, Tom II. "Announcing -- Wycross Press." Journal of the Print World 14, no. 2 (1991).

Dewey, John. *Art as Experience*. New York: Capricorn Books, 1934.

De Zegher, Catherine, Thelma Golden. Julie Mehretu: Drawings. New York: Rizzoli International Publications, 2007.

"Edward Lorenz, father of chaos theory and butterfly effect, dies at 90." *Massachusetts Institute of Technology MIT News*, April 16, 2008. Accessed December 1, 2010. http://web.mit.edu/newsoffice/2008/obit-lorenz-0416.html.

Erskine, Eleanor. *Art of Memory*. Columbia: Missouri, 2004.

Farber, Janet L. *Midlands Invitational 2000: Works on Paper*. Omaha: Nebraska, 2000.

"Fifty Years of Revelations/Alvin Ailey Dance Theatre." *www.alvinailey.org*, 2010. Accessed November 15, 2010. http://www.alvinailey.org/node/1828.

Frutiger, Adrian. *Signs and Symbols and their Design and Meaning*. Translated by Andrew Bluhm. New York: Watson-Guptill Publications, 1998.

Farling, Michael. "Coming to Terms with Time." *Santa Barbara News Press*, Jan 21, 1994.

"Fundred Supporting Operation Paydirt." *www.fundred.org*, 2010. Accessed October 12, 2010. http://www.fundred.org/about/.

Gablik, Suzi. "Connective Aesthetics: Art After Individualism," in *Mapping the Terrain, New Genre Public Art*, edited by Suzanne Lacy, Seattle: Bay Press, 1995. 82-83.

Ganson, Adelia, "Community-Studio Integration." *Review*, January, 2010. http://ereview.org/2010/01/15/community-studio-integration/.

Gaul, Emily. "Vitreography." *American Artist*, September, 1994.

Goldenthal, Jolene. "Architecture Abstracted at Trinity." *The Hartford Courant*, September 16, 1979.

Green, Gaye. "New Genre Public Arts Education." *Art Journal* 58, no. 1 (Spring 1999): 80-83.

Grosenick, Uta, Burkhard Riemschneider, eds. *Art at the Turn of the Millennium*. Köln: Taschen, 1999.

Hellman, Rick. "Wallenberg Story Inspires Artist to Produce Print Series." *The Kansas City Jewish Chronicle*, March 15, 1991.

Hinson, Mark. "Critical Impressions is Impressive." *Tallahassee Democrat*, January 15, 1993.

Hinterding, Erik. *Rembrandt Etchings from the Frits Lugt Collection*. Paris: Thoth Publishers, 2008.

Howard, Elizabeth. "Art Work in Volker Park." *Review: Art and News Features in Kansas City* 2, no. 9 (July 2000): 9.

"Institute for Children, Poverty and Homelessness." *www.icphusa.org* 2010. Accessed October 12, 2010. http://icphusa.org/index.asp?CID=1&PID=103.

Kaprow, Allan. "Success and Failure when Art Changes," in *Mapping the Terrain, New Genre Public Art*, edited by Suzanne Lacy, Seattle: Bay Press, 1995.152-158.

Kavanaugh, Lee Hill. "Space where Dreams are Built in Danger of Shutting Down." *Kansas City Star*, May 16, 2009.

Kemper Museum of Contemporary Art. *Our City, Ourselves: Portrait of a Community*. Kansas City: Missouri, 1998.

Kirsch, Elisabeth. "An Artist: The Nearer to Death the Closer to Art." *Kansas City Star*, February 20, 1998.

Koenig, Leonard. "Hugh Merrill: The Nelson-Atkins Museum of Art." *New Art Examiner*, December, 1984.

Kommun, Falu. *Falun Triennial 2007*.  Dalarnas Museum, Falun: Sweden, 2007. 138-143.

Krueger, Michael. *I'd Rather Be Drawing*. Kansas City: Missouri, 2007.

Lacy, Suzanne, ed. *Mapping The Terrain:  New Genre Public Art*. Seattle: Bay Press, 1995.

Leedy, Jim. "Creativity as Content." *Printmaking Today* 5, no. 4. (1996).

Lee, Dongeun. *Further; Artists from Printmaking at the Edge: Museum of Contemporary Photography*. Seoul: Korea, 2009.

Lippard, Lucy. *The Lure of the Local: Senses of Place in a Multicentered Society*. New York: The New Press, 1997.

Luijten, Ger, Erik Hinterding, Ernst van de Wetering. *Rembrandt the Printmaker*. London: British Museum Press, 2000.

Lustfeldt, Heather. "Teaching Art and Making Art for the Real World." *Review*, (March 2000): 8-9.

Mai, Josie. *Face, Africa: 2006-2007*. Kansas City: Missouri, 2007.

Manchester Craftsmen's Guild. *Art Within: Twenty-Year Commemorative Exhibition*. Pittsburg:  Pennsylvania, 2007. 10.

Mandel, Charles. "The Death Zone." *Edmonton Journal*, June 23, 1995.

Martin, Chris, Rackstraw Downes, William Conlon, Judy Pfaff. "Al Held (1928-2005)." *Brooklyn Rail*, September 2005. Accessed December 16, 2010. http://www.brooklynrail.org/2005/09/art/al-held-1928-2005.

Massachusetts MoCA. *Billboard Art on the Road: A Retrospective Exhibition of Artists Billboards of the Last 30 Years*. North Adams: Massachusetts, 1999.

McCracken, David. "Gallery Scene, The Wallenberg Suite." *Chicago Tribune*, Feb 1, 1991.

McKenna, George L. "Prints by Hugh Merrill." *Nelson-Atkins Museum of Art*, Kansas City: Missouri, (1985).

Miller, Cynthia. "Hugh Merrill." *Contemporary Impressions: The Journal of the American Print Alliance* 9, no. 2 (2001): 16-19.

Merrill, Hugh. "A Standard for Community Art." *Review* 3, no. 3 (1999).

Merrill, Hugh. "Educating the Next Generation of Printmakers." *Artist's Proof: The Journal of the Print Consortium* 5, no. 2 (1991): 1-4.

Merrill, Hugh. "Educating the Next Generation of Printmakers." *Printmaking Today* 4, no. 1 (1995): 8-9.

Merrill, Hugh. "Empowerment of Craft and Craft Organizations: A Two-Front War." *The California Printmaker: The Quarterly Journal of the California Society of Printmakers* 2 (Spring, 1993): 8-9.

Merrill, Hugh. "For Karen." *Graphoion European Review of Contemporary Prints*, Book and Paper Art 3, no. 4 (1998): 30.

Merrill, Hugh. "Free Speech: Audience Not Included." *Review* 3, no. 6 (April, 1999): 13.

Merrill, Hugh. "Martin Buber's Cat." *New American Paintings* 17 (1998): 78-79.

Merrill, Hugh. "New Inferno: Poems from Hell, Auschwitz Sky, Photographs and Writing by Hugh Merrill." *New Letters; A Magazine of Writing and Art* 64, no. 4  (1998): 95-100.

Merrill, Hugh. "Post Print." Paper presented at the 19th annual conference of the Southern Graphics Council, March 20-23, 1991.

Merrill, Hugh. "Professor Hugh Merrill Responds to Karl Moehl Bradley." *International Journal of the Print World* 19, no. 1 (1996): 4-5.

Merrill, Hugh. "Staking Claim." *MAPC: Journal for the Mid America Print Council* 1, no. 1 (1992): 7-8.

Merrill, Hugh. "The March of 'isms': Thoughts on Progress, Pluralisms and Boundaries." *Speck Magazine: The Midwest Magazine for Art and Culture* 1, no. 1 (2001): 51-56.

Merrill, Hugh. "Turning Art Upside Down" *Review* 2 no. 7 (May 2000): 16-19.

Merrill, Rebekah. "Exploring Life's Possibilities" *Review* 4, no. 1 (November 2001)

Museum of Fine Arts, Boston. "Fairfield Porter: Realist Painter in an Age of Abstraction." Medford Massachusetts: Acme Printing Company, 1982.

"Nelson-Atkins Museum celebrating – Art Print Lovers at 30." *Artknowledge News*, June 9, 2008. Accessed December 24, 2010. www.artknowledgenews.com/Nelson_Atkins_Museum.html

Noland, Garry. "Hugh Merrill: Nelson-Atkins Museum of Art." *Forum: A Visual Arts Publication* 10, no. 1 (1985): 13-14.

Noyce, Richard. *Printmaking at the Edge*. London: A&C Black, April 2006. 106-108.

Nugent, Bob L. *Imagery: Art for Wine*. San Francisco: Wine Appreciation Guild, 2006.

"Points, Plots, and Ploys." *Southern Graphics Council*. Kansas City: Missouri (2007): 18.

Pronko, Michael. "Art, the Artist and Politics." *Forum: A Visual Arts Publication* 17, no. 2 (1992): 1, 3.

Raverty, Dennis. "Martin Buber's Cat." *Art Papers*, (1998)

Ross, Mike. "Death Works." *Edmonton Sun*, June 23, 1995.

Sandler, Irving. *Al Held*. New York: Hudson Hills Press, 1984.

Seaton, Liz. "These Aren't Regular Books, Bookworks: Nelson-Atkins Museum." *Kansas City Star*, April 29, 1992.

Stoddard, Leah. "On View Indianapolis: Hugh Merrill." *New Art Examiner* 22, no. 3 (November, 1994): 36.

Thorson, Alice. "A Life Etched in History." *Kansas City Star*, February 22, 1993.

Trustees of the Nelson Gallery Foundation. *Print Lovers at 30: Celebrating Three Decades of Giving*. Kansas City: Missouri, 2008. 2, 8-11.

Young, Joan, Brian Dillon, Alan Balfour. *Julie Mehretu: Grey Area*. New York: Guggenheim Museum Publications, 2009.